trips & trivia

An Architectural, Educational,
Historical, and Recreational
Guide to Western Massachusetts

trips & trivia

An Architectural, Educational, Historical, and Recreational Guide to Western Massachusetts

Linda K. Fuller

THE
DONNING COMPANY
PUBLISHERS
NORFOLK/VIRGINIA BEACH

Original edition Copyright © 1978 by Springfield Magazine, Inc.

Second edition published June 1983 by Trips & Trivia, Inc.,
P.O. Box 3450, Springfield, MA 01101

Third expanded and revised edition Copyright © 1988
by Linda K. Fuller, Ph.D.

All rights reserved, including the right to reproduce this work in any form whatsoever without permission in writing from the publisher, except for brief passages in connection with a review. For information, write:

       The Donning Company/Publishers
       5659 Virginia Beach Boulevard
       Norfolk, Virginia 23502

Edited by Denise J. Grosskoff

Library of Congress Cataloging-in-Publication Data

Fuller, Linda K.
  Trips & trivia.

  1. Berkshire County (Mass.)—Description and travel—Guide-books. 2. Franklin County (Mass.)—Description and travel—Guide-books. 3. Hampden County (Mass.)—Description and travel—Guide-books. 4. Hampshire County (Mass.)—Description and travel—Guide-books. 5. Massachusetts—Description and travel—1981-   —Guide-books. I. Title. II. Title: Trips and trivia.
F72.B5F8   1987   917.44'20443   87-22297
ISBN 0-89865-552-8 (pbk.)

Printed in the United States of America

This book is dedicated to Eric and our sons—William, Keith, and Alex—who tripped all around Western Massaschusetts with me collecting trivia...

MICHAEL S. DUKAKIS
GOVERNOR

THE COMMONWEALTH OF MASSACHUSETTS
EXECUTIVE DEPARTMENT
STATE HOUSE, BOSTON 02133

Welcome.

From Agawam to Williamstown, from Mt. Washington to Warwick, western Massachusetts is a quiet paradise. In Springfield, Holyoke, Pittsfield, North Adams, and other urban centers it's a dynamic, fascinating mix of everything that makes Massachusetts unique-- ethnic diversity, cultural activity, and economic progress.

I hope you will enjoy it as much as we do.

Sincerely,

Michael S. Dukakis

Acknowledgments by County

Berkshire County

Becket: Jacob's Pillow—Nancy Tutco, Communications Manager and Photographer-in-Residence; **Dalton:** Crane Museum of Papermaking; **Great Barrington:** Olga Dance Company; Albert Schweitzer Friendship House—Antje B. Lemke, President; Southern Berkshire Chamber of Commerce—Isaline L. Bouteiller, Executive Secretary; **Hancock;** Hancock Shaker Village—Joan D. Clemons, Director of Marketing and Public Relations; Jiminy Peak—Ariane Blanchard, Marketing Department; **Lee:** Berkshire Scenic Railway Museum—John H. Staber, Promotions Director; Historic Merrell Tavern—Charles A. Reynolds; **Lenox:** The Bible Speaks—Colleen Szazynski; Canoe Meadows Wildlife Sanctuary and Pleasant Valley Wildlife Sanctuary—R. Laubach, Massachusetts Audubon/Berkshire Sanctuaries; Kripalu Center—Tom Litzinger, Advertising/Public Relations; Lenox Library Association—Denis J. Lesieur, Head Librarian; Tanglewood—Bernadette H. Horgan, Promotions Assistant/Publicist, Boston Symphony Orchestra; Edith Wharton Restoration/"The Mount"—Scott Marshall, Associate Director; **North Adams:** North Adams State College—Stephen M. Long, Jr., Assistant to the President; Northern Berkshire Chamber of Commerce—Sharon A. May, Administrative Assistant; Northern Berkshire Council of the Arts; Western Gateway Heritage State Park—Ms. Dale E. Kurlander; **Pittsfield:** Arrowhead—Colleen Bucher, Administrative Assistant, Berkshire County Historical Society; Berkshire Atheneum—Ruth T. Degenhardt, Department Head, Local History and Literature Services; Berkshire Community College—Sarah Novak, Publications Assistant; Miss Hall's School—Daniel G. Lee, Jr., Headmaster; **Sandisfield:** Sandisfield Historical Society—Myrtle A. Mazzaferro, President; **Sheffield:** Colonel Ashley House and Bartholomew's Cobble—Delphine M. Phelps, Administrator, Trustees of Reservations; Berkshire School—Patricia E. Squire, Director of Public Relations; **Stockbridge:** Berkshire Theatre Festival; Chesterwood—Paul W. Ivory, Director; the Normal Rockwell Museum of Stockbridge—Virginia H. Schwartz, Development Associate; Shrine of the Divine Mercy—Reverend Roger L. Wojcik, M. I. C. Rector; **Tyringham:** Tyringham Galleries and Gingerbread House; **Williamstown:** Potter's Wheel—Adelaide England; Williams College—James G. Kolesar, Director of Public Information; Williamstown Theatre Festival—Sarah Fargo.

Franklin County

Deerfield: The Bement School; Deerfield Academy—James Marksbury; Eaglebrook School—Arthur D. Levin, Business Manager; Historic Deerfield, Inc.,—Grace T. Friary, Public Relations Officer; Pocumtuck Valley Memorial Association/Memoral Hall Museum—Tim Neumann, Director; Woolman Hill—Jean Semrau, Director; **Greenfield:** Greenfield Community College—Robert L. Merriam, Assistant to the President; Historical Society of Greenfield—Alice Crawford, Curator; Mohawk Trail Concerts—Barbara Ansbacher, Managing Director; Stoneleigh-Burnham School—Mary Kay Hoffman; **Leverett:** Leverett Craftsmen & Artists; **Montague:** Carnegie Library Museum; Montague State Hatchery—Ralph Taylor, Manager; **Northfield:** Northfield Historical Commission—Rosa Johnston, Chairman; Northfield-Mount Herman School—Kim Nelson, Public Relations Department; Northfield Utilities—George B. Brosky, Manager; **Rowe:** Rowe Historical Society; Yankee Atomic Electric Company—Mr. McGee.

Hampden County

Aqawam: Lieutenant William Allen House—D. Thorpe; Riverside—Mary Ann Stebbins, Advertising and Public Relations Assistant; **Brimfield:** Balloon School of Massachusetts, Inc.,—Clayton L. Thomas; Brimfield Public Library—B. Robertson, Librarian; **Chester:** Hamilton Memorial Library—Nancy A. Meacham, Librarian; **Chicopee:** Edward Bellamy Homestead—Rita Thormeyer and Steven Jendrysk; Elms College—Mary Lou Lacey, SSJ; **East Longmeadow:** East Longmeadow Historical Headquarters—Richard Clark, Town Clerk; **Hampden:** Laughing Brook Education Center and Wildlife Sanctuary—Jo Benton; **Holyoke:** The Children's Museum—Martha Gray, Program Coordinator; Church of the Blessed Sacrament—Father Laughran; Holyoke Community College—Keith O'Connor, Director of Public Relations; Mount Tom—David Moore and Laura Radwell; Mountain Park—Walt Marek; Wistariahurst Museum; **Longmeadow:** Bay Path Junior College—Joanne I. Guernsey, Coordinator of Publicity; Storrs House—Peggy House, Publicity; Storrs Library—Linda Drummery; **Ludlow:** Our Lady of Fatima FESTA—Reverend David M. Farland, Administrator; **Springfield:** American International College—Craig Greenberg, Director of Public Relations; Basketball Hall of Fame—Jerry Healey, Promotion Director; City of Springfield—Richard E. Neal, Mayor; Forest Park; Greater Springfield Chamber of Commerce; Indian Motocycle Museum and Hall of Fame—Charles Manthos, President; Jewish Community Center—Joel Gross; Mayor's Office—Jeannie Barnes; Pioneer Valley Convention and Visitors Bureau; The Shops at Baystate West—Dolores Reis, Marketing Director; Springfield Adult Education Council—Edie Montgomery Kerrigan; Springfield Armory National Historic Site—Larry Lowenthal, Historian; Springfield Civic Center; Springfield College; Springfield Indians Hockey—Bruce Landon, General Manager; Springfield Library and Museums Association—Marianne Gambaro, Director of Public Relations; Springfield

Orchestra Association—Richard A. Frevert, Director of Marketing and Nancy Crowley, Assistant Director of Marketing; Springfield Technical Community College—Setta McCabe, Coordinator of Publications; Stage/West—Mark G. Auerbach, Public Relations and Marketing Consultant; Thronja Gallery—Janice S. Throne; Western New England College—Carey Downs Jack, Director of Public Relations; **Wales:** Norcross Wildlife Sanctuary; **Westfield:** Barnes Airport; Concerts on the Green; The Stanley Park of Westfield, Inc.; Strathmore Paper Company—Murray E. Grant, Manager of Advertising and Sales Promotion; Westfield State College—Jeanne M. Julian, Staff Associate, Institutional Advancement; Western Hampden Historical Society—Barbara Bush, Chairman; **West Springfield:** Eastern States Exposition—Noreen P. Tossinari, Communications Manager; **Wilbraham:** A Child's Place—Carol Dernavich; Wilbraham and Monson Academy—Chris Skypeck.

Hampshire County

Amherst: Amherst College and Dickinson Homestead—Public Affairs Office; Amherst Historical Society—Mary K. Steinway, President; Hampshire College—Russell Powell, Director of Public Information; Hitchcock Center for the Environment—Donna Rowe, Administrative Coordinator; Jones Library; University of Massachusetts—Joan F. Ashwell, News Editor; **Belchertown:** Belchertown State School—Haskell O. Kennedy, Jr., Director, Office of Employee Services; Clapp Memorial Library—Marie B. Munro, Librarian; Stone House Museum—Helen F. Lister, Curator; **Chesterfield:** Edwards Memorial Museum; **Cummington:** William Cullen Bryant Homestead; **Easthampton:** Arcadia Nature Center and Wildlife Sanctuary—Jud Pierce, Director; Daily Hampshire Gazette—Peter DeRosa; Northampton Historical Society; The Williston Northampton School—Nancy Slator, Acting Public Relations Director; **Granby:** Granby Dinosaur Museum—Mrs. Gingras, former owner; St. Hyacinth College and Seminary—Franciscan Friars; **Hadley:** Hadley Farm Museum; Porter-Phelps-Huntington House—Susan Lisk, Curator; **Hatfield:** Baracca Gallery; **Northampton:** Childs Park—William E. Dwyer, Secretary, Board of Directors; Clarke School for the Deaf—Sharianne Walker, Director of Public Relations; Forbes Library; Northampton Airport; Smith College—Mary B. Reutner, Acting Director of Public Relations; Tri-County Fair—Hampshire, Franklin, and Hampden Agricultural Society; **Pelham:** Carkhuff Institute of Human Technology; Pelham Historical Society—Robert Lord Keyes, Curator; **South Hadley:** Dinosaurland—Carlton S. Nash, President; Mount Holyoke College—Alix deSeife, Director of Press and Communications; Joseph Skinner Museum—Mount Holyoke College, Director; **Southampton:** Clark-Chapman House—Frank P. Conant, Treasurer, Southampton Historical Society.

Other Acknowledgments

The Appalachian Mountain Club; New York and New England Apple Institute—John O'Donnell, Vice President of Marketing; Commonwealth of Massachusetts, Department of Commerce and Development—Ms. Loren Hackett, Division of Tourism; Massachusetts Audubon Society; Massachusetts Aeronautics Commission; Massachusetts Boating Program; Massachusetts Council on Arts and Humanities; Massachusetts Department of Environmental Management, Division of Forests and Parks; Massachusetts Department of Food and Agriculture; Massachusetts Department of Public Works; Massachusetts Division of Fish and Wildlife; Massachusetts Division of Marine and Recreational Vehicles; Massachusetts Historical Commission; Massachusetts Maple Producers Association; Massachusetts Natural Resources, Parks, and Recreation; National Park Service; National Wildlife Refuge; Society for the Preservation of New England Antiquities; Trustees of Reservations; United States Department of the Interior; Old Sturbridge Village—Kristi J. Kienholz, Manager of Public Relations; Jan Grosskopf, Editor.

Table of Contents

Dedication v
Governor Michael S. Dukakis—Welcome vi
Acknowledgments ix
Photographic Credits xiii
Introduction xv

Counties:
   Berkshire County 1
   Franklin County 25
   Hampden County 41
   Hampshire County 75

Extra Ordinaries:
Airports 98
The Appalachian National Scenic Trail 98
Apple Orchards 98
Bed & Breakfasts 98
Boats and Snowmobiles 100
Campgrounds-State & Private 102
Covered Bridges 100
Fairs and Festivals 100
Fishing and Hunting 100
Golf Courses 101
Historic American Buildings 101
Maple Sugaring 102
Massachusetts Audubon Society 103
The Mohawk Trail 103
Native Sons and Daughters 103
Old Sturbridge Village 107
The Society for the Preservation of
   New England Antiquities 108
Ski Areas (Alpine and Nordic) 109
State Forests, Parks, and Reservations
   for Day Use 112
Trustees of Reservations 113

Index 114

About the Author 119

Photographic Credits

Author
(Linda K. Fuller): Anthony Connor (portrait)

Berkshire County
Beckett: Jacob's Pillow—Lois Greenfield
Great Barrington: Albert Schweitzer—Erica Anderson
Hancock: Hancock Shaker Village—Paul Rocheleau
Lee: Berkshire Scenic Railway—John Staber
Lenox: Edith Wharton Restoration/"The Mount"
  —Warren Fowler
North Adams: Western Gateway Heritage Park
  —Nick Noyes
Stockbridge: Naumkeag—Mission House, Trustees
  of Reservations Chesterwood—Paul Rocheleau
Williamstown: Williams College—Clemens Kalischer
Williamstown: Theater Festival—Bob Marshak

Franklin County
Northfield: Northfield Mount Hermon School
  —Lionel Delevingne
Shelburne: "Bridge of Flowers" oil on canvas by
  Vito Gramarossa (1986), courtesy Thronja Gallery,
  Springfield

Hampden County
Springfield: Thronja Gallery—Vincent S. D'Addario
  View of the Arch of Titus—oil on canvas by Giovanni
    Paolo Pannini
Stage/West—Gerry Goldstein
West Springfield: Eastern States Exposition
  —Vincent S. D'Addario
Methodist Meeting House—Dave Roback

Hampshire County
Amherst: The Strong House Museum
  —Richard Carpenter
Cummington: Bryant Homestead—Elsie Racz,
  House Administrator
Northampton: Smith College—Chuck Kidd,
  Shelley Rotner
Pelham: Pelham Town Hall and Historical
  Society Museum—Dave Prentiss
South Hadley: Mount Holyoke College—Glenn Mitchell

Extra Ordinaries
Old Sturbridge Village: Robert S. Arnold
Illustration by Al Pafenbach

Introduction

It has been said that if the four Western Massachusetts counties were combined, the total would exceed the populations of Alaska, Delaware, Montana, North Dakota, South Dakota, Vermont, and Wyoming. And so begins your involvement with the mega-bytes of information on the architectural, educational, historical, and recreational *Trips & Trivia* you're about to experience!

Here are the more than 100 cities and towns broken down by county in order to tell you what's happening where, when it's open, how much it will cost, and who has gone before you; and what a great adventure it promises to be! The first edition of this book came out in 1978 and sold over 10,000 copies before going into other printings. Originally targeted to tourists, it has been discovered that *Trips & Trivia* is the ideal book not only for your car, but also your cocktail table, your bathroom (yes!), your bedside table, your next party, and most of all, your gift to persons who want to share this rich heritage.

Rest assured that every single detail in this book has been corroborated with authorities; yet, if you discover any changes since publication date, please let me know. It is my family's sincere hope that communities represented here take great pride, that tourists to the area find many fun places and tidbits, that all of you will help in continuous updating, and that all this book's readers will delight in discovering the many *Trips & Trivia* about Western Massachusetts.

—Linda K. Fuller
Wilbraham, Massachusetts

Berkshire County

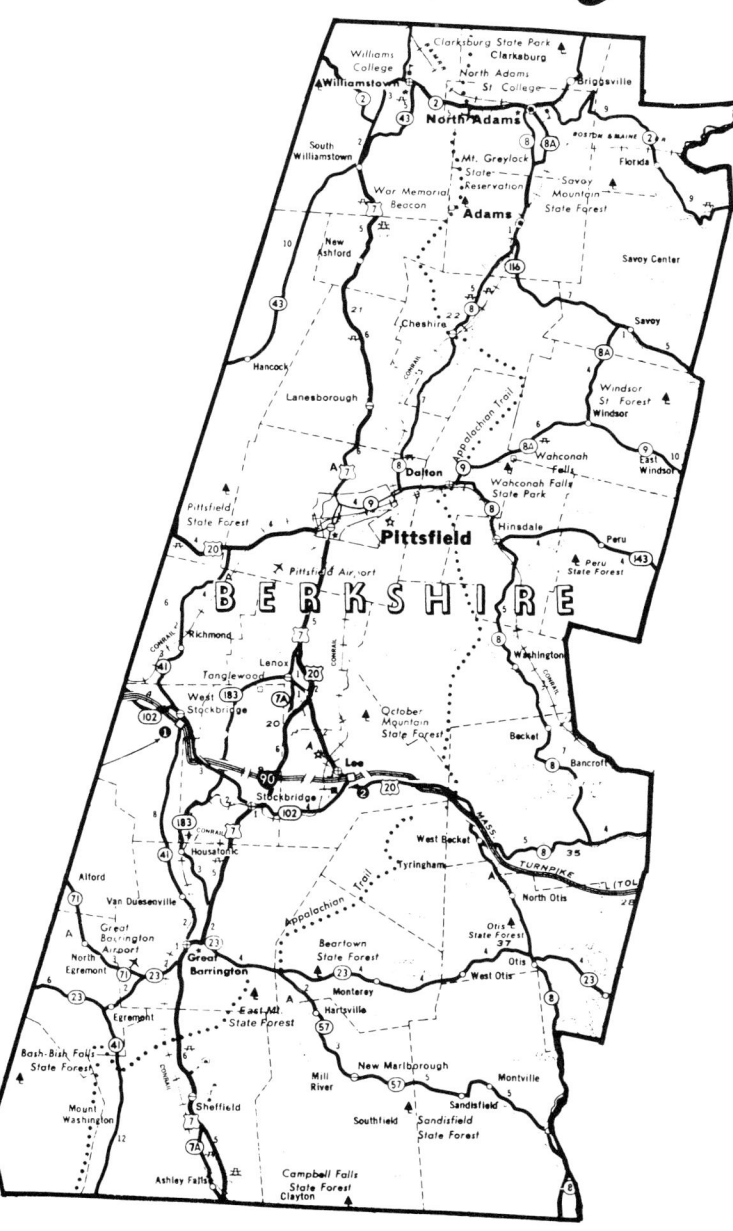

Berkshire County

ADAMS, Massachusetts
Population: 11,270   Zip Code: 01220

Originally called East Hoosack Settlement by the Quakers who settled there in the 18th century, Adams changed its name to honor Samuel Adams, American Revolutionary patriot and statesman.

Trips and trivia:
• **Anthony's Pool** on West Road, with an access from Maple Street, provides public swimming daily from 11:00 a.m. to 7:00 p.m., with individual fees or season passes available. There is provision for picnics, changing and toilet facilities, snack bar, dance pavilion, and supervised swimming.
• The **birthplace of Susan B. Anthony,** founder of the National Woman Suffrage Association, is marked by a plaque at 67 East Road. Built c. 1810, the house has maintained her favorite room with its original furnishings, and behind the house is the schoolhouse she attended as a girl. Attempts have been made in recent years to have the home, now a private home, designated as a national shrine.
• **Friends Meeting House** (1874), operated and still used by the Society of Friends, has been designated an Historic American Building. Located at the corner of Friend and Maple Streets, it is a symbol of the religious needs of the early settlers.

• **Greylock Mountain State Reservation,** with a 3,491-foot altitude, is the highest point in Massachusetts. It is reached by turning south from Route 2 just west of North Adams; a road leads to the top for cars or hikers. Telephone: 413/743-5815. At the top is **Greylock War Memorial,** with facilities for picnicking and lodging atop a spectacular panoramic view. The reservation provides areas for fishing, hiking, camping, hunting, and snowmobiling and for nature walks.
• Another good picnic/hiking area is **Mt. Prospect,** south off Notch Road on Route 2 at the Appalachian Trail crossing. Signs indicate the way to the summit of Mount Greylock.
• **Old Stone Mill,** Grove Street on Route 8, today houses a hand-screen wallpaper company in a mill built around 1850. Telephone 413/743-1015.
• The Adams Chamber of Commerce each year sponsors **summer festivals:** Polka Holiday, Susan B. Anthony Days, and agricultural fairs.
• **Winter recreation** in the area includes skiing, ice racing, tobogganing, snowmobiling, etc. Its autumn season is spectacular. The Chamber of Commerce (PO Box 215) of Adams each year sponsors a Mt. Greylock Ramble on Columbus Day, awarding certificates to all who complete the climb.

ALFORD, Massachusetts
Population: 337

This small hilly town was named for John Alford, founder of the Alford professorship of Moral Philosophy at Harvard.

Trips and trivia:
• **Tom Ball Tavern,** at an altitude of 1,930 feet, has Devil's Den on its western slope. Reached by a short footpath, the den is a large cave with an uneven floor that drips a continuous stream of cold water.
• The **Knox Trail** enters the state on Route 71 in Alford, proceeding into North Egremont.
• The old Town Hall and church along **Main Street** are of interest to the student of architecture.

BECKET, Massachusetts
Population: 1,153   Zip Code: 01223

Because it is not particularly suited to agricultural activity, Becket is a residential and recreational town that is best known for its annual summer dance festival.

Trips and trivia:
• **Becket Arts Center,** Route 8, is open July 2nd to Labor Day, Thursday through Sunday: 2:00 p.m. through 5:00 p.m., Saturday 12:30 p.m. to 5:30 p.m. Adults: $1.00
• **Becket Falls,** a 25-foot drop into a worn rock channel, has a swimming pool at the foot of the cascade.
• The only Paul Revere bell in Berkshire County can be

found on the **First Congregational Church** in Becket, dating to 1758.

• **Jacob's Pillow Dance Festival,** the oldest and foremost dance festival in America, conducts an eight-week season every summer evening, Tuesday to Saturday, with 2:00 p.m. matinees on Saturday. Established in 1932, the Pillow was the first theater in the country designed and built especially for dance. Its rustic setting, including several 18th century barn buildings, was designed by Josepf Franz, the architect of the Shed at Tanglewood. For over a half century, the Ted Shawn Theatre has featured thousands of stellar names in the dance world. It is especially famous for its premiers, unusual events, and creative work. Tickets ranging in price from $17.00 to $23.50, may be purchased through the Pillow Box Office or by writing Jacob's Pillow, PO Box 287, Lee, MA 01238. For information, group rates, and reservations, call 413/243-0745, Monday through Saturday 10:00 a.m. to 9:00 a.m., Sunday noon to 5:00 p.m. The Pillow can be reached via the Lee/Pittsfield exit off the Massachusetts Pike; follow signs from Route 20, going left on George Carter Road.

CHESHIRE, Massachusetts
Population: 3,199   Zip Code: 01225

Historically known as the town that made the "big cheese" for President Thomas Jefferson in 1802, Cheshire has in its center a replica of the press in which the 1,235-pounder was made.

Trips and trivia:
• **Cheshire Barn Flea Market** on Route 8 offers antiques and plants for sale every Sunday from 9:00 a.m. to 5:00 p.m. during the milder months.
• The replica of the **Cheese Press** can be found on the corner of Church and School Streets at Leland Park. A

commemorative sign gives these statistics about the cheese: "Weighing 1,235 lbs., One Day's Product of the Town's Dairies, Moulded in a Cider Press. It was drawn by oxen to Hudson, N.Y. And Shipped by water to Washington. It was presented at the White House to President Thomas Jefferson As a Token of Regard from the Citizens of Cheshire."
• **Cole House** (1804), opposite the Baptist Church, has a Christian door of eight panels forming a double cross, believed to protect the house against witchcraft. At one point in the early 1800s, the house was used as a meeting place for the Masons and their emblems (the beehive, Royal Arch, Bible-balance, and square and compass) have been discovered under the wallpaper in one of the rooms.
• Some other **highlights** in the town include: Big Rock on Pork Lane (Outlook Avenue), Stove Bridge on Route 8, Stafford Hill Memorial, and some unusual gravestones in the local cemetery.
• **Hoosac Lake,** on Route 8 between North Adams and Pittsfield, has picnic facilities, camping, and boating at Horn's Beach on Farnam's Road. It is open daily during the summer from 10:00 a.m. to 8:00 p.m.

CLARKSBURG, Massachusetts
Population: 1,958

Clarksburg was settled by Scotch people who worked in its many small textile mills. Today it is the archetype of a New England town.

Trips and trivia:
• **Clarksburg State Park,** Routes 2 and 8, is open daily from 10:00 a.m. to 8:00 p.m. at a cost of $2.00 per car or $15.00 for a season pass. Facilities for picnics, camping swimming, boating, and fishing are available at Mausert's Pond, complete with scenic views of Mt. Greylock and the Hoosac Range.
• **Musterfield House** (1805) on Middle Road has been designated a Historic American Building.

DALTON, Massachusetts
Population: 7,504   Zip Code: 01226

First known as the "Ashuelot Equivalent," Dalton is famous as the town where U.S. currency has been made since 1879.

Crane & Co., Inc.
Paper Makers
Dalton, Massachusetts
01226

Trips and trivia:
- Housed in Crane and Company's Old Stone Mill, built in Dalton in 1844, the **Crane Museum of Papermaking** has been open since 1930 to exhibit to the public the evolution of American papermaking from Revolutionary times to the present. Exhibits emphasize the company's distinctive all-rag papers used in currency, bonds, stock certificates, social and business correspondence, and carbon papers. The museum itself resembles the Old Ship Church in Hingham, Massachusetts, and it contains a scale model of the vat room of the first Crane mill and some of the hand molds used by Zenas Crane from 1801 to 1831, when paper was made by hand. There are demonstrations of how the paper is used today in government currency. The museum is located five miles east of Pittsfield, off Route 9. Take a right at the second light in Dalton, go to the foot of the mill, and turn right again. There is plenty of parking at the end of the road. The Crane Museum is open 2:00 p.m. to 5:00 p.m. Monday through Friday from June 1 to October 16 and is free. Special group tours can be arranged. Telephone: 413/684-2600. Adult visitors get a sample package of some of Crane's fine paper!
- **Wahconah Falls State Park,** at Routes 9 and 8A, has picnic tables and fireplaces, fishing, snowmobiling, a horse trail, skiing, and scenic spots. It is open daily from 10:00 a.m. to 8:00 p.m. at a cost of $2.00 per car or $15.00 for a season pass.

EGREMONT, Massachusetts
Population: 1,220

Egremont was named for Charles Windham, the Earl of Egremont, who worked with his brother-in-law, George Grenville, and the Earl of Halifax in negotiating peace settlements with Spain and France in 1762. Egremont was virtually the first white settlement in Berkshire County.

Trips and trivia:
- The Dalzelle **Axle Factory,** one of the first two in America (1845-1909), was situated on Main Street in South Egremont. The **Baldwin Chair Factory** (1843-c. 1900) was built by an old stone mill a mile west of South Village; the few Baldwin chairs still in existence are true heirlooms and collectors' items.
- The largest *balsam poplar* in the country is situated on Main Street in South Egremont. It measures a height of 70 feet; spread of 60 feet, and girth of 54 feet. Egremont is known to many as "the town of ancient trees."
- **Crystal Caves,** also known as Bats' Dens, are situated on private property just under Jug End Mountain and are documented to contain the most beautiful example of flow-stone in New England. Spelunkers will need a guide and permission.
- **Egremont Academy,** doubling since 1882 as Town Hall and library, was built in 1832. It is located on the east side of Route 41, just north of South Egremont Road. The old windows and bell tower have recently been restored, the upstairs meeting room has been refinished into an archive room, and a collection of historical memorabilia of the town and area has been installed there. The building has been designated a Historic American Building.
- **French Park,** a lovely park just east of Prospect Lake, was deeded to the townsfolk by a deceased resident. Here the visitor may enjoy a horse show, Little League game, tennis match, town picnic, or the wooded camp grounds.
- The Francis **Hare Tavern** (1780) was situated just behind the present location of the old Egremont Inn, a charming place filled with nostalgia.
- The **Indian grinding store,** just off Route 23 on Taconic Lake (about one mile west of Phillips Road), is preserved in a residential development. The Indian stone boundary wall that runs along Jug End Road marks the western side of what, in the old deeds of the area, is called **"Indian Land,"** the settlement of Umpachene, "War Chief/Hero" of the Ouestenuck Tribe of Mohican Indians that inhabited the region.
- Today the Benjamin Clark **Insole Factory** (1879-1895) on Egremont-Sheffield Road has been replaced by an apartment house, but is believed to be the site on which a method was developed to manufacture the first standard-sized shoes in America: 500 dozen pairs a day in 1885.
- On Route 23, or Route 41 via South Egremont, is **Mount Everett,** which has a path to the summit where a fire tower provides views of New York and Connecticut. the 1,000-acre reservation, with a 2,624 foot peak, is free to the public.
- Be sure to check out **Old Egremont Tower,** dating from 1762, on Main Street across from the church in South Egremont. Four buildings to the east is the notable Blacksmith Shop from the 1730s, located on the Egremont-Sheffield Road by the village common, today an antiques shop.
- **Oldest Private House** (1761) on Sheffield Back Road in South Egremont, has the initials of the original owners, John and Mary Tuller (although some histories say Fuller), with a huge heart inlaid at one end.
- **Prospect Lake,** in Prospect Lake Park off Route 71 via Hillsdale Road from North Egremont center, is open until 10:00 p.m. daily in the summer. There are facilities for swimming and a campground for trailers and motor homes.
- The **Smiley Wildlife Pond** is situated at the junction of Route 23 and Route 41 in South Egremont. At various times of the year, one may see birds of almost every ilk; it is a regular migration resting point on the north-south corridor.
- One of the first recorded mixed marriages between an Indian and a white in the Bay State occurred in Egremont more than 200 years ago when John Konkapot **Vanquilder** married the sister of the local tavern owner.

FLORIDA, Massachusetts
Population: 720

- Florida marks the start of the **Hoosac Tunnel,** nearly five miles along tracks of the Boston and Main Railroad through the heights of the northern Berkshires to North Adams. Its construction, started in 1856 and taking 17 years to complete, was very costly in money and lives.

Trips and trivia:
- **Bear Swamp Project** Visitors' Center on River Road has exhibits and displays explaining the operation of the New England Electric Company's pumped storage station for provision of hydroelectric power during peak use hours. The center is open daily from 9:00 a.m. to 5:00 p.m. and is free to the public.
- Drury Village on Route 2 features **Elks' Monument,** a chunk of granite surrounded by a huge bronze elk that was erected in 1923 by Massachusetts Elks to honor their World War I fellow lodge members.
- **Savoy Mountain State Forest,** with access from Route 2 in Florida and Route 116 in Savoy, is open daily from 10:00 a.m. to 8:00 p.m. at fees of $2.00 per car or $15.00 for the season. North Pond has picnic facilities, swimming, boat and beach houses, hiking and horse trails, fishing, hunting, tent and trailer sites, snowmobiling, and nature trails.
- **Whitcomb Summit,** on the north side of Route 2, has an observation tower called Raycroft Lookout that affords a view for miles in all directions from an altitude of 2,100 feet.

GREAT BARRINGTON, Massachusetts
Population: 7,068   Zip Code: 01230

- Home of the American poet and editor William Cullen Bryant, Great Barrington today combines literary, cultural, and recreational opportunities for its residents and tourists.

Trips and trivia:
- **Arts Action/Point One,** 10 Castle Street, is the exhibit and sales center for Berkshire handicrafts, books, and art; tickets for performing events can be purchased there. Headquarters of the Southern Berkshire Community Arts Council, Inc., it is open Monday through Saturday 10:00 a.m. to 5:00 p.m. Telephone: 413/528-4747. Volunteers help the tourist with all his art needs, from reservations to information. Interesting art galleries in Great Barrington include the Hayloft Art Gallery on Route 23 and the Tamarack Art Gallery.
- **Aston Magna Foundation for Music,** 30 Berkshire Heights Road, was established in 1972 "for the study and performance of 17th and 18th century music" and baroque and early classical music and is under the direction of artistic director Albert Fuller, noted harpsichordist virtuoso. For their fifth season of summer concerts, for example, Aston Magna presented the six Brandenburg Concerti of J. S. Bach on original instruments before sold-out audiences of nearly 500. For information or ticket reservations, call 413/528-3595 or write during the months of June and July to the above address. In the winter address mail to Aston Magna Foundation for Music, 27 West 67th St., New York, NY 10023.

the Barrington Fair

- **Barrington Fair** on Route 7, generally acknowledged to be the oldest fair in continuous operation in the country, is usually held in mid-September, with attractions ranging from general exhibits to horse racing. Telephone: 413/528-3030 in Great Barrington or 786-9300 in Springfield.
- Benedict Pond in **Beartown State Forest's** 8,207 acres has swimming facilities. Follow signs from Route 23 or from South Lee, Route 102. Swimming is also available at the Barn Swim Club on Route 7, open 10:00 a.m. to 12:00 p.m. In addition to the two outdoor pools, there is a golf range open to the public.
- The **Bill of Rights** of 1781 marked Great Barrington as the site of the freeing of the first slave under due process of law.
- The **William Cullen Bryant House,** also known as the General Joseph Dwight House (1739), has been designated a Historic American Building. It is located near the junction of Routes 7 and 23.
- Ezra **Cornell** (1807-74), financier and founder of Cornell University, ran the first telegraph line with a local station through Great Barrington in 1848.

- The **Olga Dunn Dance Co.,** founded in 1977, features an exciting repertory of modern dance and jazz. The company is available for full-length concerts, workshops, master classes, lecture demonstrations for all age groups, children's performances, and outreach programs adapted for community groups. It is located at 7 Alford Road. Telephone: 413/528/9674.

- **East Mountain State Forest** on Route 23 has trails for hiking and horseback riding, skiing, and snowmobiling, as well as areas for scenic views.
- The **Great Barrington Pottery,** Route 41 in Housatonic, has daily demonstrations of training and production of pottery in an educational institution. It is open from June 1 to September 15, 8:00 a.m. to 5:00 p.m. Telephone: 413/274-6259.
- Check out **Indian Ford** on Bridge Street, near the Housatonic River.
- Great Barrington boasts the birthplace of **Anson Jones** (1798-1858), last President of the Republic of Texas.
- The tourist can't miss **Joneses,** on Route 7, renowned for its amazing accumulation of trash and treasure.
- **Monument Mountain Reservation,** 260 acres north of town, features the 1,642-foot mountain for picnics, hikes, and a panoramic view. Other **monuments** throughout the town include "First Resistance" on the Town Hall lawn to commemorate the Revolutionary War, plus one for Shays Rebellion on Sheffield Back Road in South Egremont.
- **Mt. Everett State Reservation** covers 1,000 acres and is situated in both Great Barrington and Mount Washington. At its peak is Guilder Pond, at an altitude of 1,075 feet, which is believed to be the highest body of water in the state. It is surrounded by great boulders, forests of evergreens, and the most abundant June display of mountain laurel to be found in the Berkshires.
- The **Newsboy Fountain Statue** was given to the town of Great Barrington by the editor of the *New York Daily News,* William L. Brown, in 1895 as a tribute to the role of newsboys. It can be seen on Route 23W.

- The **Albert Schweitzer Center** on Hulburt Road (off Route 71), was founded in 1966 by the late Erica Anderson to promulgate the life and philosophy of Albert Schweitzer. It contains a library, archives, and film programs. Dr. Schweitzer built his hospital in Lambarene, in the present State of Gabon, Africa, in 1913 and devoted more than 50 years of service to the village population in what was then French Equatorial Africa. Schweitzer was a philosopher, theologian, medical scientist, and musician. His famous organ recitals—particularly of the music of Bach—helped finance his humanitarian projects. Schweitzer was awarded the Nobel Peace Prize, as well as many other awards, and died at the age of 90 without ceasing his efforts toward world peace, nuclear disarmament, and "reverence for life." Hours of the center vary seasonally. Individuals and groups are welcome; call in advance. Telephone: 413/528-3124. Free admission.
- **Searles Mansion** on Main Street, now used as a training center by the Home Insurance Company of New York, was built in 1886. The Roosevelt organ in the First Congregational Church was a gift from Mrs. Searles, and is considered one of the finest of its kind in the country. It is occasionally used for public concerts.
- Established in 1966, **Simon's Rock Early College** is a fully accredited coeducational four-year residential college that is designed especially for students 16 to 20 years old. Anyone who has completed the tenth grade is eligible to apply at the Admissions Office. Telephone: 413/528-0771.

- The **Southern Berkshire Chamber of Commerce,** encompassing the 13 towns around Great Barrington, is located at 362 Main Street. Telephone: 413/528-1510. It maintains a year-round information booth on Route 7 and is open every day except Monday during the winter and seven days a week during the summer.
- William **Stanley's** electrical power transformer helped Great Barrington in 1886 to become the first town in the world to be practically lighted by electricity.

HANCOCK, Massachusetts
Population: 697   Zip Code: 01237

- Named for John Hancock, the American Revolutionary statesman who was the first governor of the Commonwealth and first signer of the Declaration of Independence, Hancock blends its historical ties with present-day Berkshire recreation.

Trips and trivia:
- The **Alpine Slide** at Jiminy Peak offers a 3,150-foot scenic chairlift ride with a view of the Jericho Valley and then a 2,890-foot, bobsled-style descent on a plastic sled complete with a brake that can be adjusted to provide the desired speed. The sled is large enough to accommodate a solitary rider or an adult and a child. (Children under age six ride free, but must ride with an adult.) Dual tracks

consist of 25 twists and banked turns, with rides lasting from five to seven minutes, depending on the driver. Operating schedule goes from 9:00 a.m. to dusk, mid-June to mid-September; the slide will not operate after dusk or in the rain. It is also open weekends and holidays from Memorial Day into November, weather permitting. Price is $3.50 for a single ride, $8.75 for a one and a half hour ride, and $12.00 for a five-ride book. Group rates are available on request. In the first few months after its opening in the spring of 1977, over 30,000 people used the Alpine Slide.

THE MOUNTAIN RESORT
Jiminy Peak

Jiminy Peak, a famous ski area with 24 slopes and trails, operates five lifts by day and three by night from mid-November to April, thanks to its extensive snowmaking and lighting. It also features mountainside patios, a ski shop, a health club, and four restaurants and cafeterias. Follow signs off Route 43 or 7 in Hancock. Telephone: 413/738-5500 or 458-5500.

• **Birch Acres** is a 130-acre nudist resort in Hancock.

• First settled in 1790, **Hancock Shaker Village** is a restored original Shaker community based on the utopian ideal that men and women should work and live separately but contribute equally to the commmunity. The settlement was organized according to the Shakers' four fundamental principles: separation from the world, common property, confession of sin, and celibacy. Except for trading some herbs and remedies with the outside world, they were mainly self-sufficient. The village stands amidst 1,000 acres of unspoiled woodland and contains 20 fascinating buildings, including the famous Round Stone Barn, brick Dwelling House, Sisters' and Brethren's shops, Ministry Wash House, tan and ice houses, printing office, cemetery, schoolhouse, Meeting House, laundry and machine shop, plus an herb garden and farm. Craftspeople demonstrate 19th century craft techniques. Guides are stationed throughout the buildings. Hancock Shaker Village is certified as a Massachusetts Historic Landmark, registered as a National Historic Landmark, and is operated today by a nonprofit educational organization. Its open season is Memorial Day weekend through October 31 and is open daily from 9:30 a.m. to 5:00 p.m. Admission is $6.50 for adults, $2.50 for children, with special group rates available. There are picnic facilities in addition to the village shop. Situated at the junction of Route 20 and Route 41, the village is five miles west of Pittsfield. Telephone: 413/443-0188. Write PO Box 898, Pittsfield, MA 01202.

• **Historic American Buildings in Hancock** include:
Hancock Shakers, U.S. Route 20 (see Hancock Shaker Village)
Hancock Shakers' Brethren's Shop
Hancock Shakers' Dairy and Weave Shop
Hancock Shakers' Main Dwelling
Hancock Shakers' Meeting House
Hancock Shakers' Ministry's Shop
Hancock Shakers' Round Barn
Hancock Shakers' Shop, Laundry, and Waterworks
Hancock Shakers' Sisters Shop
Hancock Shakers' Tan Shop
Hancock Shakers' Trustees' Building
Hancock Shakers' Wash House

• **Smith Mountain,** where the Taconic Skyline Trail crosses Lebanon Springs Road, is a great spot for hikers and picnickers. Drive west on West Street from its junction with Route 9 at the Pittsfield Common to Lebanon Springs Road.

HINSDALE, Massachusetts
Population: 1,749 Zip Code: 01235

• Hinsdale's history has included the textile industry, sheep raising and a brief spell in 1895 when gold was thought to have been discovered there. Today there is an emphasis on tourism. Hinsdale is remarkable for its large number of summer camps—more than any other town in the Berkshires.

Trips and trivia:
• **Ashmere Lake** on Route 143 and Plunkett Lake at Lions Club Beach, reached via Church Street and Long View Avenue, has favorite swimming spots.
• **Atelier Stritch Art Gallery** at Shady Villa, a 1819 house on Maple Street, features the artist's own paintings and sculpture. Telephone: 413/655-8804.
• The grave of **Israel Bissell,** who retraced Paul Revere's famous ride to Philadelphia in 1776, is found at the Hinsdale Cemetery.
• The town's most famous native son is **Francis Warren** (1844-1929), two times Republican governor of Wyoming Territory, father-in-law of General John "Black Jack" Pershing, the Wyoming cattle baron.

LANESBORO, Massachusetts
Population: 3,327 Zip Code: 01237

• Said to be named for the Countess of Lanesborough, England, who was a friend of the Massachusetts' governor. Lanesboro is a suburb of Pittsfield.

Trips and trivia:
- **Balance Rock,** on Balance Rock Road, is a huge rock (25 feet by 15 feet by 10 feet) resting on a small stone, balanced on a small point.
- **Constitution Hill,** built by the town founder in honor of Jonathan Smith, a local spokesman for ratification of the Constitution, is located in the center of town.
- The First Baptist Church, now called the **Federated Church,** was built c. 1827. It is located on Summer Street at Route 7 and has been designated a Historic American Building.
- There are many **picnic areas** along Route 7, and some interesting caves to be found throughout the town.
- The old **Registry of Deeds Building,** on the site of the first meeting house, can be found on Route 7. Dating to c. 1827 like the church, it can be visited by appointment only. (Historic American Building)

LEE, Massachusetts
Population: 6,319   Zip Code: 01238

- Lee was incorporated in April 1777 and became a town six months later, naming itself for General Charles Lee, who at that time was reputed to be the best officer in the American army. It retained the name even after Lee was dismissed from Washington's troops in 1780 for disobedience and disrespect. The town is located in the geographical center of Berkshire County, at the junction of the Housatonic and Tyringham Valleys.

Trips and trivia:
- **Berkshire Scenic Railway** is a not-for-profit museum that operates over a portion of the historic New Haven Housatonic Valley Line with vintage railroad equipment. Passengers may board at Lee, Great Barrington, Stockbridge, or Housatonic, which is a flag stop; simply signal the engineer. The 30-mile excursion follows the Housatonic River, with views of historic mills, waterfalls, rapids, bridges, meadows, mountains, and wetlands abounding in wild flowers. There are two daily round-trips, rain or shine, from Memorial Day weekend through October, at 10:30 a.m. and 2:00 p.m., weekends and holidays. The 6:00 p.m. Cabaret Special is on Friday evenings during July and August. Adults $7.00, seniors $6.00, children (5 to 12) $4.00; group rates available. Contact PO Box 298, Lee, MA. Telephone: 413/243-2872.
- Check out the lovely **Congregational Church,** which dates from 1857 and is located on Park Place. Its walls and ceilings were decorated in fresco by an itinerant German painter.
- **Ferncliff** on Orchard Street is the location of Peter's Cave, the hiding place of Peter Wilcox, Jr., who was condemned to die for his participation in Shays' Rebellion; he was captured but eventually pardoned.
- There are many interesting **houses** in town. The first frame one was built on the banks of Hop Brook by Isaac Davis in 1760. The Lee Library marks the spot of Peter Wilcox's house, where the first town meeting was held. The first two-story house in Lee was the Red Lion Tavern, built in 1778. Many of the early houses were destroyed by the flood of 1886 when the dam at Mud Pond burst.
- Lee Chamber of Commerce maintains an **information booth** in the park on Main Street from late June through Labor Day, as it has been doing since 1940. The schedule: Tuesday, Wednesday, and Thursday from 1:00 p.m. to 5:00 p.m.; Friday and Saturday 10:00 a.m. to 8:00 p.m.; closed Sunday and Monday.

- **Merrell Tavern** on Main Street in South Lee was built during the American Federal period of 1810-15. Owned by the Society for the Preservation of New England Antiquities until 1981, the original structure consisted of the first two floors built as a home by Joseph Whiton. In 1871, the Merrell family turned it into a tavern and kept it for 60 years. A third-floor ballroom and front porch were added in 1837 in the then-popular Greek Revival style. The building was run as a tea room during the Depression, and today it is owned by Charles and Faith Reynolds, Innkeepers. Telephone: 413/243-1794.

• **October Mountain State Forest,** located in Lee and Lenox, is the state's largest state forest. Its 14,000 acres contain hiking trails and areas for fishing, hunting, snowmobiling, and campsites.

• Lime and marble **quarries** are found on Marble Street. Marble in Lee was first quarried in the latter part of the 18th century. Almost one million dollars worth of marble was shipped to Washington in the middle of the 19th century for the expansion of the Capitol. Of superior quality, Lee marble also was used for St. Patrick's Cathedral in New York City, City Hall in Philadelphia, and headstones for soldiers at Arlington Cemetery.

• In 1942 **Queen Wilhelmina,** exiled from her native Netherlands, chose the John B. Lloyd estate on Stockbridge Road as a summer home for her daughter and two grandchildren, a choice that caused quite a bit of local excitement.

LENOX, Massachusetts
Population: 5,718   Zip Code: 01240

Named for Charles Lenox, the third Duke of Richmond, friend of the colonists, who pronounced himself in favor of universal suffrage. Lenox today calls itself "The Town for All Seasons."

Trips and trivia:

• **Bellefontaine,** at 91 Kemble Street, is the former estate of Giraud Foster, inventor of clothing snaps; he built it in 1898 at a cost of $2.5 million, designing it after the Petit Trianon at Versailles. The original estate was over 400 acres of beautifully gardened terraces, employing nearly 100 servants while in full operation during the "Great Gatsby" era. There is talk that the "ghost of Bellefontaine" still haunts the beautiful woods and winding paths around the property.

• Founded in 1946, **Berkshire Country Day School** is located on Route 183 between Lenox and Stockbridge (mailing address: Box 867, Lenox, MA 01240). It is a coeducational day school for preschool through grade 9 for some 200 students. Its 23-acre campus and six buildings (once Brook Farm of the famed Shadowbrook estate, at one time the largest summer "cottage" in the country) are used in summer for a six-week remedial session; day camps for children four to twelve; and one week of intensive workshops for teachers. Telephone: 413/637-0755.

• **The Bible Speaks,** part of a worldwide Christian ministry, is located at 40 Kemble Street. Focusing on biblical literature and pastoral and Christian service, it operates Stevens School of the Bible. Telephone: 413/637-1520.

• The **Church on the Hill** is a famous landmark dating to 1805.

• **Hawthorne College,** where American novelist Nathaniel Hawthorne wrote several of his books, is on the grounds of Tanglewood.

• **John D. Kennedy Park,** on the grounds of the former Aspinwall Hotel, offers hiking trails and picnicking. It is off Route 7A.

• "For Yoga and Health," **Kripalu Center,** located in the many wings and 400 rooms of a former Jesuit monastery on a hillside overlooking Lake Mahkeenac, offers year-round personal growth workshops, in-depth yoga retreats, or comprehensive training programs. It offers eight ways to experience total relaxation: Kripalu bodywork, polarity therapy, Shiatsu, yoga, facial skin care, foot care/reflexology, a flotation tank, and personal counseling. Accommodations include deluxe or standard/dormitory rooms ranging from $40.00 to $85.00 a day. Write PO Box 793, Lenox, MA. Telephone: 413/637-3280.

• The Lenox Chamber of Commerce maintains an **Information Center** in the historic academy building on Main Street from 10:00 a.m. to 5:00 p.m. daily in the summer months. The year-round mailing address is Box 648, Lenox, MA.

Lenox Library Association
LENOX, MASSACHUSETTS 01240 / (413) 637-0197

• The **Lenox Library** on Main Street, housed in a building erected in 1815 as a county courthouse and library, features a reading room, art gallery, exhibits and displays, and an outdoor garden. The library is on the National Register of Historic Places and is open from June to September; Monday through Saturday from 10:00 a.m. to 5:00 p.m. From October to May it is open Tuesday through Saturday 10:00 a.m. to 5:00 p.m.; Thursday until 8:00 p.m. The library has an extensive music collection,

with listening equipment available.

• **Lenox Memorial** is memorable for the 360-degree view from the fire tower on its summit. Follow directions for the Pleasant Valley Wildlife Sanctuary.

• **Lenox Open House,** an annual event usually held mid-October, features crafts demonstrations, street festivals, artists, and musicians.

• The **Ella Lerner Gallery** on 17 Franklin Street, open 10:00 p.m. to 6:00 p.m. daily year-round, features 19th and 20th century European and American artists' work. Telephone: 413/637-3315.

• Edith Wharton Restoration/**"The Mount"** was the summer estate of the first woman to receive the Pulitzer Prize as the celebrated author of such works as *Ethan Frome, The House of Mirth, The Age of Innocence,* and *The Old Maid.* Built in 1901-2 by Francis L. V. Hoppin, the "cottage" at Plunkett Street offers tours, summer matinees of Wharton's stories, periodic photographic exhibitions, and a book/gift shop. Tours cost $3.50, $2.00 for youth (13 to 18); group discounts are available. It is open May 30 to Labor Day. Telephone: 413/637-1899.

• The **Music Inn** on West Hawthorne Street calls itself "The Berkshire Performance and Entertainment Center," and features twilight lawn concerts from June to September. For futher details, write PO Box 476, Lenox, MA 01240. Telephone: 413/637-2970.

472 West Mountain Road
Lenox, Massachusetts 01240

Massachusetts Audubon Society

Berkshire Sanctuaries

• **Pleasant Valley Wildlife Sanctuary,** 720 acres of the Massachusetts Audubon Society, offers hiking trails, fields, beaver ponds, streams, and a trailside museum of natural history. Sanctuary grounds are open dawn to dusk daily except Mondays. The museum is open daily from 10:00 a.m. to 4:00 p.m. during the summer; weekends only in the spring and fall. Admission is $2.00 for adults, $1.00 for children and persons over 60. The sanctuary can be reached on Route 7 opposite the Holiday Inn in Lenox, onto West Dugway Road at the sign. Telephone: 413/637-0320.

• **Tanglewood,** the summer home of the Boston Symphony Orchestra, currently under the direction of Seiji Ozawa, Music Director, is renowned as the oldest major music festival in the U.S. Founded in 1934, the concerts take place on a 210-acre estate with enclosed seating in the Shed and room on the lawn for music lovers to sit on blankets. Boston Symphony Orchestra concerts are scheduled Friday and Saturday evenings and Sunday afternoons during July and August, and chamber music concerts take place most Thursdays and selected weekends. Admission to the lawn is $6.00 (on sale two hours before each concert), while tickets to a theatre-concert hall performance cost $50.00 for a box seat for a special event concert in the Shed, with a wide variety of price options in between. For further information and a free schedule of summer events, write Tanglewood c/o Lenox, MA 01240. Telephone: 413/637-1940 June through August; September through May write Symphony Hall, 301 Massachusetts Ave., Boston, MA 02115. Telephone: 617/266-1492. Tanglewood can be reached from New York via the Taconic State Parkway or New York throughway or from the Massachusetts Turnpike, exits 1 or 2. Signs are clearly marked, and ample free parking is available on the grounds. For concert information May through August, call the Tanglewood concert line. Telephone: 413/627-1666.

MONTEREY, Massachusetts
Population: 758   Zip Code: 01245

Named for the American victory at Monterey during the Mexican War, Monterey today blends recreation with the arts in the typical Berkshire tradition.

Trips and trivia:
- The town's many **artists and artisans** include Leonard Weber, whose paintings in all media can be found at the Hayloft Art Gallery; Fred Lancome, who shows his sculpture at his Sun-Side Inn; Fred Leuch, whose stained glass is seen in many neighboring homes; and Alan and Sharon Steinberg, who have the Stone Mountain Workshop, a pottery and weaving studio-gallery in their home. Telephone: 413/528-4115.
- **Beartown State Forest** off of Route 23 has facilities for boating, fishing, hiking, hunting, camping, swimming, and picnicking. Telephone: 415/528-0904.
- **Bidwell Park,** just off the village center on the banks of Konkapot Rivers, is a nice spot for picnics.
- The Berkshire National **Fish Hatchery** on Hatchery Road, between Routes 23 and 57, is open for free visits 8:00 a.m. to 4:00 p.m. weekdays. Operated by the U.S. Fish and Wildlife Service, it is one of the most important Atlantic salmon hatcheries in the Northeast. Telephone: 413/528-4461.
- Monterey is located on the scenic General **Knox Trail.** In 1976, the Bicentennial reenactment of General Knox's winter trek from New York to Boston to bring cannons for General Washington included an overnight stop in Monterey. In honor of the 200 years, the town built a historical museum wing onto its library.
- **Lake Garfield's** swimming beach can be reached by Tyringham Road at Kinne's Grove off Route 23. Boats are available for rent, and admission is free. There are also swimming and picnicking at Beartown's Lake Buel, plus good hiking territory along the Appalachian Trail there.
- The rural atmosphere of the town is enhanced by the Langdon Store, established in 1780. At sap time the **Monterey Maplers** produce maple syrup in the old tradition. The town meeting of 1968 was filmed for Japanese television to show the workings of a typical New England democratic government.

MOUNT WASHINGTON, Massachusetts
Population: 78

Located in the extreme southwest corner of Massachusetts, Mount Washington has the smallest population of any Bay State town, but can boast one of its most spectacular sights. For many years it was known as the first town to vote in presidential elections.

Trips and trivia:
- **Bash Bish Falls State Forest,** located in a deep gorge adjoining Taconic State Park, has dual streams of water gushing down from a high rocky cliff into a small wilderness pool. This gorge is the actual tri-state demarcation point. The waterfall can be reached most easily from the New York State side (Copake Falls, off Route 22), then followed by foot. If you're the adventuresome type and want to walk on the rocks, bring sneakers.

NEW ASHFORD, Massachusetts
Population: 160

- Known at various times for its valuable quarries of blue and white marble, or as the spot where humorist Josh Billings summered, New Ashford today is mainly a quiet farming community.

Trips and trivia:
- The **Berkshire Indoor Tennis Club** on Route 7 welcomes guests on its four sport-face courts from October to May. Telephone: 413/458-9577.
- **Red Bat Cave,** four chambers 100-feet long and 150-feet deep, named for the tiny redheaded bats found on its walls, has been coverted to a house.

NEW MARLBORO, Massachusetts
Population; 1,087

Gunpowder and paper were once important industries in New Marlboro's principal village, Mill River. New Marlboro itself was a stop on the famous Red Bird Stagecoach line.

Trips and trivia:
- **Campbell Falls,** off of Route 272, is one of the most spectacular sights to behold; the Whiting River drops over a split-rock ledge into a 100-foot gulch.
- **Cookson Property,** on Route 183, has an access from Blackberry Pond, and has fishing, hiking, horseback riding, skiing, and hunting facilities.
- The Lieutenant **Harmon House,** built in the early 19th century, has been designated a Historic American Building.
- The **Kolburne School, Inc.,** at Southfield Road is a private coeducational residential treatment center for emotionally disturbed and learning disabled children and adolescents, ages 7 to 21. Approximately 120 children are enrolled in the 12-month psycho-educational program. Telephone: 413/229-8787.
- **Tipping Rock** on Rock Ledge, just southwest of Southfield, is a 40-ton boulder balanced so precariously that pressure of the hand will actually sway but not dislodge it. It is located on private property.

NORTH ADAMS, Massachusetts
Population: 18,424   Zip Code: 01247

The only city located on the Mohawk Trail, North Adams is both a good base from which to make trips throughout the Berkshires and a fascinating place for the tourist.

Trips and trivia:

• Each year North Adams sponsors a **Fall Foliage Festival** at the end of September or the beginning of October, depending on the conditions.

• **Fort Massachusetts,** one of a chain of forts built during the mid-18th century by the Massachusetts Bay Colony to protect early settlers from frequent attack by Indians, is located on Route 2; it was the only portion of land in the state taken under conquest for the French government by General deVaudreuil in 1746.

• The **Gunboat Monitor** of Civil War fame is located on West Main Street. The Monitor Monument marks the site of the Beckley Iron Furnace, the foundry that made the plates for the gunboat, the first iron-clad vessel to be used in the U.S. The *Monitor* was sunk during a storm off Cape Hatteras on New Year's Eve, 1862.

• **Houghton Memorial Library-Blackinton Mansion** on Church Street was built in the late 19th century in the Second Empire or Grant Style for industrialist Sanford Blackinton. It was later purchased by the city's first mayor, Albert C. Houghton, and donated to the city for use as a library. Inside are many lovely antiques and finishing touches.

• North Adams made the *Guiness Book of World Records* under the food feat of "greatest amount of **ice cream** ever consumed at one sitting" when Ronald Long of that town had 51 scoops of Friendly Ice Cream on May 2, 1975.

• The Charles H. **McCann Technical School** at Hodges Crossroad is a trade and technical school of approximately 430 undergraduates and 90 graduates. Admissions are competitive to this first regional vocational school in the commonwealth. Telephone: 413/663-5383.

• New England's **Natural Bridge,** located on Route 8 at the foot of the Mohawk Trail (with plenty of signs guiding you there), is the only natural marble water-eroded bridge in North America. It is said to be about 550 million years old. A 60-foot chasm winds through 475 feet of rock formation with numerous potholes and fractures along the walls. At an elevation of 1,100 feet above sea level, the bridge and chasm depict marine life from the early Cambrian and Ordovician periods of geography in the U.S. The marble formation, made of mud, sand, and sea shells, dates to pre-Cambrian times when the earth was created. The marble dam, the erosion-worn potholes, the glacial striations, and the 30-foot waterfall down the startling white rock inspired Nathaniel Hawthorne to enter this description in his "American Notebook" of 1838: "The cave makes a fresh impression upon me every time I visit it . . ." Now owned by the Commonwealth of Massachusetts, Natural Bridge is open daily from 10:00 a.m. to 6:00 p.m. on weekdays and from 10:00 a.m. to 8:00 p.m. weekends and holidays from May 15 to October 30. There is plenty of parking ($3.00 per car). A Junior Ranger Program is available for youths ages 10 to 14. Telephone: 413/663-6392.

north adams state college
north adams, massachusetts, 01247

• **North Adams State College** on Church Street (Telephone: 413/664-4511) provides a multifaceted curriculum for its approximately 2,100 full-time undergraduates and nearly 600 part-time graduate and continuing education students. A fully accredited, co-educational institution of higher education, it was established in 1894. The college offers a number of unique programs, including the recently created College Resource Center and its long-running Winter Study Program. More information on the college is available by writing or calling the Director of Admissions.

Expanding the Berkshire Economy

- The **Northern Berkshire Chamber of Commerce,** located at 69 Main Street, maintains an information booth at Union Street (Route 2, Mohawk Trail) that is open from June through October. Telephone: 413/663-3735.

- A nonprofit organization funded in part by the **Northern Berkshire Council of the Arts** (12 Berkshire Plaza) brings arts resources to the schools and community. Its program includes an Arts & Crafts Fair in July, summer outdoor concerts, children's performances, and an evening performance series. Hours are Monday through Friday 9:00 a.m. to 5:00 p.m. Telephone: 413/663-3651.
- **Pine Cobble,** with a panoramic view that takes in Mt. Williams, Mt. Greylock, the New York Taconics, and the towns of North Adams and Williamstown, is one mile west of the North Adams-Williamstown line off of Route 2.

- Celebrating the city's proud industrial past, **Western Gateway Heritage State Park** is located at 9 Furnace Street Bypass/Route 8. Telephone: 413/663-6312. Developed and maintained by the Department of Environmental Management, it comprises seven acres of land and 43,000 square feet of building space. In an area known as the "Freight Yard," the park has six turn-of-the-century wood frame warehouses restored to house restaurants, specialty shops, and a visitors' center. Children can ride through the freightyard on a miniature train, complete with locomotive, weather permitting, May through October. The park is open Friday through Wednesday 10:00 a.m. to 6:00 p.m., Thursday 10:00 a.m. to 9:00 p.m. Admission is free.
- **Windsor Lake** is a free city-run swimming area in Historic Valley Park, reached via Bradley Street from North Adams State College or by Kemp Avenue from East Main Street. It is supervised daily from 10:00 a.m. to 8:00 p.m.

OTIS, Massachusetts
Population: 898   Zip Code: 10253

In 1810, the town decided to name itself for American statesman Harrison Gray Otis, Speaker of the House, delegate to the Hartford Convention, U.S. Senator, and mayor of Boston in the early 18th century.

Trips and trivia:
- In honor of the **Bicentennial,** Otis published its *History of Otis, Massachusetts: 1773-1899,* which is available at Town Hall.
- The **Otis Reservoir** at Tolland State Forest can be reached from Route 8 south of Otis Center. The above-mentioned book gives an interesting account of the reservoir's beginnings.
- **Otis State Forest** on Route 23 offers recreational boating, fishing, hunting, snowmobiling, hiking, skiing, and horseback riding trails.
- The **Pyenson Family** in town, owners of the Otis Poultry Farm on Route 8, offers tours of their "eggcentric" facilities. Telephone: 413/269-4438.
- The home of *Squire Filley,* noted lawyer and member of the legislature, dates to 1800.
- There are some interesting churches in Otis. **St. Paul's Episcopal Church** (1828), one of the earliest churches of the Anglican Faith in Berkshire County, is noted for the beautiful simplicity of its Gothic design. Also, don't miss the First Congregational Church in the Center Village.
- **Tolland Otis State Forest** on Routes 23 and 8 has facilities for boating, swimming, hiking, fishing, skiing, snowmobiling, horseback riding, and picnicking.

PERU, Massachusetts
Population: 464

The highest inhabited town in the commonwealth, Peru reaches a height of 2,064 feet at its center, on the Green Mountain Range.

Trips and trivia:
- **Peru State Forest** on Route 143 offers fishing, hiking, hunting, snowmobiling, and skiing.
- At one point in the early 1800s, Peru's poor people were sold off at **public auction!**
- When it **rains** on the Congregational Church in Peru, water on the west side drains off into the Housatonic River, while rain on the east side goes into the Connecticut River.
- The Dorothy Frances **Rice Sanctuary** on South Road, off of Route 143 in the center of town, offers 273 acres of woodland walking trails that are enjoyed by birdwatching enthusiasts. Owned by the New England Forestry Foundation, the sanctuary is free to the public, but contributions are appreciated. It is open daily from the end of May to mid-October.

PITTSFIELD, Massachusetts
Population: 55,299   Zip Code: 01201

Named for British statesman William Pitts, Pittsfield is

located in the center of Berkshire County, seven miles from the New York State border on the west and 150 miles from both New York City and Boston.

Trips and trivia:

• **Arrowhead,** the home of Herman Melville, author of Moby Dick, from 1850-1863, is located at 780 Holmes Road, accessible off of Routes 7 and 20. Designated a registered National Historic Landmark, Arrowhead is headquarters of the Berkshire County Historical Society. It features a collection of South Seas artifacts and other Melville mementos. The museum is open Memorial Day weekend through October 31, Monday through Saturday 10:00 a.m. to 5:00 p.m. Sundays, 11:00 a.m. to 3:30 p.m.; otherwise by appointment only. There is an admission charge of $3.00 for adults, $2.50 for senior citizens, $1.50 for students; free to members. Telephone: 413/442-1793.

serving the entire Berkshire area. Founded in 1960, it is the first of 15 such colleges operated by the commonwealth. In 1971, it moved to its current location, a 180-acre campus with nine buildings around a central core: the Ralph Hoffmann Environmental Center, Koussevitzky Arts Center (with a 500-seat theater said to be the finest one in Western Massachusetts), and the Jonathan Edwards Library. In 1984, BCC opened its South County Center in Great Barrington. There are currently more than 3,000 students attending day and evening classes. It is accredited by the New England Association of Schools and Colleges. Telephone: 413/449-4660.

• **The Berkshire Athenaeum,** Pittsfield's Public Library, is a modern structure at 1 Wendell Avenue, near Park Square. It features the **Herman Melville Memorial Room** with books, photographs, and personal memorabilia of the American novelist. The museum is open Monday, Wednesday, Friday, and Saturday from 10:00 a.m. to 5:00 p.m. Tuesday and Thursday from 10:00 a.m. to 9:00 p.m., with evening hours subject to change. Telephone: 413/499-9480.

• **Berkshire Community College** (BCC) on West Street is a two-year comprehensive community college

• Berkshire County's Museum of Art, Natural History, and History, the **Berkshire Museum,** located at 39 South Street in the center of Pittsfield on U.S. Route 7, has been free to the public since its founding in 1903 by Zenas Crane of nearby Dalton, Massachusetts. The permanent collection features a strong selection of American 19th century landscapes and portraits, early American abstract painting and sculpture, English and European Old Masters, and objects from ancient civilizations. The natural history galleries offer exhibits on birds, mammals, reptiles, shells, biology and minerals, and includes 15 Louis Paul Jonas dioramas of *Animals of the World in*

Miniature. A newly opened aquarium presents a variety of aquatic ecosystems from around the world, ranging from the county's own Housatonic River to an Atlantic tidepool or Amazon River Basin. In addition, the museum maintains an active education department, presents first-run foreign and American films throughout the summer, and a year-round program of concerts, performances, lectures, films, workshops, trips, and classes. The museum shop is auxiliary-run. Supported by endowments, gifts, grants, and memberships ($15.00 individual, $25.00 family, and $50.00 sustaining), the museum is open Tuesday through Saturday, 10:00 a.m. to 5:00 p.m., Sundays, 1:00 p.m. to 5:00 p.m. It is closed Mondays except in July and August, plus holidays. Telephone: 413/443-7171.

- **Canoe Meadows Wildlife Sanctuary** at Holmes Road is a Massachusetts Audubon Society sanctuary consisting of 257 acres of fields, woods, ponds, and marshes. The trails are open year-round from 9:00 a.m. to dusk, daily except Monday. Admission is $1.00 for adults. Telephone: 413/637-0320.
- The **Central Berkshire Chamber of Commerce** operates an information booth, run by retired senior volunteers, daily except Sunday 10:00 a.m. to 5:00 p.m. June through September at Park Square.
- **General Electric,** the largest single employer in the area, is open for plant tours. Telephone: 413/494-1110.
- In addition to Arrowhead, the Berkshire County Historical Society also maintains the Major Butler **Goodrich House** (1793) at 823 North Street on Route 7. Preserved as a furnished historic house, the museum is open Thursday through Sunday, 1:00 p.m. to 4:00 p.m. during July and August, otherwise by appointment only. Another project is **Headquarters House** (1855) at 113 E. Housatonic Street, which is open year-round.
- **Historic American Buildings** in Pittsfield include:
  1. Arrowhead (also called the Bush-Melville House), built 1794, originally a tavern, then owned by Melville.
  2. William Brattle, Jr. House, 626 Williams Street, built 1762.
  3. Bulfinch Church, corner of North Street and Maple Avenue, built in 1789-93, with Charles Bulfinch the architect.
  4. Colt-Pingree House, built early 19th century.
  5. First Bank Building, 800 East Street, built in 1806.
  6. Peace Party House, corner of East Street and Wendell Avenue, built mid-18th century.
  7. West Park School, corner West Street and Churchill Street, built early 19th century.

- **Miss Hall's School.** Established in 1898, this is a preparatory boarding and day school for girls and is located on Holmes Road in Pittsfield. The school is a successor to an earlier institution (founded 1806) that was the first boarding school for girls incorporated in Massachusetts. It offers a fully accredited, traditional education for 210 students from 24 states and 11 foreign countries. Telephone: 413/443-6401. Contact Daniel G. Lee, Jr., Headmaster.
- **Holmesdale,** a private home on Holmes Road, is the former residence of Dr. Wendell Holmes.
- The **Site of the Old Elm** in Park Square is marked by a sundial; under its branches have stood such famous people as Longfellow, Hawthorne, Holmes, Melville, and Lafayette. At its location much of the history of Pittsfield has taken place: celebrations, mustering and honoring of soldiers, and general announcements of crucial importance of the townspeople.
- **Onota and Pontoosuc Lakes,** both have free municipal beaches with supervision and are open summers 10:00 a.m. to 8:00 p.m. daily. Pontoosuc charges $.75 for non-Pittsfield cars on weekends. Follow the signs from the center of town.
- The **Pittsfield Historical Commission** is located at 14 Kenwood Street. Telephone: 413/445-5039.
- **Pittsfield State Forest,** Cascade Street from Churchill off West, is marked by signs. Swimming, picnicking, hiking, and nature trails are available. Don't miss Berry Mountain's pond, the highest body of water in the state (2,000 feet), resplendent in azaleas and blueberries in season. Fees are charged for picnic tables or campsites.
- The **Department of Public Park and Recreation Programs** in Pittsfield maintains a wide and varied program including everything from archery to square dancing for senior citizens. Telephone: 413/448-8274. It sponsors **band concerts** during the summer months at Park Square, Pontoosuc and Onota Lakes, and Springside Park, Mardi Gras and Halloween parades, city-wide Easter Egg Hunts, Christmas Tree Lighting, Memorial and Veterans' Day observances, and Firemen's Muster in July. There are year-round programs for the **elderly,** including a Drop-In Center at 349 North Street (open Monday through Friday 9:30 a.m. to 4:30 p.m. Saturday 11:00 p.m. to 4:30 p.m. Golden Age Club meetings Tuesdays at 2:00 p.m. at the Center, and special group activities. A **Children's Zoo** is located at Springside Park, open from mid-April to mid-October. In addition, hiking and bird-watching are available at **Brattlebrook's** 148 acres; **Wild Acres** has picnic facilities and a stocked trout pond for children ages 6 to 14 and is open daily from 7:00 a.m. to sunset. Playgrounds, including a special playground at Highland School that accommodates handicapped children, are open during the summer months at 10:00 a.m. Beaches and pools daily from 12:00 p.m. to 8:00 p.m.
- **South Mountain,** at an elevation of 1,870 feet, is located one mile south of Pittsfield on Routes 7 and 20.
- Situated on a wooded slope in the midst of the Berkshires, **South Mountain's Concert Hall** has been the scene of distinguished music since 1918. The hall, famous for its acoustics, is listed in the National Registry of Historic Buildings. Among the internationally renowned

South Mountain Association
Box Twenty-three
Pittsfield, Massachusetts 01202

artists that have appeared here are Leonard Bernstein, Alexander Schneider, Leontyne Price, Rudolf Serkin, the Juilliard Quartet, the Guarneri Quartet, Gary Graffman, and the Beaux Arts Trio. South Mountain also arranges Young Audiences Concerts in the Berkshires, which are annually attended by over 10,000 students. Musical programs of the nonprofit educational organization are maintained by tax-deductible contributions. For more information, contact the **South Mountain Association**, Box 23, Pittsfield, MA. Telephone: 413/442-2106.

RICHMOND, Massachusetts
Population: 1,689   Zip Code: 01254

Like the town of Lenox, Richmond is named for Charles Lenox, the third Duke of Richmond, who was a defender of rights of colonists.

Trips and trivia:
- **Peirson Place** (1790) and Kenmore (1792), both on Route 41, are handsome Georgian houses open in the summer as guest houses.
- The 1,003-foot **Richmond Furnace** was named for the large iron smelter that operated in the town until 1922. The remains of the stone furnace exist, but are now in private hands and not open to the public except by special request.
- **Steven's Glen,** a deep ravine with a brook running through it, is also now privately owned.
- There are fine **views** of distant mountains from side roads east and west of the valley through which Route 41 runs.

SANDISFIELD, Massachusetts
Population: 660   Zip Code: 01255

- Originally an industrial town for the manufacture of clothing, Sandisfield is the largest township in Berkshire County, with many fine old houses along its streets. Rumor holds that it is really a "ghost town," that it doesn't really exist, as Sandisfield proper is hard to find.

Trips and trivia:
- The **New Boston Inn** is a town landmark, one of America's oldest continuing hostelries—dating back to the 1750s.

- The **Sandisfield Historical Society** holds its monthly meetings in The Meeting House (1909), the fourth edifice constructed by the Congregational Society which first organized in Sandisfield in 1756. It is located on Sandy Brook Turnpike in South Sandisfield. For more information, contact Myrtal A. Mazzaferro, President, at PO Box 74, Sandisfield, MA 01255. Telephone: 413/258-4438.
- **Sandisfield State Forest** on Route 57 has facilities for boating, swimming, hunting, picnicking, fishing, skiing, and horseback riding. York Lake is a special feature.
- The Christmas carol "It Came Upon a Midnight Clear" was written in 1849 by native Edmund H. **Sears,** the Unitarian clergyman who was editor of "Religious Magazine and Monthly Review."
- **Spectacle Pond** on Cold Spring Road has picnic tables available.
- **West Lake Recreation Area** on West Road offers fishing, hunting, horseback riding, skiing, boating, and snowmobiling.

SAVOY, Massachusetts
Population: 467   Zip Code: 01256

Savoy, whose chief export is Christmas trees, is generally associated with all the woodland it encompasses.

Trips and trivia:
- **Savoy Mountain State Forest** actually covers Savoy, Florida, North Adams, and Adams in over 11,300 acres. Accessible from Route 2 in Florida or Route 116 in Savoy, the forest is a fisherman's dream, with four ponds and numerous streams, including campsites at the South Park area. The fire tower on **Borden Mountain** provides a spectacular view. Also of note in the forest are Tannery Falls and Balance Rock on Tannery Road.
- **Spruce Hill** (Mount Busby) is also part of the thousands of acres of woodland to be found in Savoy. Follow signs from Route 2 to the Savoy State Forest sign, then go right onto Shaft Road nearly three miles to the North Pond Recreation Area.
- In **winter** Savoy offers cross-country skiing and snowmobiling over many miles of trails and unplowed roads.

SHEFFIELD, Massachusetts
Population: 2,723   Zip Code: 01257

The only town in the Bay State with two *covered bridges* (both spanning the Housatonic River), Sheffield was the first town chartered in Berkshire County.

Trips and trivia:

• The oldest complete house in Berkshire County is the **Colonel John Ashley House** on Copper Hill Road in Ashley Falls. Built in 1735, the house has "unexcelled original Early American paneling and furnishings of the period" in a restored and preserved house. Maintained by the Trustees of Reservations, as is the nearby Bartholomew's Cobble, the house is open from Memorial Day to Columbus Day, Saturday through Sunday, 1:00 p.m. to 5:00 p.m.; Wednesday through Sunday, 1:00 p.m. to 5:00 p.m. in July and August. Some of the furnishings include pottery, tools, kitchen utensils, and furniture. An herb garden grows next to the house. Colonel Ashley was a pioneer, lawyer, officer in the French and Indian wars, legislator, judge, and patriot who furnished iron and supplies during the American Revolution. In 1781, the slave Mum Bett fled from this house and won her suit for independence. By dropping his appeal, Colonel Ashley was the first in Massachusetts to recognize abolition by the new state constitution. The house is reached via Routes 7 and 7A to Ashley Falls center; follow signs west one mile. An admission fee is charged for the guided tour. Telephone: 413/229-8600.

• Located west off Route 7 in the village of Ashley Falls in Sheffield Township is the charming sanctuary of **Bartholomew's Cobble.** A National Natural Landmark, the reservations' 277 acres form a wild rock garden where many rare ferns and flowers are kept in a natural state. Bordering the winding Housatonic River at the southern end of the Berkshire County, the sanctuary features marble and quartzite over 500 million years old, seven miles of hiking trails, the Bailey Museum of Natural History (open daily 9:00 a.m. to 5:00 p.m. except Monday and Tuesday), and areas of picnicking and bird-watching. The reservation is open daily April 15 through October 15, 9:00 a.m. to 5:00 p.m., with a warden-naturalist available daily except Monday and Tuesday to interpret the plants, geology, and wildlife of the area. As its purpose is the preservation of scenic, scientific, educational, and conservation goals, Bartholomew's Cobble encourages nature study and recreational enjoyment on its premises. The Trustees of Reservations own and operate the Cobble and adjacent Colonel Ashley House. There are guided group tours on request by advance reservation; admission is charged. Follow the signs west from Ashley Falls. Telephone: 413/229-8600.

• **Berkshire School,** an independent coeducational, college-preparatory school for boarding and day students grades 9-12, currently enrolls approximately 265 boys and 165 girls. Founded in 1907, it is accredited by the New England Association of Schools and Colleges and is affiliated with Independent Schools Association of Massachusetts and the National Association of Independent Schools. Telephone: 413/229-8511.

• **Historical American Buildings** in Sheffield include:
Colonel John Ashley House, Copper Road, built in 1735 (see above)
General John Ashley House, built early 19th century
The Congregational Church on main Street (1760), also known as "Old Parish Church."
The Parker L. Hall Law Office on Route 7, built c. 1826.

• Cows at the **Riverlea Milk Farm** in Sheffield are milked each day from 8:00 a.m. to 9:00 a.m. and 5:00 p.m. to 6:00 p.m.—a stopover the kids will adore.

• **Westenhook Gallery** on Route 7 features graphics, paintings, photographs, sculpture, crafts, miniatures, and etchings and seriagraphs of local subjects. It is open daily except Tuesday. Summers 11:00 a.m. to 5:00 p.m., otherwise by appointment. Telephone: 413/229-8101.

STOCKBRIDGE, Massachusetts
Population: 2,228   Zip Code: 01262

At one point called *Wnahktakook,* meaning Great Meadow, by the Indians, Stockbridge was eventually named for an English village. It is perhaps the most popular Berkshire town, due to its wide offering of history, music, theater, and outdoor recreation in a beautifully peaceful setting.

Trips and trivia:

• Beautiful gardens of flowers and trees are free for all to enjoy at the **Berkshire Garden Center** at the junctions of Routes 102 and 183, two miles west of Stockbridge. One of the earliest nonprofit horticultural centers of its kind, the center was incorporated in 1936 with the purpose of "educating its members and the public in the art of enjoyment of growing things." Featured at the garden center are labeled trees and flower shrubs, trial vegetable plots, perennial borders, annuals, rose and rock gardens, naturalistic planting, tuberous begonias, an educational greenhouse, a small greenhouse with exotic plants, a pond area, indoor plant windows, herb-and-garden gift shops. Although there is no admission charge, memberships are encouraged, and members receive the center's quarterly magazine, *Cuttings,* a spring plant distribution, and free admission or discounts to certain lectures and demonstrations. Major events sponsored by the Berkshire Garden Center are its annual antique and flower shows, the Harvest Festival held annually the first Saturday in October, and Open House each fall. The center is open daily May 1 through September 30 from dawn to dusk; the shops and office are open from 10:00 a.m. to 3:00 p.m. Telephone: 413/298-5530.

Berkshire Theatre Festival
Stockbridge ☆ Massachusetts 01262

- The **Berkshire Theatre Festival,** (BTF) on East Main Street, brings the finest American artists to the Berkshires each summer season. The historic Stanford White-designed Playhouse offers four American plays, including an American musical favorite. The Unicorn Theatre features the resident acting company performing new and/or experimental works, and the Children's Theatre is performed out-of-doors, weather permitting. Established in 1928, the BTF is one of the oldest theatres in the country, and the only one dedicated exclusively to American drama. Telephone: 413/298-5536; box office after June 1st: 413/298-5576.
- **Chesterwood** is the 1920s summer estate and studio of American sculptor Daniel Chester French (1850-1931), considered America's foremost traditionalist sculptor. His works, depicting national figures, ideals, and events, reflected the mood of an America emerging as a world power in the late 19th century and early 20th century. His most famous works are the seated Abraham Lincoln in the Memorial in Washington, D. C. (1922) and the Minute Man, North Bridge, Concord, Massachusetts (1875). French also sculpted: John Harvard for the University yard (1884); the bronze doors for the Boston Public Library (1894-1904); the Dupont Memorial Fountain, Washington, D. C. (1921); and Alma Mater for Lower Library, Columbia University (1903). He fashioned the statue of Lincoln at Chesterwood, and the plaster casts for this national symbol still dominate the studio. A property of the National Trust for Historic Preservation and a designated Massachusetts Historic Landmark, Chesterwood provides guided tours of the colonial revival mansion and studio and special exhibits in the barn gallery. Visitors also enjoy strolling through the English-style flower garden and nature walks planned by French and shopping in the Museum Gift Shop. Chesterwood is open daily from 10:00 a.m. to 5:00 p.m. May through October. Admission is $4.00 for adults, $1.00 for youths 6-18, and free to members of the Friends of Chesterwood and the National Trust. Group rates are available. Chesterwood is located off of Route 183 in the Glendale section of Stockbridge; signs mark the route from the west end of Main Street. Telephone: 413/298-3579.
- **Children's Chime Tower** was erected by David Dudley Field as a memorial to his grandchildren. It is the site of the original Indian Mission established in Stockbridge in 1734, where the Reverend John Sergeant taught and preached to the Stockbridge Indians in their own language until Reverend Jonathan Edwards succeeded him at his death in 1749. The chimes were meant to be played "from apple blossom time 'til frost."
- **Historic American Buildings** in Stockbridge include:

  Congregational Church (1824), built by Ralph Bigelow. Located on Main Street, it is the oldest church in Berkshire County. Among its noted ministers was Reverend Jonathan Edwards, the revivalist theologian who wrote "Freedom of the Will" here.

  Mark Hopkins House, built early 18th century.

  Housatonic National Bank, built early to mid-19th century (now the Berkshire Bank & Trust Company).

  Yale-Duryea Walter Mills on Yale Hill, built in 1823 as a grist, planing, and saw mill.
- *Image Gallery* on Main Street features contemporary paintings, graphics, sculpture, and photography in constantly changing one-man shows. Telephone: 413/298-5500.
- An **Indian burial ground,** one mile west on Main Street, is a large obelisk bearing the inscription "The Ancient Burial Place of the Stockbridge Indians, Friends of Our Fathers."
- **Franklin Jones House,** an artist's home and gallery, is available for visiting by appointment. Telephone: 413/298-3275.
- **Nathaniel Hawthorne College,** also called Hawthorne's Little Red House, is on Hawthorne Street near Tanglewood, the place where the famous author collected material for *Tanglewood Tales* and where he wrote several books.
- **The Lenox Arts Center** at Citizens Hall in Interlaken has musical and theatrical premieres weekends from July 4 through mid-August. Telephone: 413/298-9463.

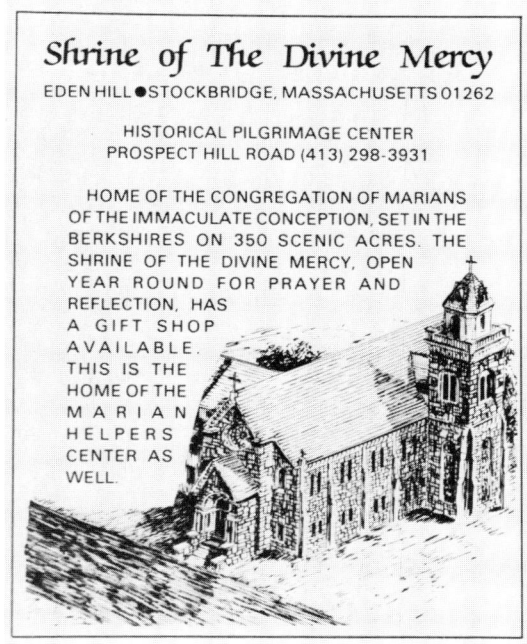

- Shrine of The Divine Mercy on Prospect Hill Road is a historical pilgrimage center for the **Marians of the Immaculate Conception.** Towering atop the crown of the hill on 350 scenic acres, the shrine is open year-round for prayer and reflection. A gift shop is also available. Telephone: 413/298-3931.
- **Merwin House** (also called Tranquility) is located at 39 Main Street in the center of town. Built c. 1825, with an ell added later, the house reflects foreign travel and cultural interests of the 19th century in its furnishings and paintings. The house is the property of the Society for the Preservation of New England Antiquities. Open Tuesday, Thursday, and Saturday afternoons, 1:00 p.m. to 5:00 p.m.; an admission fee is charged.

- **Mission House,** designated as a National Historic Landmark, is located at Main Street and Sergeant Street. Built by the Reverend John Sergeant, first missionary to the Stockbridge Indians, the house is the oldest one in town, dating from 1739. Colonial furnishings, tools and utensils, and gardens in which may be found only plants known to have been grown in the period are all part of the unique charm of the house. It is open from Memorial Day to mid-October, Tuesday through Saturday, 10:00 a.m. to 4:30 p.m. Sunday, 11:00 a.m. to 3:30 p.m. Admission is $3.00 for adults, $1.00 for children. Telephone: 413/298-3239. A property of the Trustees of Reservations, Mission House offers guided tours only.

- **Naumkeag** on Prospect Hill, one-half mile from the center of Stockbridge, is the former estate of Joseph H. Choate, American lawyer and diplomat who was ambassador to England 1899-1905. The house was designed by Stanford White and built in 1885 in a Victorian style. It contains fine antiques, Chinese Lowestoft procelain, and formal gardens with water displays on the grounds. There are guided house tours available for $2.50, garden tours for $2.50, or $4.50 for both. Naumkeag is open May 23 through October 12, Saturday, Sunday, and holidays; June 30 through September 7, Tuesday to Sunday, 10:00 a.m. to 4:15 p.m. The gardens close at 5:00 p.m. There are picnic accommodations available. A property of The Trustees of Reservations. Telephone: 413/298-3239.
- **Austen Riggs Center** on Main Street is noted for its psychiatric research and treatment.

- The **Norman Rockwell Museum at Stockbridge** is the permanent home for the only significant collection of the paintings of Norman Rockwell, the American painter and illustrator famous for his covers of the *Saturday Evening Post.* A magnificent 18th century Georgian house is the home of the collection, which includes the famous *Four Freedoms* and *Main Street of Stockbridge at Christmas.* There is a fully stocked museum shop where books, prints, memorabilia, etc. are available. The museum is open year-round except for Thanksgiving, Christmas, New Year's Day, and Tuesdays from November 1 until Memorial Day. Continuous guided tours are given from 10:00 a.m. to 5:00 p.m. Admission charge is $3.00 for adults; $1.00 for children. Telephone: 413/298-3822.

- **Squaw Peak,** at the summit of Monument Mountain, offers a nice picnic area. Follow signs two and a half miles south from Stockbridge on Route 7.
- The Kiwanis Club of Stockbridge and West Stockbridge maintains an Information Booth on Main Street in the center of town during July and August at these hours: Monday through Wednesday, 11:00 a.m. to 3:00 p.m.; Thursday, 11:00 a.m. to 8:00 p.m.; Friday and Saturday 10:00 a.m. to 8:00 p.m.; and Sunday 12:00 p.m. to 3:00 p.m. The Laurel Hill Association, the oldest village improvement society in the country, has been preserving and improving the beauty of **Stockbridge** since 1853. Each year Laurel Hill's annual meeting features a prominent speaker, the Stockbridge Bowl Association holds an August regatta, and the Berkshire Garden Center holds its flower festival.
- The **Stockbridge Library,** in the center of town on Route 7, is open to the public Tuesday to Saturday, 10:00 a.m. to 5:00 p.m., and contains exhibits in its museum of Stockbridge Indian artifacts, inventions by Anson Clark, and American financier Cyrus W. Field memorabilia. Founded in 1864, the library contains 45,000 volumes. The **Historical Society** of the Stockbridge Library Association is also located on Main Street.
- **St. Paul's Episcopal Church,** on Main Street across from the Red Lion Inn (1834), was designed by the noted architect Charles McKim and features a chancel window by John LaFarge, baptistry by Louis St. Gaudens, and a nave window by Tiffany.
- **St. Joseph's Roman Catholic Church,** on Elm Street, has been the parish church in Stockbridge for over 100 years.
- The **Village Cemetery** on Main Street contains the graves of early settlers, including John Sergeant, Chief Konkapot, and Deacon Peter Puaquannqupeet.

TYRINGHAM, Massachusetts
Population: 328　　　　　　　　　Zip Code: 01264

Lord Howe named the town for Tyringham, England, where he owned an estate. Once an important Shaker community, Tyringham Valley is considered to be one of the most beautiful areas in the Berkshires.

Trips and trivia:
- The book *Daddy Longlegs* was written in what is known as "Orchard House" on Tyringham Main Road.
- **Fernside,** on the west side of the valley, has many of the old Shaker homes located in it, most converted to summer homes.

- **President Taft** used to visit the Valley, and after **Mark Twain** spent the summer of 1903 in Tyringham he decided to donate a complete set of his works to the library there.
- **Tyringham Galleries** and Gingerbread House are located in the former story-book studio of sculptor Sir Henry Hudson Kitson who created the *Minute Man* at Lexington; *The Puritan Maid* at Plymouth; *Music of the Sea* in the Boston Museum of Fine Arts; *Chris* in the Drexel Museum in Philadelphia; *Indian Blessing* at Lebanon Springs, New York; and many memorials found throughout the nation. It is set among beautiful rock and sculpture gardens and woodland trails. Leading contemporary artists are featured by paintings, graphics, glass, sculpture, ceramics, objets d'art, oceanic art, and etchings and lithographs. Open days, 10:00 a.m. to 5:00 p.m. weekends; evenings by appointment. Telephone: 413/243-3260. It is located four miles south of the junction of the Massachusetts Pike and Route 20, four miles along Tyringham Road. Admission to the combination gallery and museum is $.50, children under 12 free. See Santarella Sculpture Gardens and Sickle Shed Antiques.

WASHINGTON, Massachusetts
Population: 486

One of the first towns in the nation to name itself after "The Father of our Country," Washington is situated in the Green Mountain Range at the eastern end of Berkshire County.

Trips and trivia:
- As the United States was celebrating its **Bicentennial,** the town of Washington was preparing for one of its own in 1977. The Congregational Record of May 25, 1977, quotes the Honorable Silvio O. Conte's tribute to the town occasion: "It is the scenic small town, like Washington, Massachusetts, that makes New England the beautiful place that it is."
- Currently, the town's most famous **citizen** is singer Arlo Guthrie, who makes his home there with his family. Actor Wendell Corey used to live there, and his family still maintains a residence in town.
- **Eden Glen** is a popular swimming spot. Other **recreation** can be found at the October Mountain State Forest, a 17-acre park along Route 8 that has two baseball diamonds and tennis courts. The Appalachian Trail goes through the town.
- 78-year-old **St. Andrew's Chapel,** a classic building in the Gothic style, is the object of a current local preservation effort.
- The old **Town Hall** and one-room schoolhouse are being preserved by the Washington Historical Commission. The Town Hall and its records are open on request. The annual meetings of Sons and Daughters of Washington is held the first Sunday after Labor Day.

WEST STOCKBRIDGE, Massachusetts
Population: 1,255　　　　　　　　Zip Code: 01266

A well-known summer resort town, West Stockbridge was once the eastern end of the Hudson and Berkshire

Railroad. Its first settler was William Bryant. The town center was once a prosperous marble-quarrying area.

Trips and trivia:
- **Crane Pond,** a breeding place for several species of fish, and **Shaker Mill Pond,** where speckled trout can be found, are well known to area fishermen.
- **Historic American Buildings** include:
  Engine House Ruins, near the end of Mills Street, built in 1838 by the Hudson and West Stockbridge Railroad
  Marble House, built early 19th century
  Marble Hill, also built early 19th century
  Old Bank Building, called the Greek Temple House, built early 19th century
- The **Square Rigger** is a barn with live entertainment and food. Telephone: 413/232-8565.
- **Old Stone Gristmill** is open to the public.

WILLIAMSTOWN, Massachusetts
Population: 8,247   Zip Code: 01267

Begun as "West Hoosuck" in 1750, Williamstown today is called the Village Beautiful. It was named for Colonel Ephraim Williams, who had commanded the northern line of defense in the French and Indian War and who, before his death in 1755, left a donation for the founding of a free school that became Williams College in 1793. The college, the industry, an art museum, and other cultural and recreational attractions have all combined to make Williamstown a four-season community.

Trips and trivia:
- **Buxton School** on Stone Hill Road is a coeducational boarding and day school for grades 9 through 12 of about 100 students. Telephone: 413/458-3919.

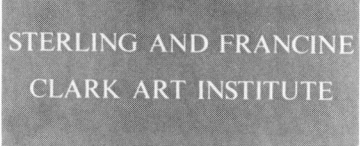

- The Sterling and Francine **Clark Art Institute,** housed in a classical white marble museum, contains one of New England's finest art collections. In exhibits ranging from the Renaissance through the 19th century, many of the great masters are included: Botticelli, Cassatt, Constable, Corot, Courbet, Daunier, Degas, Gainesborough, Gericault, Goya, Hobbema, Homer, Inness, Manet, Memling, Millet, Monet, Pissaro, Rembrandt, Remington, Renoir, Rubens, vanRuisdael, Sargent, Sisley, Toulouse-Lautrec, Turner, etc. Its special strength is the collection of 19th century art, including old silver spanning nearly five centuries. A recent gallery has been set aside for prints and drawings, with constantly changing exhibits. Open year-round, the Institute is closed only on Mondays; otherwise its hours are 10:00 a.m. to 5:00 p.m. Tuesday through Sunday, including all holidays except Thanksgiving, Christmas, and January 1. There is no charge for admission. Public gallery talks are scheduled at intervals during the summer months, special guided tours can be arranged, and a recorded tour is available at a cost of $.75 per person. A Children's Treasure Hunt is especially fun for youngsters being introduced to art. Postcards, slides, photographs, catalogues, jewelry, books, and reproductions of art are on sale. Telephone: 413/458-9545.
- The Yellow House on Spring Street is also known as the **Gallery in Williamstown,** where paintings and sculpture by area artists are featured. Open daily from 10:00 a.m. to 5:00 p.m. (Sunday and Monday according to the season); tea and pastries served Wednesday to Saturday from 1:30 p.m. to 4:30 p.m. in the Danish Tea room. The address is 85 Spring Street, off of Route 2; mailing address is PO Box 195, Williamstown. Telephone: 413/458-8531.
- **Green River Park** on Water Street (Route 43) bills itself as "a linear park made up of trails, picnic tables, play equipment, toddler play area, and more."
- **Haystack Monument** at Mission Park on the Williams College campus marks the site where, under the shelter of a haystack, five Williams College students founded the American Foreign Missionary Society in 1806.
- **Hopkins Memorial Forest** on Northwest Hill Road contains an experimental forest operated by Williams College's Center for Environmental Studies, which is a "living Laboratory for nature walks, bird-watching, cross-country ski trails, and deer hunting by permission." Contact C.E.S., Box 632, Williamstown. The forest also has a Farm Museum with authentic farm tools and implements of the late 19th century and 20th century. Located in the Moon family barn are exhibits of the contrast between subsistence and gentleman farming. Also nearby are Buxton Garden and the Hopkins Memorial Nature Trail. Open daily, year-round. Telephone: 413/597-2346.
- Margaret **Lindley Park,** at the corner of Routes 2 and 7, is open daily from 10:00 a.m. to 7:00 p.m. from June 16 through Labor Day for swimming and picnicking. There is a seasonal charge of $3.00 per family for residents, $2.00 per person each time for nonresidents. **Mount Hope Park** also has picnicking areas, with fireplaces, and is found on Route 43 at Hooper and Green River roads. **Mount Williams,** off of Route 2 on Notch Road, crosses the Appalachian Trail in an ideal spot for hikers and picnickers.

- The **Pine Cobble School** on Main Street is a coeducational day school established in 1937 for 100 boys and 50 girls from nursery to grade 9. Telephone: 413/458-4680.
- A craft gallery, **The Potter's Wheel** on Water Street (Route 43) represents the world of artist-craftsmen in media of stoneware, gold and silver jewelry, glass, cloisonne, weaving, metal sculpture, leather, etc. It is open seven days a week, year-round. The owner is Adelaide England. Telephone: 413/458-9523.
- **Sand Springs** Mineral Springs on Sand Springs Road, a bubbling spring with water at a constant 74 degrees year-round, is a 50 feet by 75 feet pool that reminds one of a health spa. The pool is located off of Route 7 near the Vermont State line. Open from 10:00 a.m. to 7:30 p.m. It was once the tribal health ground of the Maquon Indians and is the site of the oldest public resort in the U.S. There is a charge of $1.75 for adults; $1.25 for children. Seasonal rates available. Telephone: 413/458-5305.
- The **Taconic Trail State Park** on Route 2 has facilities for hiking, horseback riding, skiing, hunting, snowmobiling, and scenic viewing.

- **Williams College,** founded in 1793, is one of the oldest and most distinguished liberal arts colleges in the country. The college is private, co-educational, and nonsectarian, and has a student enrollment of approximately 2,000 men and women in the undergraduate division and under 50 in graduate study. Telephone: 413/597-3131. Located on 450 acres, it offers the following features:

Adams Memorial Theater—offers productions during the academic year under the aegis of Williams Theatre and during the summer under the aegis of the Williamstown Theater Festival (see below).

Bronfman Science Center is a unique modern science laboratory, lecture, and classroom building located on Science Quad.

Chapin Hall is a handsome, wood-lined 1,100 seat auditorium where college and community concerts, recitals, lectures, and special events are held.

Chapin Rare Book Library at Stetson Hall contains one of the world's foremost collections of old books and manuscripts—30,000 in all. It is the only place in the world where originals of the four founding documents (the Declaration of Independence, the Articles of Confederation, the Constitution, and the Bill of Rights) are on permanent display. The library is free to the public. 9:00 a.m. to 12:00 p.m., 1:00 p.m. to 5:00 p.m. year-round.

Hopkins Forest, the college's 2,000-acre experimental forest, open to the public.

Taconic Golf Club, the college's 18-hole course on which several amateur championships have been played, is open to the public from mid-April to early November.

Music performances are offered throughout the academic year, most of them free, in a variety of series from recitals to symphonies. Telephone: 413/597-3146 for recorded concert information.

Sawyer Library contains over 600,000 volumes and more than 3,000 periodicals.

Thompson Memorial Chapel, a landmark of the college, is a superb example of Gothic architecture and is especially noted for its stained-glass windows. Colonel Ephraim Williams, the founding father, was interred here with full military honors in 1920, 165 years after his death in the French and Indian War.

West College, the oldest building on the campus (1793), still stands on Main Street, and is used today as a dormitory.

Hopkins Observatory is the oldest astronomical observatory in the country. It is open by appointment through the Department of Physics and Astronomy and offers free planetarium shows each Friday during the academic year. The building also contains a small museum of astronomy.

The Williams College Museum of Art emphasizes 18th century through 20th century American art, modern and contemporary art, and ancient and non-Western art. It contains a large and varied collection of paintings, sculptures, decorative arts, prints and drawings, and furniture. Postmodern additions designed by architect Charles Moore and completed in 1986 have dramatically enlarged the original museum building, and 1846 octagonal rotunda. Free admission. Open to the public Monday through Saturday, 10:00 a.m. to 5:00 p.m.; Sunday 1:00 p.m. to 5:00 p.m.; closed Thanksgiving, Christmas Day, and New Year's Day.

- The **Williamstown Board of Trade** maintains an information booth daily in the summer on Route 2 at the corner on Main Street and North Street.
- The **Williamstown House of Local History** is located at 169 Main Street. Telephone: 413/458-3652. The **Williamstown Historical Commission** is right down the street at 148 Main Street.

- **Williamstown Theater Festival,** entering its 33rd season in 1987, has been called "the best of all American summer theaters" by *Newsweek*. Many of the American theatre's most distinguished actors, directors, and designers return year after year for productions of modern classics on the Festival's Main Stage and new plays on the Other Stage, as well as for nightly cabarets, staged readings, and literary events. The season runs during July and August each year. For information, write PO Box 517, Williamstown, MA 01267 (New York address: Williamstown Theatre Festival, 820 Second Ave., Suite 901, New York, NY 10017). Telephone: 413/597-3377.
- The Williamstown Historical Commission, as part of the Bicentennial celebration, put out a booklet in 1976 called "Williamstown: A Walk Along Main Street" to Points of Historical and Architectural Interest. Samples from these styles are included: the Regulation House (1752-1760), gambrel roof (late 1760s, early 1770s), early colonial (1770-1790), Federal, or Late Georgian (1790-1810), domestic brick (1820s and early 1830s), Greek Revival (early 1830s), Gothic Revival (1850-1870), Mansard (1870-80), Victorian Gothic (1880-90), Richardson Romanesque (1880s), Academic Classical and Colonial Revivals (1900-1940), and contemporary.
- The **Women's Exchange** of Williamstown is a unique organization in that it completely supports the work of the local Visiting Nurses Association.
- The **Williamstown Annual Report** of 1976 adds this interesting notation: "Williamstown, over 220 years old, still operates on the principles of the old New England Town Meeting. Every voter has the right to attend, to have his or her say and to vote according to his or her convictions."
- A book by Robert R. R. Brooks, et. al. called *Williamstown: The First Two Hundred Years and Twenty Years Later* reviews some places along Main Street of architectural interest, including:

Site of First Meeting of West Hoosac Proprietors, December 5, 1793
Site of Fort West Hoosac, 1756
1753 House, a replica of the first house in town, built in 1953 with 1753-style tools, materials and methods
West College, the first Williams College building, built in 1790
Haystack Monument, site of the thunderstorm meeting at which American Foreign Missions were initiated in 1806
Smedley House, built in 1772, an early Colonial house where Benedict Arnold slept
Simonds House, built 1770, an early Colonial where Ethan Allen drank
Steel's Corners in South Williamstown, an excellent example of commercial Green Revival, built 1820
- Buildings of interest to the historian include:

Red Saltbox House, built c. 1765, an early tavern
Ben Simond's Grave (a founder of West Hoosac in 1752-3)
Dr. Meack House, late Colonial built in 1760s, rebuilt in 1790s
First house on the north side of Glen Street, Richardson Romanesque
Pine Cobble School, 1979
Williams Inn, 1974
Town Hall, formerly Phi Gamma Delta Fraternity, 1928
Center for Development Economics, formerly Delta Psi Fraternity, 1886
Greylock Quadrangle, 1967
Wood House, formerly Zeta Psi Fraternity, 1908
Weston Language Center, formerly Alpha Delta Phi Fraternity, 1869
Adams Memorial Theater, home of Williams College and Williamstown Summer Theater, 1941
Perry House, formerly Phi Delta Theta Fraternity, 1908
Mather House, Williams Admissions Office, c. 1800
Spencer House, formerly Delta Kappa Epsilon Fraternity, 1960
Faculty Club, 1938
Carter House, 1875
Park Hall, Center for Environmental Studies, 1854
President's House, built by General Samual Slone, 1802
Congregational Church, 1869
Hopkins Hall, Williams Administration Building, 1890
Thompson Memorial Chapel, 1904
Griffin Hall, 1828
Hopkins Observatory, 1836, oldest extant observatory in the U.S.
Dewey House, 1798
Friendship Hall, Mason's Hall, 1820
Botsford Memorial Library, 1810
Samuel Duncan House
Murray Smith House, 1817
White-Smith House, 1880s
Bissel Sherman House, 1797
Judah Williams House, 1778
- Also, the **Titus Deming House** (c. 1800), on the road to New Ashford in South Williamstown, has been designated a Historic American Building.

WINDSOR, Massachusetts
Population: 569   Zip Code: 01270

Although the town was established in 1771 as Gageborough in honor of General Thomas Gage, the last royal governor of Massachusetts, the townspeople later settled on the name Windsor.

Trips and trivia:

- Through the years the town has had a number of farms and small **industries,** such as charcoal-making, spruce oil distilling, and sawmills. One of the most interesting industries was that launched by Charles H. Ball, who patented and manufactured a tubular truss iron ring in East Windsor in the 1890s. He sold several to neighboring towns, and four survive today. Ball later established a woodworking mill, which by the early part of this century was a major supplier of such items as wooden meat skewers to meat packing plants in his country, Argentina, and Australia; wooden lollipop sticks; and wooden coat hangers.

- **Notchview Reservation** includes 3,000 acres of spruce and hardwood forest, hayfields, and rambling hills. Located in the Hoosac Range, much of the reservation is over 1,900 feet in elevation; the highest point is Judge's Hill: 2,297 feet. Notchview Reservation is free to the public. The Visitors' Center is open Friday through Sunday and holidays and offers a waxing room, picnic tables, and rest rooms. The property has several miles of trails for hiking, picnicking, cross-country skiing, and snowshoeing. The land was bequeathed to the Trustees of Reservations by the late Lieutenant Colonel Robert D. Budd, U. S. Army Retired, in 1965. The entrance is off Route 9, one mile east of the junction of Routes 9 and 8A, three miles west of the Cummington/Windsor line.

- In 1975 the active **Windsor Historical Commission** moved a 19th century farmhouse to a new site on Route 9 in the center of town and has been working to restore it as a museum for town and local history. Three-dimensional models of past town industry and a full-size replica of a 19th century summer kitchen are featured.

- **Windsor Jambs,** a natural land and water formation (gorge) is owned by the state forest. **Windsor Pond** is accessible via Route 116.

- **Windsor State Forest** has facilities for swimming, camping, picnicking, and hiking. Follow signs from Route 9 in West Cummington or Route 116 in Savoy.

Franklin County

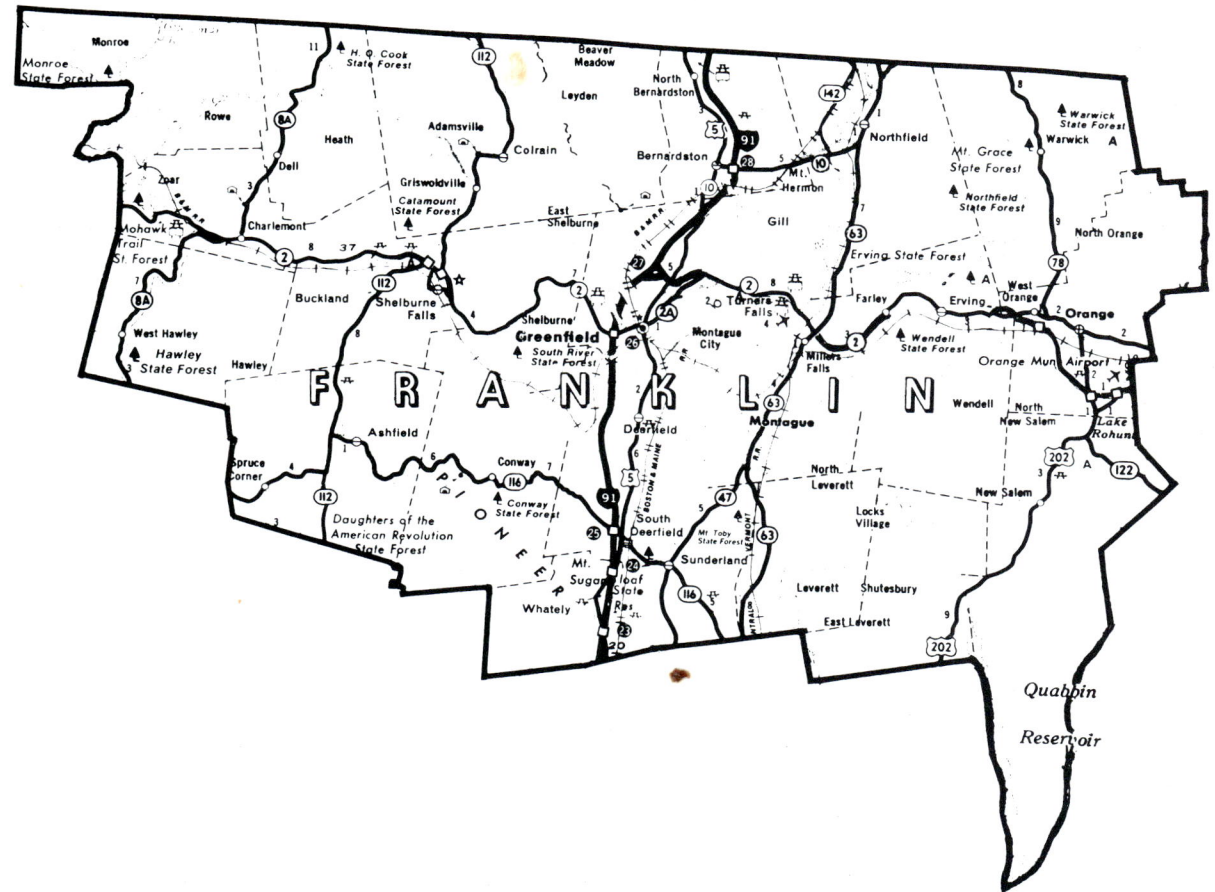

Franklin County

ASHFIELD, Massachusetts
Population: 1,274   Zip Code: 01330

Called "Little Switzerland" because of its many hills and dales, Ashfield is famous mainly as Maple Sugaring Country, with many antique and gift shops for the tourist.

Trips and trivia:
- The **Ashfield Historical Society,** headquartered on Main Street, is open Sunday afternoons and by appointment. It displays its collection of antique farm tools, early school articles and items, and the largest known collection of Howes Brothers Glass Plate Negatives. There are prints on display, and for sale, plus a microfilm reader that can be used to view some 23,000 images.
- **Ashfield Lake,** a popular summer resort area, has a public swimming area, golf, and picnic facilities.
- **Chapel Falls** is a 128-acre cascade off Route 116 in South Ashfield.
- **Chapelbrook,** a 128-acre reservation, is owned and operated by the Trustees of Reservations, complete with streams and waterfalls and Pont Mountain. Picnicking also available. Take Williamsburg Road off Route 116 at South Ashfield.
- There is a **Civil War marker** on Baptist Corner Road.
- Movie producer Cecil B. **DeMille** (1881-1959) was born in Ashfield. President of his own production company, DeMille was responsible for such all-time greats as *The Ten Commandments, Cleopatra, The King of Kings,* and *The Crusaders.*
- **Historic American Buildings** in Ashfield include:
  1. Town Hall (1814), on the south side of Main Street near the village center, was originally built during 1812-4 as a Congregational Meetinghouse. It has a remarkable spire.
  2. St. John's Episcopal Church, at the southwest corner of Main Street and Baptist Corner Raod, was built 1824-7 by Jonathan Lilly.
- **Lesure's Sugar House and Maple Museum,** near Watson Spruce Corner Road, is open year-round.
- **Sanderson Academy,** a two-story building with an octagonal belfry that was constructed in 1888, was founded in 1816; it is now a public school.
- **Spruce Corner** is a crossroads settlement in Ashfield.

BERNARDSTON, Massachusetts
Population: 1,659   Zip Code: 01337

Originally called "Falls Flight Township" to commemorate its participation in early settler wars with the Indians, the town later was named for provincial governor Sir Francis Bernard. Bernard served as governor from 1760-69, and named the town by means of a petition that he initiated himself.

Trips and trivia:
- The **cemetery** has outstanding examples of old tombstone art and epitaphs for the gravestone rubbing enthusiast.
- There are many areas for **camping and picnicking** along the roadsides.
- Historical markers in Bernardston:
  1. **Burke Fort** on Route 5, built 1738-39, sheltered 50 people during the French and Indian War.
  2. **Connable Fort,** also on Route 5, was erected in 1739.
  3. **Deacon Ebeneezer Sheldon's Fort,** built 1740-41, is on the road to Hickle Hill.
  4. **Lieutenant Ebeneezer Sheldon's Fort,** on the road to Northfield, was built in 1740. It marks the place the place where the first Proprietors' Meeting in Fall Town was held.

BUCKLAND, Massachusetts
Population: 1,829   Zip Code: 01338

Some say Buckland received its name from Samuel Taylor's Deer Park on the banks of the Deerfield River where he captured bucks who jumped into the park from atop a steep bank, but then couldn't jump back; Taylor killed the bucks and let the does go safely. Others say the town was named by early settlers from Buckland, England. The town celebrated its Bicentennial in 1979.

Trips and trivia:
- **Buckland Historical Association** has converted an old schoolhouse on Upper Street of Buckland Center, off Route 112 into a museum to preserve local artifacts. Organized in 1957, the Association has a collection of early furnishings, crafts, ledgers, costumes, guns, etc. that were used in the town since 1797. It is open Sunday afternoons during the summer. Free. Telephone: 413/625-6472.
- **Buckland Recreation Area** on Route 112 is open afternoons throughout the summer for swimming and picnicking. There is an admission charge for nonresidents.
- Below the dam on the Deerfield River is **Lamson and Goodnow Cutlery,** in existence since 1835. Of architectural interest is an elevated, circular walk of wood from one building to another.
- The village's most famous native is **Mary Lyon,** founder of Mount Holyoke College in South Hadley in 1837, the first women's college in the United States. Her birthplace, in the southeastern end of town, is marked by a bronze tablet. Mary Lyon's classroom, located in what is known as the Major Joseph Griswold House (1818) on Upper Street, is listed on the National Register. It is open Tuesday afternoons during the summer at no charge. Telephone: 413/625-2031.

- Buckland also claims several famous resident **painters,** including:
  1. Edwin R. Elmer, whose *Lady of Baptist Corner, Ashfield, Massachusetts* was exhibited in 1950 at the Corcoran Gallery. Smith College owns his widely shown *Mourning Picture* of his home built in Shelburne Falls.
  2. Robert Strong Woodward, an artist famous for his rural scenes around New England, lived on Upper Street.
- The Clesson and Deerfield **Rivers** offer popular fishing spots.
- There are many architecturally interesting houses throughout Buckland that are not open to the public, such as the **LeBaron Ruddock House** (1796) on Upper Street across from the museum.

CHARLEMONT, Massachusetts
Population: 897   Zip Code: 01339

At various times called Boston Township number 1, Chickley's Town, then Charley Mount, Charlemont today is widely popular for winter sports. It is the central point of the Mohawk Trail.

Trips and trivia:
- **Bissell Covered Bridge,** one of the Commonwealth's four covered bridges still in use, is located north of Route 2. There is a direction sign at the junction of Routes 8A and 2.
- **Buttonball Tree**—the watering trough there was built in 1760 as a token of friendship to the Indians.
- Historic landmarks:
  1. Site of the **Captain Rice Home**
  2. **Charles Dudley Warner House** (see Famous Native Sons and Daughters)
  3. Grave of **Captain Moses Rice**

- **Hail to the Sunrise Monument** is a memorial to the Mohawk Indian, which faces east on the Mohawk Trail looking across the Deerfield River. Located at the site of the old Indian Fordway, the statue has uplifted arms in supplication to the Great Spirit, calling for hope and peace in the country. The eight-foot bronze statue, carved by Joseph P. Polia, stands on an eight-ton boulder. It has become a symbol of the Mohawk Trail since its unveiling in 1932. Each year, early in October, a pilgrimage is made to it by Red Men and Pocahontas Association members and their families.
- **Mohawk Trail State Forest** on Route 2 has camping facilities, fishing, hiking, hunting, snowmobiling, swimming, picnicking, and facilities for the handicapped. Telephone: 413/339-5504.
- For those families playing the alphabet game, it should be of interest that there is a town called *Zoar* in Charlemont, just north of Route 2.

COLRAIN, Massachusetts
Population: 1,420   Zip Code: 01340

Settled in the early 18th century by Scotch-Irish, Colrain was named for Irish peer Lord Coleraine; later it drew many French-Canadians to handle its farming and industry.

Trips and trivia:
- A **boulder** in the Lyonsville cemetery commemorates Amasa and Rhoda Shippee who were responsible, in 1812, for raising the first flag to fly over a school in the U. S.
- Catamount (wildcat) dens are found at **Catamount State Forest** on Routes 2 and 112.
- **Colrain State Forest,** 1,244 acres of woodland, contains some of the oldest trees in the commonwealth. **H. O. Cook State Forest** on Routes 2 and 112 has facilities for fishing, hiking, riding, and hunting.
- **Colrain Historical Society** on Main Street, located at the Old Methodist Church in the center of town, is open Sunday 2:00 p.m. to 5:00 p.m., May through October.
- There are historical markers for:
  1. The **site of Fort Morris** (1754-63)
  2. **Harp elm** at the entrance of the North River Cemetery
  3. Site of the first church (1740) at Chandler Hill, the first village in Colrain. Just east of it is the **first burying ground,** dating back to 1736, including the ancestors of steamboat builder Robert Fulton.
  4. Arthur Smith **covered bridge**
- **Old Fort Trail,** a marked tour, guides the visitor to interesting places throughout Colrain.

CONWAY, Massachusetts
Population: 998   Zip Code: 01341

Popular as both a winter and summer resort and residential area, Conway was named for Major General Henry S. Conway, British minister and leader of the House of Commons. Conway was popular with the colonists because he helped secure repeal of the Stamp Act in 1766.

Trips and trivia:
- **Conway State Forest** on Route 116 has facilities for fishing, hiking, horseback riding, hunting, and recreational vehicles. Telephone: 413/268-7098.
- **Joe Herrick House** (Historical American Building), also called the Joel Parsons House, on Poland Road, was built in 1755.
- Located at the South River crossing at the junction of Route 116 is **Burkeville Bridge,** a typical New England covered bridge.

• Marshall Field, Conway's most famous native son, founder of the famous Chicago department store that bears his name, donated the **Field Memorial Library** to the town in 1901. The many historical collections of the library can be seen Monday, Wednesday, and Friday, 2:00 p.m. to 5:00 p.m. and 7:00 p.m. to 9:00 p.m. except during holidays. Telephone: 413/369-4646.

• **South River State Forest** on Route 116 has fishing, hiking, hunting, and facilities for recreational vehicles. Telephone: 413/268-7098.

DEERFIELD, Massachusetts
Population: 3,850   Zip Code: 01342

Deerfield, destroyed by Indians in the Bloody Brook Massacre of 1675 and the Deerfield Massacre of Feburary 29, 1704, today distinguishes itself for its historic restorations and educational institutions.

Trips and trivia:

• **Bement School** on Main Stret is a coeducational boarding and day preparatory school for grades K through 9. Established in 1925, Bement enrolls 140 students in a full academic and sports schedule, plus extra opportunities in art, crafts, and music. Telephone: 413/774-7061.

• The Frank L. **Boyden Collection of Carriages** is housed in the Cowles Barn across the street from the Sheldon-Hawks House. It is open occasionally on Saturday and Sunday afternoons, but not on any regular schedule.

• The **Broom Shop** is an appendage to the Pratt House situated between the Post Office and the Deerfield Inn aross from the Hall Tavern. Although it is seldom open to the public, visitors can see the whole display through the front windows.

• Children will enjoy reading *The Boy Captive of Old Deerfield* by Mary P. Wells Smith, published in 1967 by the Pocumtuck Valley Memorial Association in Deerfield. The story of the 1704 massacre is told as it relates to Stephen Williams, ten-year-old son of the village minister.

• A **Civil War monument** is located on the Town Common.

• **Deerfield Academy** is a boys' residential school, national in scope, of 500 boarding and 50 day students, grades 9 through 12. Established in 1797, Academy students come from most of the states of the Union and many foreign countries. All of the students go on to college. The Academy is located on 200 acres in a setting that John Quincy Adams described as "not excelled by anything I have ever seen, not excepting the Bay of Naples." The Hilson Art Gallery, in the west wing of the Academy auditorium, has changing art exhibits; it is open during the school year, 2:00 p.m. to 5:00 p.m. Telephone: 413/772-0241.

• **Eaglebrook School** on Pine Nook Road is a boys' boarding school for grades 6 through 9 for 240 students. The school was established in 1922. Telephone: 413/774-7411.

• All of the houses that are part of Historic Deerfield are listed as **Historic American Buildings.** Others in the town include: Captain Thomas Dickinson House (1762-4), David Dickinson House (also called the Smith House, c. 1790), Augustus Lyman House (c. 1803), Godfrey-Nims House (1718), Old Manse (1768 Barnard-Willard House), Benjamin Ray House (1835), Joseph Stebbins House (c. 1772), and Parson John Williams House (c. 1760). Others in the vicinity include Allen House (Fuller studio, c. 1730), Locke-Fuller House (c. 1790), and Wapping School House (1839), moved in 1967 to The Street.

• **Indian House Memorial** on Main Street (Route 5) in Deerfield is a reproduction of a building that withstood an Indian attack in 1704. The original house was torn down in 1848 when efforts to restore it were turned down by the townspeople, but the famous door is preserved at Memorial Hall. The door shows the mark where an Indian tomahawk went through wood to kill a resident of the building. Today the reproduction houses antiques, rooms furnished in colonial style, Indian relics, handwoven items, pottery, and exhibits of handicrafts by local artists. Handweaving is demonstrated there on old looms. The memorial is open to the public May through November weekdays, except Tuesday, 9:30 a.m. to 12:00 p.m., 1:30 p.m. to 5:00 p.m.; Sunday 1:00 p.m. to 5:00 p.m. There is an admission charge. Telephone: 413/772-0845. **Old Bloody Brook Tavern** is located in the rear yard of the Indian House Memorial. The long frame building was probably built prior to 1700 and was moved to its present location from South Deerfield. It houses a pottery shop and provides demonstrations to visitors during the same hours as the Indian House Memorial.

• **Historic Deerfield, Inc.,** The Street (PO Box 321) is a "nonprofit organization devoted to preserving Deerfield, Massachusetts, and fostering an appreciation of its history and colonial American artifacts." Founded in 1952 by Mr. and Mrs. Henry N. Flynt for the historic preservation of Western Massachusetts culture, the educational organization was awarded National Landmark status in 1962. Historic Deerfield, Inc., maintains architecturally significant museum houses that span dates from the early 1700s to the early 1800s. Most of the houses are on their original sites, and all are located within the one-mile village "street." The museum houses are open year-round except Thanksgiving and Christmas. Hours are Monday through Saturday, 9:30 a.m. to 4:30 p.m.; Sunday, 11:00 a.m. to 4:30 p.m., with specific hours for certain buildings available at the Information Center. Guided tours are available at the various houses, with prices of admission varying: combination rates, group tours, and tours-by-appointment are available. Telephone: 413/774-5581. The houses include:

1. **Ashley House** (c. 1730), home of Tory preacher Jonathan Ashley from 1732-80. Its remarkable 17th century and 18th century furnishings depict the elegant lifestyle of the early New England minister.
2. **Sheldon-Hawks House** (1794), residence of Deerfield historian George Sheldon and his family for two centuries, where the original paneling and fine family china are seen along with English ceramics, and the Potter collection of furniture.
3. **Dwight-Barnard House** (c. 1725), moved from Springfield, Massachusetts shows a doctor's office, an elegant parlor, and other rooms decorated with furniture from the Connecticut Valley.
4. **Wright House** (1824), one of two brick buildings in Deerfield, built for Asa Stebbins, Jr. by his father. Today it houses the Cluett collection of Chippendale and Federal furniture, American paintings, and Chinese export porcelain.
5. **Helen Geier Flynt Textile Museum** (1872), housed in a Victorian barn, contains needlework, costumes, bedspreads, and textiles of fine American and European fabrics, plus a collection of needlework and elegant period furniture.
6. **Parker and Russell Silver Shop** (1814), the shop of an early American silversmith, contains a country parlor of the Federal era, clocks, and a collection of silver by Revere, Dummer, Coney, Onckelbag, Myers, deLamerie, and two Deerfield silversmiths—Isaac Parker and John Russell.
7. **Asa Stebbins House** (1799), the town's first brick house, built for the wealthiest landowner in Franklin County. Today it features Sheraton and Hepplewhite furniture, portraits by Gilbert Stuart and other period painters, French wallpapers, freehand wall painting and decorative plasterwork, Chinese export porcelain, and a hallway display of Captain Cook's South Sea voyages.
8. **Hall Tavern** (c. 1760), formerly an 18th century eating and drinking establishment on the Boston-Albany highway in Charlemont. Today it contains an Information Center for Historic Deerfield, Inc., and a seven-room museum of New England furniture.
9. **Frary House** (c. 1720), with its location on the Town Common, served as a refuge for the Frary family in pioneer days, and later was enlarged to serve as a tavern for the Barnard family. General Benedict Arnold is reported to have stayed there in 1775 when he purchased 15,000 pounds of meat for his troops before going to Fort Ticonderoga. The enormous L-shaped, two and a half story building contains an elegant ballroom, country furniture, and domestic items of Miss C. Alice Baker, who restored the house in 1890. This house is especially recommended for children visiting Historic Deerfield; they enjoy the "touch-it" room.
10. **Wells-Thorn House** (1717), home of settler Ebenezer Wells, is recommended for the first-time visitor to the Village, as it contains a bit of everything: fine furniture and furnishings, needlework, English ceramics, a pantry, a buttery, a garret, and a lawyer's office. Some rooms have the original paneling.

- **Allen House** (1710) is one of the earliest surviving houses in Deerfield. It was restored in 1946 to show the house of an early settler (originally the home of Mrs. Hannah Beaman, the first schoolmistress of the town) with feather-edged paneling and massive fireplaces. From 1944-75 it was the home of Mr. and Mrs. Henry Flynt, the founders of Historic Deerfield, and contains their exquisite collection of Connecticut Valley furniture, textiles, paintings, prints, and decorative accessories.

Historic Deerfield also maintains a research library and carries on many active education programs.

- The **Liberty Pole** is a replica of a pole originally erected on July 29, 1774 by a group of patriots in Deerfield. The replica was erected in 1947 as a tribute to those early inhabitants and flies a liberty flag each day.
- **Meeting House** (1824), designed by Isaac Damon and Winthrop Clapp, is the fifth such structure, this one built for the First Church of Deerfield. Constructed of brick, it has a gilded cock weathervane that dates to 1729.
- The **Museum of Architectural Fragments** is located in the Hawk's Barn (1864). It is situated behind the Dwight-Barnard House and is open to the public only on special occasions or by prior arrangement.
- **Mount Sugarloaf State Reservation,** just west of the Connecticut River off Route 116, offers a dramatic view of the river winding through the valley. The entrance road is open daily, May through October, for picnics and hiking trails that lead to the 652-foot summit.
- There is an **old burying ground** on Albany Road.
- The **Old Fort Well** is on the Town Common directly in front of the Civil War monument.
- **Pocumtuck Valley Memorial Association,** headquartered at Frary House, is a historical society that was established in 1870. Telephone: 413/773-3294. It maintains **Memorial Hall Museum** on Memorial Street. Designed in 1798 by Asher Benjamin as Deerfield Academy's first building, it was renovated and opened as a museum in 1880 by town historian George Sheldon, who wrote in its first catalog: "the collection is founded on purely historical lines, and is the direct memorial of the inhabitants of this valley, both Indian and Puritan." When the museum opened, it included what are believed to be the oldest permanent period rooms in the U. S.—an old family

kitchen, parlor, and bedroom. The museum now contains a remarkable collection of local furniture, pewter, paintings, tools, textiles, and Indian artifacts. Its special collections include: Allen Sister photographs 1880-1920 (considered among America's most gifted early glass-plate camerawomen); carved and painted chests 1650-1720 (examples of an important Connecticut River Valley furniture style, illustrating one of the earliest American folk art expressions); Deerfield embroidery 1896-1926 (from the Society of Blue and White Needlework); and musical instruments 1680-1886 (including a 1680 Keene Spinet, an 1807 Clementi square piano, an 1820 Pratt chamber organ, and a 1775 church base and pitchpipe by Justin Hitchcock of Deerfield). Memorial Hall is especially famous for its "Indian House Door" that survived attack by the Indians on the 1698 homestead of Ensign John Sheldon. The museum is open May 1 through October 31, weekdays 10:00 a.m. to 4:30 p.m.; Saturday and Sunday, 12:30 p.m. to 4:30 p.m.; by appointment April and November. Admission is $2.00 per adult, $1.50 for students. It is located on the corner of Memorial Street and U.S. 5 and 10. From the south, take I-91 north to exit 24, then six miles north on U.S. 5; from the north, I-91 south to the Greenfield 2-A exit, and follow signs for U.S. 5 to Deerfield.

- The **Sheldon-Hawks Shed** is located behind the Sheldon-Hawkes House. It contains the Lucius Potter Memorial Collection of toys and antique furniture. The Shed is open to the public only ocasionally or by prior arrangement.
- The **Village Street** is marked throughout with inscriptions depicting Deerfield's history.

- **White Church,** a Greek Revival-style building dating to 1838, has recently been restored to serve as a community center and Sunday school.

- **Woolman Hill** on Keets Road is a Quaker conference and retreat center on 100 acres of beautiful woods and farmland. The center includes a comfortable old farmhouse and several cabins that are rented to groups and individuals. Also on Woolman Hill are Traprock Peace Center, a small sheep farm, a homestead, and a few residences. Check in at the office before using trails and facilities, and please do not bring dogs, as they frighten the sheep! Telephone: 413-774-3431.

ERVING, Massachusetts
Population: 1,260　　　　　　　　Zip Code: 01344

Named for John Erving of Boston, who bought land there in 1752, the town of Erving is now said to be the world's largest producer of printed paper napkins.

Trips and trivia:
- **Barndoor Cave,** left from Farley Village, cuts through 50 feet of rock and comes up on top of the cliff.
- **Erving State Forest,** on Route 2 surrounds Lake Laurel and includes facilities for boating, swimming, fishing, hiking, riding, picnicking, hunting, and camping.

GILL, Massachusetts
Population: 1,276　　　　　　　　Zip Code: 01376

Historically-oriented enough to name itself for Moses Gill, a lieutenant governor, Gill keeps turning up prehistoric footprints for dinosaur track seekers.

Trips and trivia:
- **Barton Cove Nature Area** on Route 2, a Northeast Utilities project, is unique in both natural and cultural

history. Its mile-long ridge of rocky outcropping is covered with hemlock, maple, oak, and hickory trees, a perfect setting for imagining prehistoric life there millions of years ago. It is an ideal spot for bird-watching, picnicking, tent camping, and hiking along nature trails. The campground opens Memorial Day weekend daily through September 14; day-use areas remain open until October 19. Telephone: 413/659-3714 prior to the camping season, 863-9300 once the campground has opened. A night's deposit is required to secure your reservation, refundable only with a 24-hour notice. Rates are $8.00 per night, $48.00 per week for the tent sites. Canoe and small boat rentals are available on a first-come basis for $4.00 per hour, $20.00 per day.

• Near Barton Cove is a state-owned **boat ramp** leading to the Connecticut River.

• There is an unusual monument in one of Gill's **cemeteries,** and also a perfectly shaped arrowhead with only the name "Smith" at its base.

• The site of **Falls Fight,** a famous old Indian battle, is commemorated by a monument located at the end of the Turners Falls-Gill Bridge on Route 2 west of Barton Cove.

• **Mount Hermon School for Boys** was founded in Gill in 1881 by evangelist Dwight L. Moody. See Northfield.

• **Red House,** a Historic American Building, on French King Highway in Riverside was built c. 1745.

GREENFIELD, Massachusetts
Population: 19,010   Zip Code: 01301

Taking its name from the fertile Green River Valley where it is located, Greenfield is the seat of Franklin County. It is known as the site of the largest manufacturer of taps and dies in the world.

Trips and trivia:

• **Arena Civic Theatre, Inc.,** a nonprofit organization founded in 1971 to further live theatre in the area, plays summer stock at the Roundhouse of the Franklin County Fairgrounds. Telephone: 413/773-9891.

• Examples of the architecture of **Asher Benjamin** can be seen at the Greenfield Public Library on East Main Street and the McCarthy Funeral Home at Court Square. The library has changing exhibits of rocks and minerals, art and sculpture; it is open Monday through Friday, 10:00 a.m. to 8:30 p.m.; Saturday, 10:30 a.m. to 5:00 p.m.

• There is a **covered bridge** on Eunice William Drive, off Leyden Road.

• The first **cutlery factory** in America was established here in the early 19th century.

• **Cheapside Landing** is where canal boats anchored in 1792.

• The **Franklin County Chamber of Commerce** operates at 395 Main Street. Telephone: 413/773-5463. Summers it maintains an Information Booth at the junction of I-91 and Route 2 at exit 26.

• At **Fort Square** the old colonial fort burned in 1810.

• **Greenfield Community College** (GCC) located at One College Drive, was founded in 1962, one of 15 community colleges in the state. It has approximately 1,400 students in its day division and 2,500 students in the Division of Continuing Education. Fully accredited by the New England Association of Schools and Colleges, GCC offers a general liberal arts program as well as career programs in accounting, art, computer information systems, criminal justice, early childhood education, electronics technology, engineering, graphic design, management, marketing, media communication, office administration, and recreation and leisure services. One year certificate programs are offered in computer-aided drafting, fire science technology, graphics communications, office assistance, outdoor leadership, Pioneer Valley studies, studio arts, and word processing. Open to the public during regular class hours, the college has a library of 60,000 units, classrooms, labs, and a computer laboratory. It boasts a full-time faculty of 70 men and women and offers over 500 courses. Telephone: 413/774-3131.

Greenfield, Massachusetts

• **Greenfield Historical Society,** 43 Church Street, founded in 1907, offers tours by appointment, May 15 through October 17, of its nine-room museum located in a three-story, 15-room Victorian mansion built in 1850 and purchased in 1914. The society preserves local historical and industrial items, genealogical books, and other records.

Telephone: 413/772-6992.
- **Greenfield Mountain,** on the Mohawk Trail, offers a panoramic view of the Connecticut Valley from its observation tower.
- Historic American Buildings include:
  1. **Gould-Potter House,** 486 Main Street at the corner of High, a private home built in the Greek-revival style of 1822.
  2. **Hovey-Leavitt House** (now the Greenfield Public Library), 402 Main Street, built in 1797.
  3. **Reverend Roger Newton House** at Newton Place, built in 1793.
- **Highland Park's** Sachem Head has picnic facilities, ice-skating at Highland Pond, and a rocky cave formation at Bear's Den.

- **Mohawk Trail Concerts** take place at the Charlemont Federated Church, Friday and Saturday evenings during July and August. Founded in 1970 by Arnold Black, composer for film, theatre, television, and symphony and chamber ensembles, the concerts are admired for their unique blend of excellence and informality. Ticket prices range from $3.50 to $7.00, with discounts for seniors and students. For information, contact Mohawk Trail Concerts, Box 843. Telephone: 413/625-2566.
- The **municipal swimming pool,** open daily during the summer from 10:00 a.m. to 8:00 p.m., is free to residents, with a nominal fee for out-of-towners. It offers a natural pool with a beach and picnic area. **Rocky Mountain Park** is another nice picnic choice.
- The **McHard House,** (Historic American Building) two and a half miles away on Route 5, was built before 1730.
- **Poet's Seat Tower,** off of Route 2, was named for local poet Francis Tuckerman and offers a wonderful view from Rocky Mountain high above the Connecticut River. There are parking facilities at the entrance for those who want to walk up to the tower.

- **St. James Church,** (1847) an Episcopal church at the corner of Federal and Church Streets, is a replica of St. Mary the Virgin Church in South Milford, Yorkshire, England.

STONELEIGH-BURNHAM SCHOOL
GREENFIELD, MASSACHUSETTS 01301

- **Stoneleigh-Burnham School,** on Bernardston Road, is an independent boarding school for young women, grades 9 to 12, which offers challenging academic experiences, as well as outstanding programs in the visual and performing arts, athletics, and riding. The school's dance and riding program are open to the community. Telephone: 413/774-2711.
- The expression **"Up to Green River,"** synonymous with being "up to snuff," derives from the top-quality Green River knives made in Greenfield that were used by the Mountain Men in the Old West.
- **Veteran's Memorial Field** on Silver Street has tennis facilities.
- An historic marker commemorates the site where **Eunice Williams,** a Deerfield minister's wife, was slain by the Indians during the Deerfield Massacre of 1704.

HAWLEY, Massachusetts
Population: 234   Zip Code: 01339

The town decided to name itself after liberal Joseph Hawley of Northampton, one of the Valley's "River Gods" who led the opposition to revivalist Jonathan Edwards, urged adoption of the Declaration of Independence, and helped unify colonial administration.

Trips and trivia:
- The **charcoal kiln** in East Hawley is a popular tourist attraction.
- **Dubuque, Kenneth Memorial State Forest,** along Route 8A, offers facilities for hiking, riding, camping, canoeing, picnicking, hunting, and scenic views. Telephone: 413/339-6631.
- There are scenic views from **Parker Hill** in East Hawley.

HEATH, Massachusetts
Population: 383   Zip Code: 01346

Honoring William Heath, Major General in the Continental Army of 1776, the town has been known as a "Christmas tree town" for all its evergreens sold for that purpose. Heath, which typifies one's visions of a New England town, has a green with a church, community hall, one-room schoolhouse (not in use), library, town hall, and lovely old houses.

Trips and trivia:
- **Old Town house,** dating to 1835 and recently restored, is maintained by the Heath Historical Society. It contains exhibits of articles of historic interest to

townspeople. The society also owns the schoolhouse.
- The **Methodist Church** has been converted to a community center.
- At one point Heath was famous for its many lovely **summer houses.**
- Today there are only about ten **working farms** left, but the town has two blueberry farms.

LEVERETT, Massachusetts
Population: 1,400   Zip Code: 01054

In a historic move, the town named itself in honor of John Leverett, a Governor of Massachusetts from 1673-79 who banished persecution from the commonwealth. Leverett today is preserving many of the artifacts and handicrafts skills of yesteryear.

Trips and trivia:
- **Charcoal kilns,** restored in 1885, are found on Old Coke Kiln Road in North Leverett. At one time, the manufacture of charcoal was a leading industry in the town.
- **Electronic chimes** of the Congregational Church (1838) play daily at 12:30 p.m., 6:00 p.m. and 7:00 p.m.

- **Leverett Craftsmen & Artists, Inc.** (LCA), on Montague Road in Leverett Center maintains a gallery and retail store open Tuesday through Sunday from 12:00 p.m. to 5:00 p.m. It is located in an old box factory that dates to 1875. LCA has 15 residents who are available by appointment for studio tours. Represented are: furniture-making, pottery, painting, weaving, silverworking, and stained glass. Memberships are available and entitle the card-carrier to a 10% discount and reduced fees on lectures and classes. To reach the building, take Depot Road out of North Amherst, approximately three miles off Route 63 to Leverett Center. Direct inquiries to Liz Canali, Managing Director at LCA. Telephone: 413/548-9070.
- Bradford Field House, better known as **Old Field Tavern,** contains an upstairs barroom and interesting old relics. Many of the items stored in this 1790 house are now kept in the Bradford M. Field Memorial Library in the center of town. Hours are 2:30 p.m. to 8:30 p.m., Tuesday and Thursday.

- **Rattlesnake gutter,** a fabulous ravine complete with steep stones, crags, and ledges, challenges even the toughest backpacker. The finish leads to the 100-foot Bourne's Cliffs. Rattlesnake Gutter is located approximately one mile north of the center of town, but the road is not always open to traffic.
- **Roaring Brook,** on the east side of Mt. Toby, is a popular fishing spot.
- The **town pound** on Montague Road has survived more than 150 years of use for impounding stray animals.

LEYDEN, Massachusetts
Population: 376   Zip Code: 01300

Pronounced "LIE-den," the town is named for Leiden, Holland, where the Pilgrims once sought refuge before coming to Plymouth. It is the northernmost community in the commonwealth.

Trips and trivia:
- The story of Leyden is the story of *people:*
  1. **John L. Riddell** (1807-65), inventor of the binocular microscope, was born here.
  2. Another famous native son is **Henry Kirke Brown** (1814-1886), who sculpted the Washington and Lincoln monuments at both West Point and the Capitol, Generals Winfield Scott and Nathanael Green in Washington, and *Angel of the Resurrection* at the Greenwood Cemetery.
  3. **William Dorrell** (1752-1846) brought some notoriety to the town as a resident who started what became the "Dorrellite Movement," which advocated "Free love and the sanctity of all life, animal and human." Dorrell lived in the town until, at the age of 94, he starved himself to death when he decided that he had lived long enough.
  4. Other famous residents include **Mary Stone,** a non-objective painter; **Masha Arms,** portrait photographer of prominent Americans such as Robert Frost; and **William T. Arms,** author of a history of Leyden and the Leyden historical novel *Salute to Courage.*

MONROE, Massachusetts
Population: 216   Zip Code: 01350

When Monroe was incorporated in 1822, it named itself for the current President of the U. S.—James Monroe, author of the Monroe Doctrine and President during the "Era of Good Feeling." It is the smallest manufacturing town in the state, paper products being its main industry.

Trips and trivia:
- **Dunbar Brook Gorge,** west of the junction with Monroe Road, has water flowing over huge boulders into a deep gorge.
- Another spectacular sight, the **Deerfield River Gorge,** can be seen from Route 2.
- **Monroe Bridge,** at an altitude of 1040 feet, is within view of Rowe's Yankee Atomic Power Plant. There is a nearby observation post.
- **Monroe State Forest** on Route 2, a 4,250-acre woodland preserve, provides hiking, riding, hunting, and scenic trails. Telephone: 413/424-7600.

- The **Old Congregational Church** in town has both historical and architectural interest.

MONTAGUE, Massachusetts
Population: 8,451   Zip Code: 01351

Montague is actually five villages in one: Montague City, Montague Center, Turners Falls, Lake Pleasant, and Millers Falls.

Trips and trivia:
- **Carnegie Library Museum** in Turners Falls has an outstanding collection of Indian relics. It is open Tuesday and Wednesday, 2:00 p.m. to 5:00 p.m., 7:00 p.m. to 8:00 p.m.
- The old **Congregational Church** in Montague Center was designed by architect Asher Benjamin.
- The **covered bridge** spanning the Connecticut River in Montague City has been declared a Historic American Building. Built in 1870, it is wood on two Masonry abutments and four piers, 770 feet long.
- **French King Bridge** in Turners Falls, 750 feet long and 140 feet above water, offers a picturesque view of the Pioneer Valley. The sandstone formations show traces of fossil footprints and marine and plant life from days gone by. The various levels of sea water, long since receded from the area, are visible from the striated lines in the sandstone.
- **Lake Pleasant,** the town reservoir, is located in Turners Falls.
- **Mayo's Point** is another scenic area.
- **Montague State Fish Hatchery,** off Montague Road midway between Turners Falls and Montague Center, propagates three species of trout: rainbow, brown, and brook trout. According to Ralph Taylor, Hatchery Manager, numbers range from 150,000 to 250,000, depending on the time of year. The hatchery is open weekdays at no charge, 9:00 a.m. to 4:00 p.m.

NEW SALEM, Massachusetts
Population: 474   Zip Code: 01355

Since most of the original proprietors who founded this town in 1737 were from Salem, Massachusetts, they decided to retain the name. At one point in its history, its location on the stagecoach Route between Brattleboro and Worcester made New Salem a busy trade center, but the population decreased with the coming of the railroad. Today it is mainly an agricultural and residential community, with many New Salemites teaching or working in some other capacity at the nearby University of Massachusetts.

Trips and trivia:
- The **Samuel C. Allen House** (Historic American Building) on South Main Street, a two-story frame dwelling with clapboarding, was built between 1809 and 1816. The Allen house is a Federal townhouse of fine design.
- Canals, dams, and mill sites can still be found representing the early sawmills and gristmills. The best example shows clearly at **Bears Den,** where a flume carried water from the falls to a gristmill. The wheel pit has withstood the test of time. The Bears Den area was also used by King Philip as a gathering place for the Nipmuck Indians for councils of war.
- **Curtis House** in North New Salem (1775), adjacent to the green, was once a tavern on the old stagecoach road. Although privately owned now and not open to the public, the house at one point was a hideaway for slaves on the Underground Railway.
- Also involved in the cause of blacks were two New Salem natives, **Sophia B. Packard** and **Harriet E. Giles,** who organized the Spelman Seminary for Negro Girls in Atlanta, Georgia.
- **Twin Spires,** consisting of the old Unitarian Church (1794) and the Congregational Church (1856) next to it, is a town landmark.

Swift River Valley Historical Society, Inc.

- **Whitaker-Clary House** (1816) on Elm Street, maintained by the **Swift River Valley Historical Society,** contains historical items and memorabilia of the lost towns of the Quabbin Valley. Here all the ghost towns—Dana, Enfield, Greenwich, and Prescott—are represented. The eight-room house also features a unique map of the old valley in topographical relief. The house is open to the public by appointment and every Wednesday and Sunday, 2:00 p.m. to 4:00 p.m. in July, August, and September. The North Prescott Methodist Church was recently moved to New Salem, alongside the Whitaker-Clary Museum. Telephone: 617/544-6807.

NORTHFIELD, Massachusetts
Population: 2,631   Zip Code: 01360

Originally called *Squakheag,* an Indian word for spearingplace for salmon, Northfield makes the best of its local educational and environmental facilities and sets an example as a forerunner in town planning.

Trips and trivia:
- **Antique auctions** are held in Ken Miller's bar every Monday night from April to mid-December. Every Sunday from 9:00 a.m. to 5:30 p.m. there is a popular Flea Market held on Warwick Avenue.

- **Clarke's Island,** a short distance south of town, is

the scene for a bit of local legend: **Captain Kidd** buried a treasure chest there, and the ghost of a murdered pirate is reputed to haunt the area.

• Built in 1784, **Captain Samuel Field House** is found opposite a marker indicating the first settlement in Northfield. The house is open by permission only.

• **Historic American Buildings** in Northfield and vicinity include:

1. Hall-Spring House at 89 Main Street, built c. 1846.
2. Captain Samuel Lane House at 33 Main Street, built 1845-7 by builder-architect George Stearns.
3. Isaac Mattoon House, 26 Main Street, built by Calvin Stearns in 1801.
4. William Pomeroy House, also built by Calvin Stearns (c. 1820), on the west side of Main Street just south of the town center.
5. Stratton House, early 18th century.
6. White-Field House, on the northeast corner of Main and Maple Streets, built in 1784.
7. Simeon Alexander House at 188 Main Street in East Northfield, built c. 1776.
8. Captain Richard Colton House (1828) on the east side of Main Street in East Northfield.
9. Elijah E. Belding House in West Northfield, on the east side of Mt. Hermon Station Road, north of the road to Northfield, built in 1840 by George Stearns.

• **Historic markers** throughout the town include:
1. Grave of Captain Richard Beers on Route 83
2. First Settlement on Route 10
3. Nathaniel Dickinson House on Route 10
4. King Philip's Hill on Route 10
5. Indian Council Fires on Route 63

• The **Kiwanis Picnic Area** on School Street is a popular recreation area for the townspeople.

• **Linden Hill School** is a boarding school founded in 1962 that has approximately 30 boys grades 5 to 9. Special emphasis is placed on language skills and other learning problems. The director, Thomas D. Scheidler, adds this tidbit about the school: "The grave of Captain Richard Beers, killed by Indians in pre-Revolutionary days, is on the property and I tell the boys that his ghost resides in our basement." Telephone: 413/498-2167.

• Northfield's most famous native son is **Dwight L. Moody** (1837-99), a noted evangelist who founded both the Northfield Seminary for Girls and Mount Hermon School for boys. His home, located at the corner of the first road north of West Northfield Road, is open by permission.

A collection of memorabilia on Moody's times and work can be seen at the Moody Museum, under the direction of Mr. William Morrow. Telephone: 413/498-2484.

• The **Northfield Historical Society Museum** is open on the second and fourth Wednesday and the first and third Sunday in July and August or by appointment with Mrs. Robert Johnston. Telephone: 413/498-2049. Three centuries of decorative arts, toys, tools, and textiles owned by Northfield families are on exhibit. The society also encourages a **Walking Tour** of its Main Street. There is a parking lot at the rear of the Town Hall; turn left from there and head south down Main Street to see these architectural styles: Georgian colonial, Federal, Greek Revival, Victorian Gothic, and Bungalows.

• The largest boarding school in the U. S. is the **Northfield Mount Hermon School.** The birthplace and grave of Dwight L. Moody are marked on its campus, the result of a merger of the Northfield School (established in 1879) and Mount Hermon School (established in 1881). It now serves as a coeducational college preparatory school for 1,000 students in grades 9 to 12. Northfield Mount Hermon has regional accreditation and is a member of the New England Association of Schools and Colleges. Telephone: 413/498-5311.

• **Northfield Mountain Pumped Storage Station** is a federally licensed plant offering the public a variety of recreational opportunities through the Northfield Mountain Recreation and Environment Center. This one-million kilowatt station pumps water from the nearby Connecticut River to a 320-acre reservoir on top of Northfield Mountain. During peak electrical demands, the water is released back through the underground power plant to generate electricity. Bus tours to the upper reservoir and underground powerhouse depart from the Center, April 22 through October 21; you are advised to call for available tour times. An exhibit area contains displays depicting the power aspects of Northfield as well as the historical use of the Connecticut River in this area. The Center is open Wednesday through Sunday, 9:00 a.m. to 5:00 p.m. spring, summer and fall. During the winter ski touring season, the Center is open seven days/week. Telephone: 413/659-3714.

- **Northfield Mountain Recreation and Environmental Center,** located at the site of the Northeast Utilities Hydroelectric Pumped Storage Station, offers hiking, cross-crountry skiing, and picnicking on its 25 miles of scenic trails.
- **Northfield State Forest,** on Route 2A, has facilities for fishing, hiking, and using recreational vehicles.
- **Old Pomeroy Place,** restored by a late principal of Mount Hermon, Elliot Speer, is privately owned by the Northfield Schools.
- An annex of the Northfield Inn, **Schell Chateau** is open for a small fee during the summer. It was built in 1890 by Robert Schell to simulate an English Country house.

- **Quinnetukut,** the Indian name for the Connecticut River meaning long tidal river, is also the name of the cruise boat used by Northeast Utilities to guide people along the river to learn about its historical, ecological, and geographical features. The one and a half-hour cruise departs from the Riverview Picnic Area, and offers interpretive riverboat rides, Wednesday through Sunday from June through October at 11:00 a.m., 1:00 p.m., and 3:00 p.m. on a modern 40-foot, 60-passenger vessel built under Coast Guard supervision. Tickets cost $5.00 for adults, $2.50 for children (14 and under); advance reservations are recommended. Write Box 377, Northfield. Telephone: 413/659-3714.
- The first **Youth Hostel** in America was founded in Northfield in 1934; members could pay an annual fee of $1.00 to have lodging throughout the U. S. and eventually Europe.

ORANGE, Massachusetts
Population: 6,104 Zip Code: 01364

Named for William, Prince of Orange, incorporated, this town has traditionally been noted for its skydiving meets.

Trips and trivia:
- Orange was the site of the first **automobile factory** in the country, established by Fred Grout in 1896 for making steam vehicles and then gasoline cars. One of the first Grouts is now at the Historical Society.
- **Lake Mattawa's** rainbow and brown trout are well known by fishermen.
- The **monument** located in Soldiers Memorial Park, which depicts a veteran explaining the futility of war to a youngster, was known nationwide following World War I. Sculpted by Joseph Pollia of New York, it bears the inscription, "It Shall Not Be Again."
- **North Orange** is responsible for some of the town's trivia, claiming native son Oliver Chapin, one of George Washington's personal guards; the second lending library in the U.S.; and the 1781 church, the first one in Orange, which still holds services regularly today.

ORANGE HISTORICAL SOCIETY

A Society for the Preservation of Records and Material Evidence of Orange's Past Which Have Influenced Its Present and Will Mould Its Future

41 NORTH MAIN STREET ORANGE, MASSACHUSETTS

- The **Orange Historical Society** maintains a museum at 41 North Main Street that has a large pewter collection, antique musical instruments, and a doll room. It is open Sunday afternoons from June through August, from 2:00 p.m. to 4:00 p.m. at an admission charge of $1.00 for adults, $.25 for children. It may also be seen at other times by appointment. Telephone: 617/544-3248 or 544-6635.
- The town used to be known as "The Sport **Parachuting** Center of the U. S.," because of all the jumps taken at the Orange Municipal Airport, but Parachutes, Inc., suspended operation there in 1984.
- Another change took place with the **Prescott Historical Society,** which disbanded in 1966 when the society gave the church and its contents to the Swift River Historical Society in New Salem.
- The **Sentinel Elm,** called the Signal Elm by the Nipmuck Indians, was felled in 1931, a monarch about 300 years old and 93 feet tall. It overshadowed the pioneers' fort.
- Orange's **Wheeler Memorial Library** was donated by the Wheeler family, who owned the New Home Sewing Machine Company.

ROWE, Massachusetts
Population: 315 Zip Code: 01367

Steeped in a tradition of historical preservation yet flexible to change, Rowe, named for a wealthy Boston merchant named John Rowe, represents the benefits of that foresight. It is located at the top of the commonwealth, bordering on Vermont.

Trips and trivia:
- **Adams Mountain,** reached by an access off Sibley Road, has a Summit Tower at 2,140 feet that affords the hiker a well-deserved view of four states: Massachusetts, New Hampshire, New York, and Vermont.
- As part of a Bicentennial project, the town of Rowe decided to relocate and restore the **Browning Bench Tool Factory** (built in 1834) for summer use as a "Community Center for the Arts and Crafts." Now a part of the Rowe Park Department, the bench tool factory offers a widely varied program to enhance the cultural, educational, and historical heritage of the town. It is open weekends throughout the summer months.
- University of Massachusetts students have been performing diggings for several summers at **Fort Pelham** and have unearthed many interesting artifacts that are in the Rowe Museum.

Rowe Historical Society Museum

- The **Helen McCarthy Memorial Museum** of the Rowe Historical Society, Inc., has been called "one of the finest small museums in New England." Since its founding in 1962, with the gift of the 1848 village school from the town of Rowe, the museum has grown to nine rooms, including the annexing of the old 1785 West School. With love and affection for her adopted community, Museum Director Helen McCarthy collected artifacts and memorabilia from well over 300 different friends of Rowe; under her efforts, the collection now contains more than 13,000 items. After her death in 1977, the Trustees of the Historical Society felt it a fitting tribute to rename the museum in her honor. It is open Wednesday and Sunday, 1:00 p.m. to 4:00 p.m. summers, by appointment year-round. Admission is free. Telephone: 413/339-4729, 339-5598, or 339-4700.
- **Pelham Lake,** site of many summer cottages, has swimming and boating facilities for townspeople.
- **Wooden bowls** for washing gold were made in Rowe during the 1850s. They were very popular during the California gold rush.
- The first atomic-powered steam-electric plant in New England, **Yankee Atomic Electric Company's** power plant in Rowe was one of the first in the nation. Completed in 1960, the plant's guiding purpose is the application of atomic power to peaceful utilization. It can generate 186,000 kilowatts of electricity and is estimated to have cost over $43 million. Tours of the Yankee Atomic Information Center are available Memorial Day through Labor Day from 9:00 a.m. to 5:00 p.m. Telephone: 413/625-6140.

SHELBURNE, Massachusetts
Population: 1,836   Zip Code: 01370

Known primarily for its falls and the beautiful flower-lined bridge that spans those falls, Shelburne was named for the Second Earl of Shelburne, Sir William Petty (1737-1805), the first Marquis of Lansdowne.

Trips and trivia:
- **Historic American Buildings** in the area include:
1. Arms House on Shelburne-Colrain Road, built in the late 18th century.
2. Daniel P. Bardwell House, on the east side of Bardwell's Ferry Road, about three miles south of Shelburne Center, built in 1842.
3. Daniel P. Bardwell, Ash House, near number two.
- There is an observation tower on **Mount Massaoment,** off Route 2, that is used by many sightseers who come to the area during the fall foliage season.
- **Pot Holes** in the Deerfield River, unusual depressions worn into the rocky bed of the river at the base of the falls, are of great geological interest. The rock formations were formed many thousands of years ago by the flooding Deerfield River. There are signs on Deerfield Avenue directing the visitor. **Salmon Falls** on the Deerfield River, so named for the large number of salmon that used to be caught there, has three distinct potholes.

- The unique **Bridge of Flowers** at Shelburne Falls welcomes its visitors with a placard reading: "Originally designed to carry trolley tracks across the Deerfield River, the 400-foot, five-arch span was converted into a pathway of flowers in 1929. A community project." The bridge itself was constructed in 1908 to connect Shelburne with Buckland, but it became an eyesore with the passing of the trolley line. Local groups united to form a pathway of beautiful shrubs and flowers across the bridge, and the Shelburne Falls Women's Club undertook sponsorship of the project. A monument to native sons who lost their lives in wartime was erected in 1948 by the American Legion at the center of the north side of the Bridge; opposite that is an American flag sponsored and maintained by American Legion Post No. 135. Special town celebrations take place nearby. At the entrance to the bridge is a gallery studio that features paintings of well-known artists. The register for guests indicates that the Bridge of Flowers has been

visited by people from all over the U.S., Canada, Australia, Europe, Asia, Africa, and Central and South America. The bridge is located just south of Route 2, off the by-pass, with directional signs. There is no charge, but contributions are appreciated. The Bridge of Flowers is floodlighted nightly until 10:30 p.m. during the summer months.
• **Shelburne Falls,** bisected by the Deerfield River, is the governmental center of the towns of Shelburne and Buckland.
• **Shelburne Summit** on Route 2 has a tower at its 1170-foot summit that overlooks Greenfield. Picnicking and hiking are available there.
• The first **Yale locks** were made in Shelburne by native Linus Yale in 1851.

SHUTESBURY, Massachusetts
Population: 788   Zip Code: 01072

Once known as "Roadtown," Shutesbury eventually named itself in honor of Samuel Shute, governor of Massachusetts Bay and New Hampshire from 1716-27.

Trips and trivia:
• **Beehive Huts** can be seen in two different places: Route 63 north from Amherst and past Lake Wyola to the first right, and Mineral Mountain.
• The Site of the Birthplace of Ithamar **Conkey,** adjacent to the General Store, commemorates the author of the hymn music of "In the Cross of Christ Is Glory."
• **Industry** in Shutesbury has been varied:
1. Basketmaking, one of the earliest industries in the town, is still carried on today. Palm leaf hats and shoes were very popular, and the town supported many cottage industries.
2. Its healthful climate has attracted many invalids and senior citizens who wanted to be like the legendary Granther Ephraim Pratt whose 1686-1800 gravestone in the center's old burying ground indicates he lived to see three centuries.
• **Lake Wyola** offers fishing, picnicking, boating, swimming, and camping. **Shutesbury State Park** has fishing and hunting. Telephone: 413/659-3797.

SUNDERLAND, Massachusetts
Population: 2,236   Zip Code: 01375

Originally called "Swampfield," Sunderland's early settlers came around 1673 to establish a lovely town amid beautiful mountains and streams and fertile farmland.

Trips and trivia:
• There is an **American Youth Hostel** on Falls Road.
• **Mohawk Brook,** in the southern part of town, is a popular local fishing spot.
• **Mount Toby,** used by the commonwealth as a demonstration forest, has an observation tower at its top. Near its base is the **Sunderland Town Park,** which has a pavilion with picnic facilities for large groups. Contact the park commissioner for reservations.
• **Sunderland Cave** has some interesting rock formations, especially Chimney Rocks.

• The giant **sycamore tree** on Main Street, the largest of its kind east of the Mississippi, is a local landmark. It can be seen just north of Town Hall.
• The **Sunderland Fish Hatchery** on Route 116 is open weekdays, 9:00 a.m. to 4:00 p.m., year-round, free to the public.

WARWICK, Massachusetts
Population: 492   Zip Code: 01378

At first Warwick was known as "Gardner's Canada" because many of its early settlers served under Captain Gardner in the Canadian campaign of 1690. A town renowned for its healthful climate, Warwick also has a great deal of civic pride—as evidenced by the big celebration of its own Bicentennial anniversary in 1963 when it drew more than 15,000 spectators to a Labor Day parade. It is located along the New Hampshire border.

Trips and trivia:
• The natural unspoiled beauty of Warwick's rugged terrain, with its many streams and ponds, can't be overemphasized. The state owns over one-third of the town's area, and its **forests** are its greatest natural resource.
• **Indian Cave,** north of Stevens Swamp and south of the old South Road to Northfield, is a spectacular rock formation entered through a 12-foot square opening.
• **Laurel Lake State Park** has facilities for swimming, picnicking, boating, camping, and fishing. **Mount Grace State Forest,** on Route 78, is open for fishing, hiking, riding, picnicking, hunting, skiing, snowmobiling, and, from its 1628-foot Fire Observation Tower, viewing New Hampshire. A trail leads from the village to the top of the mountain. Look for the "Indian Mail Box," a hole in the face of the ledge about 200 feet west of the tower.
• One of the many glacial boulders, **Warbeek,** is found on the west side of the Hastings Pond Road. The name is Indian for big rock, and it bears the inscription "In the Beginning—God."
• **Warwick State Forest** on Athol Road has facilities for fishing, hiking, riding, hunting, and recreational vehicles. Swimming is available in Moore's pond.

WENDELL, Massachusetts
Population: 405   Zip Code: 01379

The settlers of this lovely wooded town decided to name it in honor of Judge Oliver Wendell of Boston. Its woods provide Wendell with its main industries: lumbering, logging, and recreation.

Trips and trivia:
• **Miller's River** is named for a young man who drowned in sight of his beloved when his canoe struck an ice mass.
• The **State Proving Grounds** are located in Wendell.
• There are facilities for boating, swimming, and picnicking at **Wendell State Forest** on Wendell Road at Ruggles Pond; hiking, hunting, snowmobiling, and a boat-

launching ramp at Wickett Pond.

• **Mormon Hollow** is named for travelers who left a Mormon caravan to settle there or settlers who decided to become Mormon.

WHATELY, Massachusetts
Population: 1,145   Zip Code: 01093

Governor Hutchingson decided to name this town after his friend Thomas Whately of England in gratitude for political favors, and to this day it is the only Whately in the world. Throughout its 200 years it has been essentially agricultural, with salts and minerals in its geological strata bestowing superior flavor on fruits, milk, maple syrup, and tobacco.

Trips and trivia:

• The town's S. White **Dickinson Library** on Main Street was erected in 1949 with money left the town by Anna White Dickinson in memory of her father. A local history room features Whately pottery, Indian relics, and pressed glass in the Dickinson pattern. Statistics hold that the library has such an incredible circulation each year that townspeople average 50 books per year. The library has an outstanding reference section. Its hours are Monday, 2:00 p.m. to 5:00 p.m., 7:00 p.m. to 9:00 p.m.; Tuesday and Thursday, 7:00 p.m. to 9:00 p.m. (except in summer); Wednesday, 12:00 p.m. to 5:00 p.m., 7:00 p.m. to 9:00 p.m.; Saturday, 12:00 p.m. to 6:00 p.m. Telephone: 413/665-2170.

• Whately was the site of the first **gin distillery** in the state.

• The original Whately **pound** on West Lane, established in 1771 to impound stray cattle and horses, still exists. Keeper of the pound is the road superintendent. Whately is the only town in the commonwealth with both a pound and a pound-keeper.

• Due to the unique geological inheritance left the town by the Triassic era, Whately may be the only town of its size—three by six miles—to have three **reservoirs** within its borders for adjoining towns. Still, there is no reservoir for Whately—"Eminent domain's villainous 'rights' saw to that."

• Whately, in common with other New England towns, had to be **self-sufficient** to survive, so many farmers were industrialists who managed mills, smithies, potteries, cabinet-making, brick kilns, shoemaking, and wagon-making along with their farms and animals. Sixteen-hour work days and large families made it possible.

• The **Smith College Observatory,** located on a 180-acre tract on Poplar Hill, is used for research and instruction for Smith College in cooperation with the others in the Five College program: Amherst, Hampshire, Mount Holyoke, and the University of Massachusetts. There is a 16-foot reflecting telescope, found in the circular brick building with an electrically operated dome.

• A large boulder on Chestnut Plain Road marks the site of the **stockade** used throughout the French and Indian War. The stockade was never attacked but was used for many watches against surprise attacks.

• From the days of its earliest inhabitants, the Nipmucks, **tobacco** grown in Whately had superior quality, and tribes from New York, Vermont, and New Hampshire would come to barter for it. In 1940, after the invasion of the Dutch East Indies by the Japanese, the Queen Wilhelmina Company transferred its tent tobacco growing to Whately, where the product was indistinguishable from that grown in the Indies. Lemuel Graves is reputed to be the first to grow tobacco under netting in the valley, in 1901.

• **Whately Glen,** a half-century ago considered one of the most beautiful natural parks in the world, is on the drawing board for a revival by the Whately Historical Society.

Hampden County

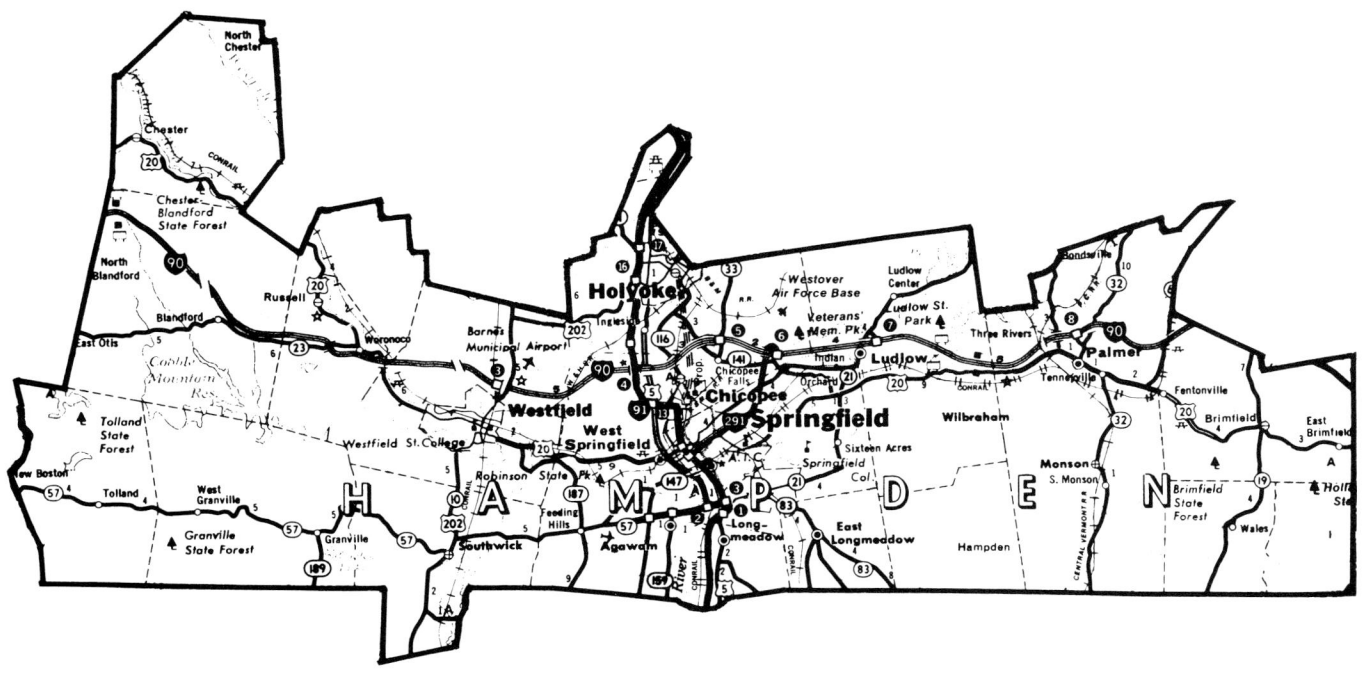

Hampden County

AGAWAM, Massachusetts
Population: 21,717   Zip Code: 01001

Agawam is an Indian word for crooked river, and in 1634 the modern site was the original settlement of Springfield. It boasts the lowest Zip Code in the continental United States.

Trips and trivia:

• **Agawam Gin** at one point in history was a nationally known product. A peppermint distillery was established on Main Street in 1810, then expanded to manufacture potato whiskey, then cider, brandy, rye, and gin.

• The **Lieutenant William Allen House** at 726 Main Street was built c. 1795. Historic American Buildings in the town include:

Colton-Cooley House at 740 Elm Street and Main Street, built in 1805.

Captain Charles Leonard House (1805-7) at 663 Main Street, a Georgian house believed to have been designed by architect Asher Benjamin. It is listed with the National Register of Historic Places; open to the public by arrangement. Telephone: 413/786-9421.

Tobacco Barn at the rear of Main Street, built in 1885.

• The **Metacomet-Monadnock Trail,** running from the Hanging Hills of Meriden, Connecticut, to the summit of Grand Monadnock Mountain in New Hampshire; crosses Massachusetts at the Agawam-Southwick line, then follows the Holyoke Range to Amherst Notch on Route 116 to Mount Grace before heading northeast. It is a popular place for hikers and backpackers.

• Two famous **natives** of the town include:

1. General Creigton W. Abrams (1914-74), Army Chief of Staff who commanded U. S. forces in Vietnam from 1968-72 and who then saw gradual U. S. withdrawal from the war. Abrams was described by President Gerald Ford as "an American hero in the best tradition." He was voted by his graduating class of 1932 at Agawam High School as "the boy most likely to succeed."

2. Anne Sullivan (Macy) (1887-1936), the famous miracle worker who taught mute, sightless Helen Keller. There is a monument in the center of town commemorating the Feeding Hills native.

• **Riverside Park,** The Largest Amusement Park in New England, is located on Route 159. It is open weekends March 28 through Memorial Day and Labor Day through September 27, daily June 1 through Labor Day, 11:00 a.m. Over 50 major rides including the number one roller coaster in the U. S. and the Riverside Cyclone. New petting zoo. Over 30 food stands, including German, Chinese, Italian, and Mexican cuisine. Many games and arcades along the midway, exciting new shows such as music revues and magic shows. Rates are $11.99 for adults (including all rides, shows, and attractions), juniors $8.99, and special rates for senior citizens and the handicapped; group rates available for 25 or more. The private Grove Pavillion is available for groups up to 5,000. Telephone: 413/786-9300. Riverside Park is accessible from the Massachusetts Turnpike by exit 4 (south on Route 5 to Routes 57W and 159S), or exit 6 (south on Route 291 to I-91S, then Routes 57W and 195S); from Connecticut, take Route 91N to Route 190W, at Route 159N. Riverside features the best leisure time in New England.

• **John C. Robinson State Park** on North Street in Feeding Hills has 1,000 acres offering recreational swimming, tennis, and picnicking in the summer and cross-country skiing and snowmobiling in the winter. Telephone: 413/786-2877.

• The Agawam *town offices* are located at 36 Main Street. Telephone: 413/786-0400. The 4th of July celebration is an annual event in the town which features a gigantic picnic and fireworks.

BLANDFORD, Massachusetts
Population: 863   Zip Code: 01008

The origin of Blandford has quite a story: its Scotch-Irish settlers named it New Glascow, and the homeland in Scotland was so touched it promised the town church a bell. However, when the provincial governor, William Shirley, opted to name the town for the ship he was coming on to the U. S., Glascow reneged.

Trips and trivia:
- The **Blandford Church** on North Street, in the center of town, was built in 1822. Designed by architect Isaac Damon, it is an oustanding example of Greek Revival architecture.
- For three days each year over Labor Day weekend, the **Blandford Fairgounds** are the scene for farming exhibits, rides, and many special events.
- The **Blandford Historical Society** on North Blandford Road at North Street maintains a historical house open by appointment. Telephone: 413/848-2823.
- **Cobble Mountain Reservoir** supplies water to Springfield; it is open to the public for picnicking and hiking. Nearby, the **Mountain Laurel Trail,** resplendent each June, is a favorite hiking area of natives and the many resort residents of the town. The course runs from Westfield through Granville to Blandford.
- The town's charm has been captured for several **movies,** including Shirley Temple's *The Littlest Rebel* and some Tarzan shots.
- The **Springfield Ski Club, Inc.,** is headquartered in Blandford. Telephone: 413/786-2732 (Springfield), 848-2860 (Blandford), or 786-4957 for a snow condition report.

BRIMFIELD, Massachusetts
Population: 1,907   Zip Code: 01010

Trips and trivia:
- The annual Brimfield **Apple Festival** is held on the town green over the Columbus Day weekend, featuring apple sales, exhibits, and shows.

BALLOON SCHOOL OF MASSACHUSETTS INC.

- **Balloon School of Massachusetts, Inc.** is located at Balloonport at Dingley Dell. Telephone: 413/245-7013. Ballooning is an all-season sport, and flights can be made year-round, weather permitting. Up to seven passengers can fly in the largest of the fleet of five balloons. The cost is $135.00 per person per flight (including breakfast for morning flights), and each passenger is presented with a flight certificate suitable for framing. Also, instruction for certification is offered.
- The **Brimfield Public Library** is custodian of the town's archives, which are in its Sherman Room, as are all local historical materials. Telephone: 413/245-3518.
- **Brimfield State Forest,** 3,158 acres of recreational offerings off of Route 20, features swimming, fishing, picnicking, and camping at Dean Pond, Dearth Hill Pond, and Woodman Pond, plus hunting, hiking, and snowmobiling in other parts of the sanctuary. Telephone: 413/245-9966.
- The **Chamberlain House** was built in the early 19th century and has been designated a Historic American Building. Other structures of architectural note in town include the Elias Carter-designed houses in the center of town next to the First Congregational Church (1848) and the Italianate Hitchcock Free Academy that dates to the mid-19th century. There are many fine buildings located around and near the lovely old town green.
- There is swimming at the **East Brimfield Dam** on Route 20. The **East Brimfield Reservoir,** with an access from Route 20, comprises 420 acres that were formed to control the flow of the Thames River and White River which pass through the town. There are recreational facilities for swimming, boating, and fishing.
- **Indian Hill** is the site of an Indian stockade and corn storehouse, the old Indian village of Ashquoach, and Quaboag Old Fort.
- The Captain **Nicholas House** in West Brimfield, now privately owned, quartered Hessian soldiers marching from Saratoga to Boston in 1777.
- **Steerage Rock,** a landmark on the Indians' Bay Path Trail, was a guidepost in 1639 to pioneer settlers. It is located four miles away from town on the summit of East Waddaquododuck Mountain.

CHESTER, Massachusetts
Population: 1,110   Zip Code: 01011

Formerly called Murrayfield, Chester at one point was a boom town as the birthplace of the abrasives industry in the nation. It is located in the northwestern corner of Hampden County.

Trips and trivia:
- The Reverend **Aaron Bascom House,** on the road to Middlefield, was built in 1769 and is an Historic American Building. Other places of interest include:

Hiram Smith's tomb in the Chester center, just a short walking distance off Maynard Hill Road—where Smith and his sister Isabel Toogood are buried; the tomb was hollowed out of a granite boulder from their farm pasture. It took two years to complete the seven feet, two inch by four feet, five inch-opening.

Also in Chester center are the old schoolhouse in the process of being restored, church, mid-20th century homes, and cemetery with burials dating from 1763.

In North Chester on East River Road is a restored old tavern, chapel, and schoolhouse.

Chester Village features a round-house off Middlefield Street that was built in 1833 and the railroad station on

Main Street.

• The **Chester-Blandford State Forest** on Route 20 has facilities for hiking, hunting, picnicking, fishing, camping, and swimming. Of particular note are Boulder Park and Sanderson Brook Falls in the 2,400-acre scenic area. Telephone: 413/532-3985.

• Hamilton Memorial Library houses the **Chester Museum** in its building on Route 20. The museum contains local artifacts and antiques, plus an outstanding mineral collection, and is open free of charge on Saturday and Sunday afternoons from 1:00 p.m. to 4:00 p.m. in the summer and by appointment. The building is in the process of being sold for senior citizen apartments, at which point the library would be moved to the first floor. Telephone: 413/354-7808.

• Deposits of **emery** were discovered in Chester during the 19th century, and the town had the first emery mine in the country.

• The **Littleville Fairgrounds** are the scene each second weekend in August of a fair that features livestock competition, exhibits, and food. Telephone: 413/354-7760.

CHICOPEE, Massachusetts

Population: 66,676   Zip Code: 01013

Chicopee was originally named by the Nipmuck Indians with the word for violent water because of the Chicopee River Falls. Now, Chicopee is famous as the site of Westover Air Force Base, at one point the largest Strategic Air Command base in the Eastern U. S.; the largest sporting goods manufacturer in the country, A. G. Spalding and Brothers; *The Wall Street Journal* publication; the College of Our Lady of the Elms; and the recently restored Edward Bellamy Homestead.

Trips and trivia:

• **Band concerts** are given throughout the summer months on Sunday nights at Szot Park on Front Street. Other public parks include the Chicopee Country Club, Chicopee Memorial, Atwater Park, and Chicopee Meadows.

• The **Edward Bellamy Homestead** at 91 Church Street commemorates the novelist and social reformer who, impelled by the injustices in the economic and social systems of 19th century society and a desire for reform, in 1888 wrote *Looking Backward,* a novel set in Boston in the year 2000. The book is a remarkable vision and had tremendous popular impact in its day. Celebration of the 100th anniversary of the book will take place with a Bellamy conference in 1988. "The Prophet of Church Street" is a 28-minute documentary available at no charge to schools and civic groups; contact John Dumont, 180 Broadway, Chicopee, MA. Bellamy was also a founder of the *Springfield Daily News.* The homestead, a National Historic Landmark, is under the auspices of The Society for the Preservation of New England Antiquities (SPNEA), and is maintained by the Edward Bellamy Memorial Association. It has two tenants: **Chicopee Chamber of Commerce** (telephone: 413/594-2101) and **Chicopee Development Corp.** (telephone: 592-4731). According to Steven Jendrysik, President of the Edward Bellamy Association, the homestead will be open to the public in the summer of 1988.

• **Chicopee State Park** on Burnett Road comprises 574 acres of land for swimming, picnicking, horse and cycle trail riding, hunting, fishing, snowmobiling, and cross-country skiing. Take exit 6 off the Massachusetts Turnpike. Telephone: 413/594-9416.

• The expression **"Chicopee Steel"** has its origin from the high quality cavalry sabres made by the Ames Manufacturing Company in the town during the Civil War and Western Indian Wars. To give someone Chicopee Steel became synonymous with a fatal stabbing.

• **Elms College** (officially the College of Our Lady of the Elms) at 291 Springfield Street is a four-year Catholic liberal arts college for women. Founded in 1928 by the Sisters of Saint Joseph the college offers liberal arts and professional programs to both traditional and non-traditional students, and continuing education courses are open to adults. Total enrollment is 1,000. The Elms has received accreditation by the New England Association of Schools and Colleges, programs in nursing and social work have received national approval, and the Education Department is a member of the Interstate Certification Compact. Situated around a quadrangle, the campus buildings are examples of both collegiate Gothic and modern architecture; playing fields, tennis courts, and tree-lined walks help make it a beautiful spot. Visitors are welcome, particularly to the Alumnae Library and the Borgia Art Gallery. Telephone: 413/598-8351.

• One of the oldest in all New England, **First Church** (1751) is located on Chicopee Street. Also of architectural note is City Hall at Chicopee Center, modeled after the Palazzo Vecchio in Florence, Italy. The City Hall was recently placed on the National Register. Other interesting buildings around town include mill structures near the canal, Market Square and Kendall Hotels, homes in the Fairview and Willimansett sections, and the Chapin Cemetary on Chicopee Street. There are efforts afoot to put the 339 Front Street home of the Father of the Automobile, Charles E. Duryea, which is on the National Historic Landmark list.

• The first **friction matches,** kitchen matches known as lucifers, were made in Chicopee in 1935. Another first in the town was the first bronze statuary to be cast in the country, established in 1853 by the Ames Company—used on the east and west doors of the Capitol.

• Chicopee's annual **Kielbasa Festival,** one of the largest ethnic festivals in New England, is held at Fairfield Mall on Route 33 each September. It features Polish dancing with authentic costumes, music, and Polish dishes made with the famous sausage, plus the "World's Largest Kielbasa."

• **Lieutenant General Arthur MacArthur** is a famous native son of Chicopee Falls—see Native Sons and Daughters.

• **Memorial State Park** on Burnett Road has facilities for picnicking, swimming, boating, fishing, and ice skating.

• The **Victor bicycle,** which at one point supplied 75% of all bikes in the U. S., was established in Chicopee by designer Albert Overman.

EAST LONGMEADOW, Massachusetts
Population: 13,300　　　　　　　　Zip Code: 01028

Though once famous for its brownstone and redstone quarries, East Longmeadow is a residential, suburban community with a balance of business and industry.

Trips and trivia:

• The **Elijah Burt House** at 201 Chestnut Street, built 1720-40, is the town's oldest dwelling. Originally a stagecoach stopover, plus the spot on the underground railroad used by runaway slaves during the Civil War, the Burt House is listed on the National Register of Historic Places. It is open by appointment—Telephone: 413/525-3452. Another place of note is the depot on Maple Street, built in 1876 for the Connecticut Central Railroad that ran from Hartford to Springfield, with many stops in East Longmeadow for its quarried stone that was shipped all over the country.

• Two **churches** of historical and architectural interest are:

The First Congregational Church (1828) at 7 Somers Road on Route 83, the oldest church in continuous use in its orginal building; first used for town meetings. Telephone: 413/525-4121.

Old First Baptist Church, at 89 Meadowbrook Road in the southeastern section of town, built 1818-33. Telephone: 413/525-7866.

• **East Longmeadow's Historical Headquarters/Museum** at 25 Maple Street holds monthly open houses from May to December and by appointment. Telephone: 413/525-2354, 525-2513, or the Town Clerk, 525-3305 (8:00 a.m. to 4:00 p.m.). It contains antique furniture and artifacts, the town's Bicentennial Quilt featuring 42 historic buildings and sites, maps and prints, costumes, and exhibits of quarrying. The 1852 house was occupied by George W. Masury, the last of the town's Civil War veterans, who is believed to have been the youngest drummer in the Union Army.

• The largest **Independence Day parade** in the area is celebrated each year in East Longmeadow, with fireworks the night before near the town rotary.

• East Longmeadow is represented by diverse **industry:**
American Saw and Manufacturing Company at 301 Chestnut Street, manufactures blades, saws, and files. Telephone: 413/525-3961.

Milton Bradley, internationally famous makers of games and educational aids, is at 44 Shaker Road. Telephone: 413/525-6411.

R. E. Phelon, Inc. ignition systems for small engines are made at 70 Maple Street. Telephone: 413/525-6471.

Sunshine Art Studios on Denslow Road makes greeting cards. Telephone: 413-5500.

• East Longmeadow is a model community for its use of land for recreational and conservation purposes. It has set aside about 270 acres for **parks,** playgrounds, and other areas open to the public.

• **Quarries,** brownstone and redstone, were in operation over 125 years in their location off Pleasant Street, but they are now abandoned and filled with water.

GRANVILLE, Massachusetts
Population: 1,183　　　　　　　　Zip Code: 01034

Granville's fame is alphabetical: apples, blueberries, cheese, drums, and educators. Its land was purchased in 1686 from Toto, an Indian Sachem, by James Cornish of Westfield for the price of a flintlock gun and 16 brass buttons. First called Bedford Plantation, it changed its name to honor John Carteret (1690-1763), Earl of Granville who was a member of the King's Council. It became a town in 1754.

Trips and trivia:

• **Curtis Tavern** on Route 57, not open to the public, has been designated a Historic American Building. It was built in 1765, and many other houses in the village were also built around that same time. The Granville Town Hall, built in the neoclassic style, is a recent addition to the town. Other interesting places around town include the Congregational Church (1778) in West Granville, a marker showing where the First Methodist Episcopal Church stood in the Beech Hill section of town, Academy Building (1837), and the Old Meeting House (1802) at Granville Center, being restored by the town as a memorial to local son Reverend Timothy M. Pastor who served as Granville's pastor for 63 years.

• This Granville is the mother of the beautiful college

town of **Granville, Ohio,** home of Denison University. A close bond exists between mother and daughter, and over the years efforts have been made to perpetuate the relationship. Every 50 years the two towns officially get together—1845, 1895, and 1945 so far—and a marble monument near the Meeting House commemorates these occasions.

• The **Granville State Forest** on West Hartland Road off of Route 57 has facilities for fishing, hunting, hiking, swimming, camping, picnicking, cross-country skiing, and snowmobiling on its 2,247 acres. Telephone: 413/357-6611.

• **Liberty Hill** in West Granville is the town's Revolutionary symbol erected in the form of a liberty pole to commemorate this country's independence from Great Britain.

• A description of Granville wouldn't be complete without its **people:**

It was mostly settled by people from Springfield, Massachusetts; Suffield, and Durham, Connecticut.

Because of its clear air and pure water, the town has gained quite a reputation for its residents' longevity.

In 1800 the population was 2,309, which was larger than the population of Springfield, Massachusetts.

Some of Granville's famous personages include native son Isaac Chapman Bates, an early U. S. Senator; Attorney Milton B. Whitney, philanthropist; native son Judge Michael H. Sullivan; the aforementioned Reverend T. M. Cooley; John Phelps, the first high sheriff of Hampden County; and Reverend Lemuel Haynes, the first ordained Negro Congregational minister in the U. S.

• **Phelon Hill,** one of the Pioneer Valley's marked laurel trails, is a favorite of spring sightseers to the area.

• The **Mable Root Room** in the Granville Public Library (Telephone: 413/357-8531) contains displays of local antiques and memorabilia, the town's Bicentennial Quilt and miniatures from the extensive collection of Mrs. Henry C. Turner. The library, designed in the Richardson Romanesque style is located at Main Street and Granby Road, off of Route 57. Its Historical Room is open Wednesday and Saturday from 2:00 p.m. to 5:00 p.m. and also by appointment. Telephone: 413/357-6671. The library was built in 1900 by 13 women who were part of the still existent Women's Library Club.

HAMPDEN, Massachusetts
Population: 4,572　　　　　　　　　　Zip Code: 01036

A residential and summer resort village for many years, Hampden has been put on the map in honor of one of its most famous residents, writer/storyteller Thornton W. Burgess. It celebrated its centennial separation from the town of Wilbraham on March 28, 1878 with a full week of festivities.

Trips and trivia:

• **Hampdenites** have included several notables:

Anice Terhune, wife of writer Albert Payson Terhune, was a famed pianist and composer in her own right. Her novels include *The Boarder Up at Em's; Eyes of the Village,* said to represent some townsfolk; and *The White Mouse.*

Thornton Burgess (1874-1965)—see Laughing Brook

• Local **landmarks** include:

Academy Hall (1850), in the center of town, where exhibits and dislays are maintained by the Hampden Historical Society. It is open Sundays in the summer, 1:00 p.m. to 5:00 p.m. and by appointment. Telephone: 413/566-8930.

A cider mill, once powered by a horse, on South Road.

The Federated Community Church, built in 1832.

Old brick kilns in the eastern part of town, used for making charcoal for the Springfield Armory.

Town House, given to the town in 1932 by Miss Elizabeth Sessions. The Sessions family had been prominent in local and state politics since the end of the Revolution, and it was said that "the legislature never had a session without a Sessions."

Laughing Brook Education Center and Wildlife Sanctuary

• **Laughing Brook Education Center and Wildlife Sanctuary** at 789 Main Street is one of 17 staffed sanctuaries of the Massachusetts Audubon Society. It consists of 259 acres of land and six buildings, all used to educate adults and children toward an awareness, understanding, and appreciation of the natural environment. The Storyteller's House is the former home of Thornton W. Burgess, author of children's nature books and the *Old Mother West Wind.* The Cape Cod-style structure, originally built by Calvin Stebbins in 1872, is the oldest house in the village, is listed on the National Register of Historic Places, and is open for guided tours. Visitors can also enjoy indoor and outdoor exhibits of live native New England wildlife over four and a half miles of walking trails, a covered picnic pavilion, and the Environmental Center, which includes an Environmental Resource Library, Audubon Shop, Solar Greenhouse, etc. Laughing Brook offers a full range of natural history and environmental education programs, including courses, workshops, field trips, a summer natural history day camp, and special programs for groups both on- and off-site. Seasonal brochures are available. The Sanctuary is open year-round, Tuesday through Sunday, 10:00 a.m. to 5:00 p.m. Admission is free to Massachusetts Audubon members; the non-member fee is $3.00 for adults, $1.50 for children under 16, $1.50 for senior citizens, and free to children under 3. Group tours and programs can be arranged. Telephone: 413/566-8034. Special family programs at 2:00 p.m. every Sunday and Monday holiday. Harvest Days, with the flavor of an old-time country fair, are held each October. Directions from Massachusetts Pike: exit 8 to Palmer, then Monson, and on to Hampden; from the south or Somers, Connecticut go north up Route 83 and follow signs; from I-91, exit 4 via Route 21 up Sumner Avenue and Allen Street to Laughing Brook.

• 17-year-old Edward Leyden of Hampden became the world's **pinball wizard** on July 30, 1978 when he set a new record in the Guiness Book by a marathon 170 hours of pinball machine play.

HOLLAND, Massachusetts
Population: 1,400   Zip Code: 01550

About four miles square, located in the southeastern tip of the Pioneer Valley, Holland was incorporated as a district in 1783 and as a town in 1836. It was named for Lord Holland, Charles James Fox (1749-1806), English statesman and orator who supported Colonialists' rights; urged the abolition of slavery; was active in literary and historical work; was removed from the privy council for his toast "Our Sovereign, the people"; served as foreign secretary in the All-the-Talents ministry during which time he revealed a plot to assassinate Napoleon; and was the author of the incomplete *History of Reign of James II*. He is buried in Westminster Abbey.

Trips and trivia:

• **Hamilton Reservoir,** located between Brimfield and East Brimfield Roads, has facilities for swimming, fishing, and boating, plus ice skating in the winter. Part of the **Holland Pond Recreation Area,** it is a man-made lake owned by the town. Take exit 6 from I-86, then Holland Road from Route 20. **Holland State Park,** off of Route 20, has 1,100 acres for swimming, fishing, hunting, and picnicking.

• Holland was once inhabited by **Indians,** and their mark was made in such places as Indian Field Hill where arrowheads and other tools that have been found, an Indian Oven that was discovered there, and by Indian names for local sites: Lake Siog (Indian name for pickerel) and the Pequiog region around it (The Lake in the Region of Cleared Land), the Quinebaug River (Long Water), Mashapaug Pond (Great Lake), Tantuisque (lead mine), etc.

• **Landmarks** in the town include:
The Congregational Church, organized in 1763, whose first pastor, Reverend Ezra Reeven, served the church for 53 years.
Town Hall, built in 1820 in classic Greek Revival style.
Webber House on Brimfield Road, a cape said to be the town's oldest structure.

• The population in Holland swells to approximately 7,500 during the summer months. Other *people* facts:
The earliest deed in the area, according to county records, was granted to Governor John Winthrop (1588-1649) for land ten miles around the Black Lead Mine in Sturbridge.
Joseph Blodgett, father of 17 children, was the town's first settler, and purchased land in an area subsequently known as the Polley Place.
Another of Holland's early settlers, Captain Benjamin Church, was revered as a member of General George Washington's Revolutionary War guards having passed the requirements of "sobriety, honesty, appearance and good behavior, 5'8" to 5'10" in height." He served his country and his town well as official and benefactor.
One of the first votes taken by the original selectmen of 1783 was "that swine run at large being properly lawed" (i.e., ringed and yoked).
William A. Robins (1805-1887), a carpenter who worked on the Hitchcock Free Academy in Brimfield and who taught singing and served in local politics as a representative in the state legislature in 1862.
The town was particularly fortunate in having Reverend Martin Lovering (1853-1941) record *The History of Holland, Massachusetts,* and his records up to 1915 have been invaluable.
Mrs. Ursula Allen (MacFarland) Chase (1842-1933) worked on many genealogies and her husband, Levi Badger Chase compiled the Vital Records of Sturbridge, discovering the route of the earliest Bay Path.

HOLYOKE, Massachusetts
Population: 50,112   Zip Code: 01040

The first planned industrial center in the nation, designed to maximize its canals for industry, Holyoke was named for Captain Elizur Holyoke who was an explorer along the Connecticut River Valley around 1633. At one point known as The Paper City of the World, it is today still a major manufacterer of fine papers and its allied products.

Trips and trivia:

• Mills and townhouses along the Holyoke **Canal** are listed on the National Register of Historic Places as The Hadley Falls Company Housing District, known locally as the Hadley Mills Townhouses. The nearby former railroad terminal on Bowers Street was designed by architect Henry Hobson Richardson. Holyoke City Hall, also on the National Register, has been the city's landmark since it was built in 1875. Of special note is the Victorian Gothic tower. The history student should also note the Goodyear House (c. 1780) on Homestead Avenue, the cemetery at the corner of Rock Valley and Keys Road, and Elmwood Cemetery on Route 5.

• The **Children's Museum of Holyoke** at 444 Dwight Street provides a unique setting in which children and adults can learn together about art, science, and the world around them. Through participatory exhibits, children can challenge themselves, discover how the world works, try on new roles, and learn by doing. Founded by the Junior League of Holyoke, the museum offers changing exhibits, workshops, school programs, birthday parties, and special

events. The museum store features educational toys, games, and books. The recycle center is a source for materials and inspiration. Open Tuesday through Friday, 10:00 a.m. to 5:00 p.m. and Saturday and Sunday 12:00 p.m. to 5:00 p.m. Admission is $3.50 for adults; children are $2.50 and children must be accompanied by an adult. Telephone: 413/536-KIDS.

• **Church in the Round,** the Church of the Blessed Sacrament on Route 5's Northampton Street, was built in 1951 as a new concept in contemporary churches. Its 16 aisles radiate from a central altar, and the stained-glass windows are unusual. The architecture has been featured in several national magazines.

• When I-91 was being built, thousands of **dinosaur tracks** were uncovered along the riverbank. Said to be one of the finest Triassic beds in the world, the site is marked on Route 5 on the west bank of the Connecticut River. Some seven acres are now devoted to protecting the 150,000,000-year old dinosaur footprints. The reserve is administered by the Trustees of Reservations.

• **Dreikorn's Bakery** Company at 322 Park Street offers tours of its facility, showing the complete process of bread-making. Telephone: 415/536-5322.

• Holyoke's **Geriatric Authority** has received national recognition. Established in 1971 in response to the needs of the city's elderly residents, it is the only quasipublic geriatric authority of its kind in the nation. The Holyoke Geriatric and Convalescent Center cares for the health and housing needs of local senior citizens through this model program.

• The **Greater Holyoke Chamber of Commerce,** a voluntary organization of the business and professional community, operates at 187 High Street, Suite 304. Telephone: 413/534-3376.

• **Holyoke Community College,** (HCC) 303 Homestead Avenue (Route 202 south of I-91), is a state college founded in 1946, and today serves about 3,000 day and 2,000 evening students on its 135-acre suburban campus. Accredited by the New England Association of Schools and Colleges, its most famous graduate is now its president, David M. Bartley, Class of 1954, former Speaker of the Massachusetts House of Representatives. Asked about facilities open to the public, Bartley said, "That's the middle name of the college—community," HCC offers a one-mile interpretive trail system, summer camp, baseball school, nursery school, and a theatre program that stages periodic productions for the general public. It is the home base of the Holyoke College Civic Orchestra. Telephone: 413/538-7000.

• Spanning the Connecticut River between Holyoke and South Hadley Falls, the **Holyoke Dam** was built at the turn of the century, but is still the source of much local hydroelectric power for the city's incredible canal system. Its full unbroken breadth of 1,020 feet makes it a major attraction. A four and a half-mile, three-level network of canals there provides hydroelectric units and water processing for the city's industrial plants. At the Second Level Canal is a towering quintet of water fountains, the focal point of Holyoke Water Power Park. The 3706-foot chimney of the Holyoke Water Power Company's Mt. Tom Power Plant, the tallest in New England, is another landmark. A fishway at the end of Holyoke Dam allows thousands of Atlantic shad to pursue their migration patterns. The annual Shad Derby, held in the latter part of May, attracts hundreds of anglers to the dam.

• **Holyoke Heritage Park,** between Dwight and Appleton Streets, is a five-acre park with permanent exhibits of Holyoke. There are walking tours and seasonal tours, including an antique rail car. Open daily, free. Telephone: 413/539-1723.

• The city's local daily afternoon newspaper, the **Holyoke Transcript-Telegram,** is located at 120 Whiting Farms Road. Telephone: 413/536-2300.

• Dedicated in 1967, the John F. **Kennedy Memorial** stands at the junction of Appleton and Suffolk Streets.

• Holyoke's baseball team, **"The Millers,"** of the Eastern League, is a farm club of the Milwaukee Brewers. The Millers bring great suspense and enjoyment to the city each summer at MacKenzie Stadium. Telephone: 413/533-7580.

• **Mountain Park** advertises itself as one of New England's finest recreational and amusement areas in 100 acres of natural beauty. Located just off of Route 5 on the Mountain Park access road (off of I-91, exit 17E), the park features a giant midway with over 28 rides, picnic pavilions, numerous concession stands, and a concert stage. Its history dates back to 1895 when it started with a merry-go-round, roller coaster, restaurant, and open air theatre and a trolley car line bringing visitors up the mountain. When ownership was transferred to the Holyoke Street Railway Company, it expanded in the early 1900s to the largest summer park theatre in New England, with record numbers coming to operas in the casino. A favorite family spot, it is 45 minutes equidistant from Worcester, Hartford, and Pittsfield. Mountain Park is open from late June through Labor Day. It opens daily at 1:00 p.m., except Saturday, when it runs from 6:00 a.m. to 11:00 p.m. Parking and admission are free; tickets can be purchased for rides, with group rates available. Write Mountain Park, PO Box 29. Telephone: 413/534-5656.

Always White Day & Night
Mt. TOM
Ski Area
P.O. Box 1158
Rte. 5, Holyoke, MA 01041-1158
(413) 536-0516

- **Mount Tom State Reservation,** entered from Route 5 out of Holyoke or Route 141 from Easthampton, comprises 1,800 acres of woodland for recreation and nature education overlooking the Connecticut River. A product of geological phenomena dating back millions of years, the land was purchased in 1903 by the State Legislature and is currently supervised and financed by the Hampden and Hampshire County Commissions. Included among its facilities are bird watching, a lookout tower, fishing, and ice skating at Lake Bray; picnicking, hiking, horseback riding, cross-country skiing, and snowshoeing. The reservation is situated 1,214 feet above the Connecticut River and is open from April through October, 8:00 a.m. to 8:00 p.m.; November through March, 8:00 a.m. to 6:00 p.m. Free to the public. It features 30 miles of trails, a wildlife sanctuary, natural science museum of geological samples, and a self-guiding nature trail with identification of indigenous plants, trees, and flowers. Reservation superintendent, telephone: 413/527-9858.

- Just minutes from the junction of I-91 and the Massachusetts Turnpike is **Mt. Tom,** a favorite ski spot in the area that also features summer attractions of an Alpine Slide and a million-dollar giant wave pool. A pioneer in the manufacture of artificial snow, the ski area claims to be "Always White, Day and Night," due to the snow-making facilities. Its two double chairs, T-bars, and rope tow open weekdays at 9:00 a.m., weekends and holidays at 8:00 a.m., and extend daily until 10:00 p.m. depending on weather. For information on skiing instruction, contact the Mt. Tom Ski School at PO Box 1156. Telephone: 413/536-0416.

- For local **music lovers** there is the Community Concert series, featuring nationally known artists, during the winter months. Weekly concerts by the city band are given during the summer at Springdale and Veterans Parks.

- The **National Invitational Women's Rowing Regatta** is an annual event held in early October. Since 1975 the regatta has had more than 40 women's crews from area schools and colleges race on the Connecticut River. Each year the regatta attracts thousands of spectators.

- There are many **parks** in Holyoke, including: Community Park, featuring Scott's Tower and the Regional Stephen Chmura Pool and Recreation Area; Minnie Dwight Tiny Tot Park at the corner of Appleton and Elm streets; Hikers Park, maintained by Model Cities; Henry J. Fitzpatrick Indoor Hockey Rink at Maple Street, operated by the Department of Natural Resources; Patrick McNulty on Lincoln Street; and O'Connell Park at Dwight and Linden streets and Prospect Street. If you'd rather go shopping, Holyoke Mall at Ingleside (off I-91) offers numerous shops and eateries in a fabulous mall setting.

- **Skinner Memorial Chapel,** located at the corner of Appleton and Maple streets, is a Congregational church in typical Gothic architecture. Its interior panel features a rendition of the conversion of the Ethiopian eunuch by St. Philip.

- Holyoke's annual **St. Patrick's Day Parade,** held since 1951 during the month of March, is the third largest in the world. The most traditional parade in the area, it attracts over 300,000 viewers and is preceded by many other special events. The two and a half hour parade starts at Route 5's Northampton Street and Whiting Farms Road, on to Beech Street, Appleton Street, High Street, and Hampden Street. More than 20 floats and many bands are represented, as well as the year's Colleen Queen.

- Holyoke is the "birthplace of **volleyball**" which was invented there in 1895 by YMCA instructor W. C. Morgan. The Greater Holyoke Chamber of Commerce conducts the William C. Morgan Invitational Volleyball Tournament each year early in April, when teams from the U. S. and Canada compete for regional championships. A volleyball hall of fame is being established.

Wistariahurst

- **Wistariahurt Museum,** listed as a National Historic Site in the National Register of Historic Places, is Holyoke's museum of natural history and art. Located at 238 Cabot Street, the museum is housed in a Victorian mansion, a family home of noted silk manufacturer William Skinner. The house highlights include architectural detailing unique to the late 19th century and early 20th century, including a leather paneled room, conservatory and music hall, period furniture, decorative arts, and changing exhibitions. Textile and archival collections are available for research scholars. Open daily 1:00 p.m. to 5:00 p.m., Sunday 1:00 p.m. to 4:00 p.m. Telephone: 413/534-2216.

LONGMEADOW, Massachusetts
Population: 15,630   Zip Code: 01106

Named for the "long meddowe" purchased from the Indians in 1636, Longmeadow reputedly has the longest green in Massachusetts; along that green are some of the loveliest and most interesting homes in the commonwealth.

Trips and trivia:
- **Bay Path Junior College** at 588 Longmeadow Street is a two-year college offering liberal arts and career programs for approximately 600 women. Accredited by the New England Association of Schools and Colleges, Bay Path is authorized to grant associate degrees in arts and sciences. All programs of study are open to adult women as part of the continuing education program, and an evening adult education program open to men and women offers non-credit courses on a variety of subjects. Full-scale theatrical productions in the fall and spring are open to the public, as well as occasional lectures and entertainment during the academic year. The 25-acre campus and its facilities are available for conferences and other programs to area service, social, and civil organizations. Telephone: 413/567-0621. The college traces its beginnings to Bay Path Institute, a well-known coeducational business school founded in Springfield in 1897. In 1945 the school moved to Longmeadow and the enrollment was restricted to women; in 1949 it became a junior college. Bay Path is located on the site of the former Wallace Estate, north of the Longmeadow Green, and Deepwood Hall, the stately Wallace mansion, serves as its administration building. It derives its name from the old Indian foot trail that ran from what is now Hartford, Connecticut, through Longmeadow and Springfield and east to Boston. The route was later used by explorers and colonists as they set out westward from the seacoast and was commonly known as the Bay Path well into the 18th century.

- **The Green,** stretching three and a quarter miles along the length of Longmeadow Street, extends from the Springfield city line to the Connecticut state line. In honor of the Bicentennial, the Town of Longmeadow put together a brochure entitled "Colonial Longmeadow: A Brief History and Guide to the 18th and Early 19th Century Homes," and the houses are marked appropriately with plaques according to century (white stars on red squares for 18th century, white stars on blue squares for 19th century. Houses where militia who fought in the Revolutionary War resided and houses of architectural interest are worth noting. In addition to the First Church of Christ (1768) at 763 Longmeadow Street, the Longmeadow Community House, and the Town Office Building, these are some of the places highlighted: No. 46—built mid-1800s, the home of Margaret Rude's Kindergarten in the 1920s; No. 70 and 76—twins of the late Victorian era; No. 220—1840 Victorian; No. 237—Caleb Field House of 1830s; No. 259—1728, one of the oldest houses on the street, built by Thomas Field; No. 260—Mason Willard House (1705-1893); No. 280—Colonel Alexander Field House (1794) in the Georgian style (Historical American Building); No. 315—Amos Parker (1820); No. 384—Cooley-Williams (1765), famous during the Civil War for its patriotically painted red, white, and blue chimney; No. 417—a school, then the Town Office, now headquarters of the American Legion; No. 418—Eveleth House of 1827 where generations of Calvin Cooleys continue to reside; No. 476—1760 Cooley Twin house, now a telephone company building; No. 492—Victorian home of 1840 owned by Bay Path College; No. 506—Stebbins-Cooley House built c. 1790; No. 536—built for Merrick Stebbins in 1845 for an artist named Blake; No. 551—gingerbread-style Victorian built in 1883 by Thomas

Watters; No. 573—original house of William Silcox in 1830; No. 577—built for Samuel Colton Booth in 1821; No. 609—wedding gift for David Booth II from his father in 1861; No. 655—Ely-Scudder House (1758); No. 663—dating from 1830 when it was built for Israel Gates, the front part was once a millinery shop; No. 664—1856 of Nathaniel Ely, Jr.; No. 674—another Ely house, this one 1785 Georgian; No. 679—a 1873 Greek Revival owned by generations of Goodmans since 1875; No. 690—built in 1720 for Ebeneezer Bliss; No. 697—Storrs House; No. 702—Gothic Revival with Tudor south wing added in 1916, the house was built in 1839 for Roderick Burnham; No. 705—early 1800s home of carpenter George Reynolds; No. 715—Greek Revival parsonage for Reverend Joseph Conit, owned by six generations of the Thomas Cordis family; No. 734—Brewer-Young house, built in the 1880s; No. 756—1775 house built by David White, a master carpenter who also built First Church; No. 766—originally called Old White Tavern, built by Samuel Bliss in 1774; No. 776—c. 1800 the country store and in 1870 the town's first post office; No. 777—The Parsonage, moved from the community house location in 1921; No. 780—The Jacob Colton House, built in 1765; No. 787—Old Red House on the Green (Colton House); No. 788—built in 1829 for Daniel Colton; No. 796—Victorian Gothic built in 1856 by Thomas Mather; No. 797—built for Justin Colton in 1833, purchased by George Adams in 1921 and used for many years as a tea room; No. 812—White-Bliss-Colton House (c. 1792); No. 822—built in 1830 for Sabin Burt; No. 826—typical Gothic Revival built in 1850 by Stephen Colton; No. 857—built for W. C. Pease early 1800s; No. 870—typical 18th century Georgian farmhouse built by Newton Colton in 1823; No. 873—1756 home of Colonel Jonathan Hale, sold in 1832 to Elias Coomes; No. 878—Stebbins-Hammatt House (1795); No. 891—1830 home of Stephen Hale, then the Longmeadow Post Office, and at one time Mathews' "Cheap Cash Store"; No. 906—built 1799 for James Coomes; No. 909—Bliss-Keep House (1790); No. 912—built 1790 for Ebeneezer Chandler Colton; No. 918—1840 Victorian built of native brick; No. 930—built for David Booth in 1795, featuring a coffin door on the south end; No. 951—Burt-Coomes House (1725); No. 977—originally owned by C. Almquist (1860); No. 1028—built in 1794 for Captain Gideon Colton with beams cut from the property; No. 1077—Bliss-Colton place (1790); No. 1124—1732 home with eight fireplaces; No. 1175—Colton-Gates house (1790); No. 1183—Gates Farm, built in 1790 by Asahel Colton with, at one time, the largest barn in the area; No. 1390—built 1785 by tanner, shoemaker, and farmer Gaius Bliss who used quarry-stone from East Longmeadow for its foundation; No. 1401—Keep Farm (1782); No. 1443—Israel Colton House of 1776 with six fireplaces and two bake-ovens in the central chimney; No. 1759—late Victorian (1883) house built by Thomas Watters for George Washington Allen; No. 1587—another Watters house (1873), much of the property owned by the Longmeadow Conservation Commission; No. 1596—small Victorian built for A. Phelps, 1840; No. 1607—1786 at one time called Tabor Farm, Jabez Colton House and once a school for boys; No. 1656—Georgian farmhouse once known as The Maples when it was a boarding house for the elderly; No. 1657—built for B. C. Knox 1835, with the original farm extending to the Connecticut line.

Other houses and streets of interest in Longmeadow include:

Chandler Avenue's No. 24—the 1774 barn of the Old White Tavern; No. 19—once the Newell Button Factory (1840-55); No. 31-33—built by Peter Ward, 1875; No. 52—built 1850 for Martin Hartigan; No. 44 **Colton Place**—Daniel Burbank home built in 1775 for Asa Colton; No. 37 Birnie Road—Birnie House, built for Thomas Hale in 1710; **Fairfield Terrace** No. 14—Patrick David House (1699); No. 253 **Bliss Road**—built 1850 by J. Tuft; and **Williams Street** No. 50—Peter Ward (1850); No. 54—another 1850 house owned by the L. Dumon family, then the Leon Moynihans over 100 years; No. 60—built for Simeon Newell in 1830, resided in by the Murray family for nearly a century.

• Registered **Historic American Buildings** of Longmeadow include:

1. Captain Gideon Colton House at 1028 Longmeadow Street, built in 1796 and attributed to architect Asher Benjamin.

2. Colonel Alexander Field House (1794) at 280 Longmeadow Street.

• The Connecticut River reaches its greatest width at the town of **Longmeadow,** expanding for a mile or more to 2,000 feet from one bank to the other. Longmeadow was the first town in the Bay State to be incorporated after American Independence was recognized. Its active Longmeadow Historical Society, organized in 1899, can be reached at telephone: 413/567-3600. Each year during the last week of May the town celebrates **Long Meadowe Days,** including an art show and sale, crafts, and lots of events for children.

• The **Old Red House on the Green,** also known as the Colton House of 1734, is a property of the Society for the Preservation of New England Antiquities at 787 Longmeadow Street. The house is architecturally interesting as an example of a typical Connecticut Valley saltbox, with a central chimney heating two rooms on each of two floors. Telephone: 617/227-3956. The house is open only by appointment.

• The **Recreation and Parks Department** of the town maintains five parks: Bliss, Greenwood, Laurel, Nature Camp, and Strople Field.

• **Stebbins Wildlife Refuge** on the Longmeadow Flats, near the Connecticut River, has a year-round calendar of events. Under the auspices of the Allen Bird Club, the refuge is used for bird-banking, demonstrations, and nature walks. It is reached via Bark Haul Road off of Route 5.

• **Storrs House,** maintained by the Longmeadow Historical Society, is located at 697 Longmeadow Street. The house, also called Storrs Parsonage, was built in 1786 by Reverend Richard Salter Storrs, the second pastor of the First Church of Christ in Longmeadow. Three generations of the Storrs family lived there, and at one time a private girls' school was conducted on its premises. Renovations have been made to the house, and the Longmeadow Gardners have restored the grounds to their original appearance. During the process of redecoration, the house's original paint colors were discovered and said to be typical of the Connecticut Valley in the 18th century; the parlor on the left was usually yellow, the parlor on the

right blue, and the dining room green, with leftovers mixed for the hall. Objects of particular interest in the house include roundabout and Chippendale chairs, a Queen Anne dropleaf table, court cupboard and chairs with original crewel seats, 17th century William and Mary chairs and table, whispering or courting stick, serving or mixing chest in the dining room, Chickering piano and stool dating to 1830, and a stretcher or refractory table in the music room, plus a pine chest with original decorations of 1718, a four-poster canopy bed, and banister-back chair with rush seat in the bedroom. Storrs House is open to the public from June to mid-September Wednesday and Sunday afternoons, 2:00 p.m. to 4:00 p.m. and by appointment. Telephone: 413/567-3600.

• The **Richard Salter Storrs Library** at 693 Longmeadow Street has a fascinating history. At first, its opening times were signaled by the ringing of the Meeting House bell, and fines for delinquency were charged according to book size. If two or more persons were desirous of getting the same book, it was put up for sale to the highest bidder. In 1839 the library came under the auspices of the Young Men's Library, housed in the old brick schoolhouse; in 1854, it merged with the Longmeadow Lyceum, and books were stored in the upper room of the chapel. In 1895 the town of Longmeadow decided to accept the state's offer of $100.00 worth of books to small towns to encourage libraries, and the official library association began. By 1898, it had a full-time librarian who was paid an annual salary of $25.00. After several more moves around town, the library finally found permanency: in 1910 architects Smith and Bassette and the W. J. Quinn building company rebuilt the bequeathed Storrs estate into a proper repository for the library. Today this public building is one of the most beautiful structures in the town. The library is open Monday through Friday, 10:00 a.m. to 8:00 p.m., Saturday, 10:00 a.m. to 5:00 p.m., closed Saturdays during July and August. Telephone: 413/567-5500.

LUDLOW, Massachusetts
Population: 17,580   Zip Code: 01056

Separated from Springfield by the Chicopee River, Ludlow was part of the city and was called Stony Hill until it became incorporated as a district in 1774 and then a town in 1775.

Trips and trivia:
• The **covered bridge** off of Center Street at Ludlow Center, recently removed and sold privately by the town, is a model of a wooden covered bridge built just downriver from its present site, called Put's Bridge after its builder, Eli Putnam. The original bridge, built in the mid-19th century of wood with two masonry abutments and one pier, has been designated a Historic American Building. The present bridge between Indian Orchard and Ludlow was built in the early 1930s to replace an iron one built in 1898 when the old Put's Bridge was removed at the instigation of the Ludlow Manufacturing Company to carry heavier traffic and to take street-car tracks into the town.

• **Haviland (or Chapin) Pond** on Route 21's Center Street has long been a favorite swimming and fishing spot. In the late 1800s it was a reservoir serving the downtown section, with water from the Ludlow Reservoir being metered into the pond, which was then owned by the Ludlow Company.

Hubbard Memorial Library
24 Center Street
Ludlow, Massachusetts 01056

• The town's **Hubbard Memorial Library,** dedicated to Charles Townsend Hubbard, treasurer of the Ludlow Manufacturing Company, is located at 24 Center Street. Known for its unique architecture, the library was built in 1889 by William Ralph Emerson, cousin of the American poet Ralph Waldo Emerson, a leader in the school of Academic Reaction that combined Colonial styles with 18th century forms. Especially noteworthy are the

Palladian windows, topped with delicate and unusually fine fan windows in the east and west facades; a bronze-green side panel, vermiculated as the hemp trade of the Ludlow Manufacturing Company; an exaggerated eyelid window above the entrance, an Emersonian feature that was widely copied; the shelf room with rare window seats; and an exposed beam of flattened arches. The library has town pictures and books available. It is a member of the Western Massachusetts Regional Library system. Open weekdays 10:00 a.m. to 8:00 p.m.; Saturday, 9:30 a.m. to 2:30 p.m. Telephone: 413/583-3408.

• **Indian Leap,** a high, rocky cliff on the bank of the Chicopee River in the Indian Orchard section, marks the spot where Roaring Thunder and his warriors leaped to escape pursuit of the army in King Philip's War.

• At one point in its history, Ludlow was the world's largest manufacturer of **jute,** the fiber imported from India and other Asian countries from which bagging and twine were made.

• **Ludlow State Park,** on Minechoag Mountain via Plumbley and Tower roads, covers 50 acres and offers a lovely scenic view from its fire tower. Facilities are there for picnicking, hiking, horseback riding, snowmobiling, cross-country skiing, and cooking out. To get to the park, take East Street from the bridge, past the corner of Miller Street to Tower Road. **Red Bridge State Park** on Plumley Street has boating, fishing, and hiking facilities. Telephone: 413/594-9416.

• A granite **monument** in the East Street Park commemorates Ludlow's veterans of three wars.

• **Our Lady of Fatima FESTA** takes place each Labor Day weekend and commemorates the dedication of the church at 438 Windsor Street. There are Portuguese handicrafts, foods, and dancing, with the highlight of the weekend being Sunday, a day of religious celebrations with outdoor masses and a twilight/candlelight procession in honor of Our Lady of Fatima.

• **Recreational facilities** for Ludlowites can be found at the Stevens Memorial Building (The Rec, run by the Ludlow Boys and Girls Club), the John F. Thompson Memorial swimming pool, Whitney Street Park, and the West Street Park.

• The **Village Green** at Ludlow Center is marked by a stone monument attesting that the location is the geographical center of the town. Of particular note are the old meetinghouse (1783-4), currently being used as a Grange; the 1845 house next door at the corner of Booth Street; the house across the street (1820) that served as the local post office from 1892-1919; and the Earby Chapel, now a private dwelling. Also, check out the Romanesque Revival First Church (1859); two cemeteries—Fuller Cemetery just south of the church, a town property since 1801 but dating back farther than that, and Sike's Cemetery at Munsing Street between Church and Lyon streets that goes back at least to 1772; and the old Ely Fuller Tavern, built in the later 18th century or early 19th century, at 943 Center Street, site of the town's first post office (1874-92) and now a private residence.

MONSON, Massachusetts
Population: 7,355   Zip Code: 01057

Named for Provincial Governor Thomas Pownall's friend, Sir John Monson, Prsident of the British Board of Trade, Monson has been an industrial community since the 19th century. Its major product has been toilet seats.

Trips and trivia:

• Architecturally, besides the nine cemeteries and one monument in the town there are many **interesting buildings,** mainly concentrated near the center, including: a hip-roofed dwelling at the corner of Maxwell and Dickinson road; an unusual Georgian home on Cushman Street; an Elias Carter-designed house on Main Street; the Romanesque Revival Congregational Church of 1873 at the junction of Main and High Streets; the Monson Library (1882); and the Methodist Church of 1850, plus several industrial and textile mill buildings around the town.

• **Conant Brook Dam** on Wales Road is open to the public for picnicking, fishing, hiking, and snowmobiling.

• In 1808 **granite quarries** were opened in Monson by the U. S. government for stone to be used by the Springfield Armory. **Memorial Town Hall,** a Victorian structure built of local granite in 1885, features a museum of town memorabilia and armaments at its location at 200 Main Street.

• **Monson Academy,** founded in 1804, was host to the first three Chinese students to come to this country; it recently merged with Wilbraham Academy.

• The **Monson Historical Society** is housed at 94 Main Street. Telephone: 413/283-8143.

• James Tufts, Monson's "Grand Old Man," was a teacher to poet Eugene Field and his brother Russell at the **Tufts House** in 1865-6.

MONTGOMERY, Massachusetts
Population: 446   Zip Code: 01071

This small, rural town was named in honor of Dublin, Ireland, native General Richard Montgomery (1736-1773), second in command under Schuyler in the expedition against Montreal during the Revolution.

Trips and trivia:

Montgomery's **town center** contains many historically and architecturally interesting buildings, including the Montgomery Community Church (1848), Town House

(1849)—home of the Montgomery Historical Society, Union Hall, and Town Hall, as well as cemeteries and over 100 cellar holes interspersed throughout the town.
- At the foot of Mt. Tekoa can be found the remains of the old **Falley Armory,** complete with grinding wheels and base walls, where rifles were made in the Revolutionary days. Nearby is an old Indian cemetery marked with pyramids of stone, plus a beautiful waterfall, hiking trails, and a view of the Mt. Holyoke range. Take Montgomery Road out of Westfield to Lower Reservoir Road, then go four miles to the Westfield Water Works.
- **Montgomery Mountain,** famous for its spectacular autumn foliage, leads to the Berkshires.
- A town character was the Reverend **Seth Nobel,** first pastor of the Congregational Church in 1797, who was dismissed by the congregation for his too frequent insistence on the hymn "Bangor." He left to preach in a Massachusetts settlement that later became the State of Maine and was instrumental in naming one of its towns—guess which one!
- **Social events** in town include an annual pancake supper, sugar eat, and harvest supper sponsored by the Historical Society, plus a chicken pie supper and strawberry festival served each year by the Thimble Club.

PALMER, Massachusetts
Population: 11,680   Zip Code: 01069

Originally called the "Elbows" when it was settled as a plantation by John King in 1716, Palmer is situated on the Quaboag, Swift, Ware, and Chicopee Rivers, which were a great source of water power for early textile industries. It is made up of four villages: Palmer (Depot Village) on the Quaboag River, Bondsville on the Swift River, Thorndike on the Ware River, and Three Rivers at the junction of all three rivers, which in turn form the headwaters of the Connecticut River.

Trips and trivia:
- The **Boston and Albany Railroad Station,** designated a Historic American Building, was commissioned in 1881 by architect Henry Hobson Richardson. Known as Union Station, it is located on Depot Street, just to the west of the Main Street overpass. Palmer was known as the Town of the Seven Railroads, and was once a thriving industrial and communication center; evidence of this heyday is reflected in the Nassawano House on Main Street, dating from 1851 when it was used as a hotel for the many visitors to the town.
- There are several mid-18th century **colonial houses** of note in the area, including the Aaron King House (1745) on Route 67, the 1750 Samuel Shaw House and Bernard McNitt House on Nipmuck Road, and the Robert Hunter House of 1745 on Route 32 near the old Fink Tavern (1795).
- A landmark of the town is the **Fishing Weir** along the Ware River in Three Rivers. Made by the Indians over 2,000 years ago, the weir is a V-shaped basket that runs from one shoreline to the other, open in the center to catch fish. It is thought to be one of only three such fishing traps in the country.
- Although today there is still much **industry** in the town, it is probably most famous as headquarters of Tambrands, Inc.
- The **Palmer Historical Commission** has become active lately in historical preservation. Telephone: 413/283-7616.
- **Recreational areas** in Palmer include the Park Commission's Burleigh Park for picnics, hikes, baseball, and miniature golf; four mini-parks, run by the state along the Quaboag River at Route 67, are excellent for fishing and picnicking; a summer YMCA Day Camp; and Forest Lake Park on Route 32, a privately owned recreational area that features swimming and boating, with rental available. Fishing is popular in the Ware and Swift rivers, which are periodically stocked with trout.

- The **State Fish Hatchery** on Route 32's Ware Road specializes in Atlantic salmon breeding. It is open by appointment. Telephone: 413/283-7440.

RUSSELL, Massachusetts
Population: 1,382   Zip Code: 01071

A small rural town that was once a farming community, Russell has had its economic base in several paper companies there since the mid-1800s.

Trips and trivia:
- Russell was on the trail of General **Henry Knox** in the winter of 1775-6 when artillery was hauled from upstate New York to Boston, and has a number of historic structures along the path of the trek, which is roughly Route 23 and General Knox Road.
- There are many interesting **structures** in town, including the Doolittle Homestead (1771) on Route 20 and the Greek Revival Russell Community Church and Town Hall (early 20th century) in the center of town.
- The **Westfield River** runs through the north and northeast section of Russell and provides recreation for both fishing and an annual spring canoe race.

SOUTHWICK, Massachusetts
Population: 6,330   Zip Code: 01077

Named after an English village, Southwick is best known as a tobacco-growing center and year-round lake resort community.

Trips and trivia:
- There are many interesting historic **buildings** scattered throughout the town, including: an Early Colonial (1734) on Route 202N, recently burned; a 1740

home on Klaus Anderson Road; and a Georgian Colonial (1765) on Route 202S. In the center is an 1824 Greek Revival Congregational Church designed by Isaac Damon whose history the townspeople have recorded; a 1762 home on Route 202; Laflin House (1805) on Depot Street; another Greek Revival dwelling on Powder Mill Road; the Methodist Church (1820) near Congamond Road; and an early 19th century cigar factory.

• **Congamond Lakes,** on Congamond Road off of Route 202, are three bodies of water linked by streams. The lakes provide year-round recreational activity for swimming, fishing, boating, waterskiing, and ice skating. At one time, ice was harvested in large quantities in the lakes. Covering some 465 acres, the lakes are stocked with trout, bass, pickerel, and panfish.

• There are two **dairy farms** that periodically allow visitors: Waterman Farm on Route 10 south of Southwick Center and Hall Farm on Sunnyside Road, off of Route 10.

• From the **Roger Moore House** in the southern part of town, two states, three towns, and three counties can be seen.

• A miniature **railroad park,** operated by the Pioneer Valley Live Steamers, is located on Route 57. Go toward Granville to Hillside Road. It is open in season, Sundays, 10:00 a.m. to 4:30 p.m.

• **Sodom Mountain,** at an altitude of 1,126 feet, is a rocky ledge rising suddenly from the roadside, forming a lovely gorge. The Sodom Mountain Resort Area, Inc., on South Loomis Road is a recreation area with facilities for swimming, picnicking, dancing, and snowmobiling. Telephone: 413/569-5291

SPRINGFIELD, Massachusetts
Population: 163,905   Zip Code: 01100

Springfield is the oldest settlement (May 14, 1636), the seat of Hampden County, and the largest city of Western Massachusetts. Named for founder William Pynchon's birthplace in England, it calls itself the "City of Homes" and "Convention City" for its excellent location at the crossroads of New England, about 100 miles equidistant from Boston in the east and Albany to the west. Noted for many innovations, Springfield is proud to be recognized as the home of the first American automobile, the first gas-powered motorcycle, the first post card, the Springfield Armory, and the birthplace of basketball. It boasts one of the finest museum and library complexes in the nation at the Quadrangle, combining four distinct museums and the Central Library at one location.

Trips and trivia:
• **Alexander House** on State Street, also known as Linden Hall, is one of Springfield's most famous houses. Built in 1811 by Simon Sanborn according to specifications by architect Asher Benjamin, the house has had many well-known owners, such as Colonel James Byers, Colonel Israel Trask, the portrait painter Chester Harding, railroad superintendent James Barnes, and Civil War Major Henry Alexander. On hand at the house is a wonderful ghost story called *The Romance of Linden Hall,* written by Julia Bowles (Alexander) Phillips in 1886. The first office of the American Red Cross outside Washington, D. C. was established at the Alexander House during Taft's presidency, and during the years 1858-1938 it was the key spot for social events in Springfield. The house was purchased by Mrs. James Storrow and offered to the Society for the Preservation of New England Antiquities in 1938; the property has been held by that organization since then.

• **American International College** (AIC) at 1000 State Street, is a small nonsectarian coeducational college offering a university-size curriculum in a small private college setting. There are more than 35 majors offered in the undergraduate Schools of Arts and Sciences, Business Administration, Psychology and Education, and the Division of Nursing. The School of Continuing Education and Graduate Studies offers advanced degrees in business, education, human resources, criminal justice, psychology, public administration, and organizational behavior and a doctoral degree in educational psychology with a concentration in learning disabilities. AIC was founded in 1885 and is located on 60 acres and has an enrollment of 2,300. Of special interest is the Curtis Blake Child Development Center, which provides diagnostic and remediation services to children with special learning needs. The Karen Sprague Cultural Arts Center and the Esther B. Griswold Theatre for the Performing Arts provide a wealth of cultural entertainment and educational services to the College and the community. The Berkshire Ballet is the resident company at the 500-seat theatre, and there is also an art gallery and seminar rooms within the complex. AIC is fully accredited by the New England Association of Schools and Colleges. Telephone: 413/737-7000.

• The World's Largest Collection of Military Small Arms is said to be found at the **Springfield Armory Museum,** located on Federal Street in an area known as

Armory Square off State Street. A National Historic Site under the administration of the National Park Service, the original museum was established in 1871. But Springfield's role in the nation's defense dates back to the American Revolution, when three local residents constructed 20 firearms for the Massachusetts Committee of Safety. The first Springfield musket, a flintlock bored for a .69-caliber ball, was produced at the Armory in 1795; in 1818 craftsman Thomas Blanchard invented the Blanchard Lathe, and mass-produced gunstocks revolutionized the industry. During the Civil War the Armory was a major supplier of military small arms; its Trapdoor Springfield models of 1865 and later were important during the Indian Wars. The Krag-Jorgensen rifle was used in the Spanish-American War. World War I brought the Armory fame with its '03 model, and over five and a half million M-1 Garand rifles were manufactured for World War II and the Korean War. The M-14 semi-automatic rifle, the last of the Springfields, was used during the Vietnam Conflict. The museum collection contains a sample of every gun made at the Armory, other rare and historic weapons, the famous Organ of Rifles (see the poem *The Arsenal at Springfield* by Henry Wadsworth Longfellow), and arms memorabilia. The museum is open daily 8:30 a.m. to 4:30 p.m., closed Thanksgiving, Christmas, and New Year's. Admission is free. Telephone: 413/734-8551.

The Arsenal at Springfield
by Henry Wadsworth Longfellow

This is the Arsenal. From floor to ceiling.
Like a huge organ, rise the burnished arm.
But from their silent pipes to anthem pealing
Startles the villages with strange alarms.

Ah! what a sound will rise, how wild and dreary,
When the death-angel touches those swift keys!
What loud lament and dismal Misere
Will mingle with their awful symphonies!

I hear even now the infinite fierce chorus,
The cries of agony, the endless groan,
Which, through the ages have gone before us,
In long reverberations reach our own.

On helm and harness rings the Saxon hammer,
Through Cimbric forest roars the Norseman's song.
And loud, amid the universal clamor,
O'er distant deserts sounds the Tartar gong.

I hear the Florentine, who from his place
Whells out his battle-bell with dreadful din,
And Aztec priests upon their teocallis
Beat the wild war-drums made of serpent's skin;

The tumult of each sacked and burning village;
The shout that every prayer for mercy downs;
The soldiers' revels in the midst of pillage;
The wail of famine in beleaguered towns;

The bursting shell, the gateway wrenched asunder,
The rattling musketry, the clashing blade;
And ever and anon, in tones of thunder,
The diapason of the cannonade.

Is it, O man, with such discordant noises,
With such accursed instruments as these,
Thou drownest Nature's sweet and kindly voices,
And jarrest the celestial harmonies?

Were half the power, that fills the world with terror,
Were half the wealth, bestowed on camps and courts,
Given to redeem the human mind from error,
There were no need of arsenals or forts:

The warrior's name would be a name abhorred!
And every nation, that should lift again
No hand against a brother, on its forehead
Would wear forever more the curse of Cain!

Down the dark future, through long generations,
The echoing sounds grow fainter and then cease;
And like a bell, with solemn, sweet vibrations,
I hear once more the voice of Christ say, "Peace!"

Peace! and no longer from its brazen portals
The blast of War's great organ shakes the skies!
But beautiful as songs of the immortals,
The holy melodies of love arise.

- There are a number of **art galleries** around Springfield worth note, including: The Art Gallery, 509 Sumner Avenue, 413/788-9261; Art in Place, 1325 Springfield Street, Feeding Hills 789-1172; Art Unlimited, South Hadley 532-7047; Avis Neigher Gallery, 1500 Main Street, 734-1844; Center Galleries, 345 Worthington Street, 734-5469; Cricket on the Hearth, 200 Center Street, Ludlow 589-9879; Doyle Richard, 157 Boston Road, 783-2644; Frame Corner, 213 N. Main Street, East Longmeadow, 525-2399; International Galleries, 132 Main Street, Northampton 586-3964; Layne Gallery, 51 Prospect Street, East Longmeadow 525-1200; The Leonard Gallery, 1067 E. Columbus Avenue, 733-9492; Print Loft, 94 Shaker Road, East Longmeadow 525-3940; Shop 286 Antiques & Things, 286 Worthington Street, 788-0297; Studio Gallery, 158

Silver Street, Agawam 789-3065; **Thronja Original Art Gallery,** 260 Worthington Street, 732-0260; Town Gallery, 52 Shaker Road, East Longmeadow 525-1292; and Zone Art Center, 395 Dwight Street, 732-1995.

- The all-new, $11.4 million Naismith Memorial **Basketball Hall of Fame** in Springfield Center commemorates the fact that this international game was founded in Springfield in 1891. It was named from peach baskets that were first used! The museum contains a replica of the original gym, showing a chronological history of the game with its original 13 rules and early game equipment. Also at the museum is Honor Court, displaying medallions of the game's immortals; displays of various uniforms; the Hickox Library (the most authoritative source for basketball history and information, including a very rare complete set of rules books); free movies shown regularly; and a gift shop for souvenirs of the visit. The annual Basketball Hall of Fame Enshrinement Dinner is held each year at the Springfield Civic Center; and other events include an NBA game between top professional teams, the Hall of Fame Game in late October, and the annual Tip-Off Invitational Tourney in November. The Hall of Fame is truly a shrine to the only major sport founded in the U. S. which is played today competitively in 162 nations. It is also a tribute to its founder, Dr. James Naismith, who wanted the museum to be erected on the site of basketball's beginnings. There is an admission charge of $5.00 for adults, $3.00 for children ages 9 to 15, free to 8 and under; group rates are also available. The Basketball Hall of Fame is open daily 9:00 a.m. to 5:00 p.m., summers until 6:00 p.m., closed only on Thanksgiving, Christmas and New Year. The world's only Basketball Hall of Fame is located adjacent to I-91. Telephone: 413/781-6500.

THE SHOPS
at Baystate West

- Towering over the Central business district of downtown Springfield is the 29-story **Baystate West** at 1500 Main Street, an ultra-modern complex of offices, a four-star Marriott motor hotel, multilevel all-weather shopping mall, and 1,200-car parking garage. Constructed by architect Eduardo Catalano in 1971, the $56-million structure is topped by Baybank Tower, allowing a spectacular panoramic view of the Connecticut River Valley. Telephone: 413/733-2171. Baystate West is also the home of the Greater Springfield **Chamber of Commerce,** open Monday through Friday, 8:30 a.m. to 5:00 p.m. Telephone: 787-1555.

There are many other malls scattered throughout the

The GREATER SPRINGFIELD Chamber of Commerce

Springfield area, all climate-controlled for the shopper's pleasure, such as Eastfield, Springdale, Ingelside, Fairfield, and Springfield Plaza.

• Abolitionist **John Brown,** a resident of Springfield from 1846-9, helped organize the Underground Railroad.

• *Pro Deo, Pro Patria* (for God and country) is the motto for Springfield's **Cathedral High School,** a coeducational Diocesan school located at 260 Surrey Road. Telephone: 413/782-5285. Founded in 1885, it is the largest Catholic secondary school in New England. Springfield's public high schools include the new Central High School (a combination of Classical and Technical), Commerce, and Putnam Vocational and Technical.

• Springfield's **Civic Center** at 1277 Main Street, near the intersection of State and Main, has been a tremendous boon to the city's reputation as a conventional center. A multipurpose facility, the Civic Center may be featuring at any time a famous singer or group, professional or amateur sporting event, showcase, etc.; in addition, it also serves as a meeting place for senior citizens' groups and other social and civic clubs. The Grand Arena covers 17,000 square feet, surrounded by a seating capacity of 7,500. Exhibition Hall has 45,000 square feet, plus seven meeting rooms. The multimillion dollar complex was built in 1972 and has focused more attention on the city as an entertainment, sports, and cultural center. The box office number is 413/787-6600. Parking is available at the nearby Civic Center Parking Garage, 41 Harrison Avenue, with facilities for 1,200 cars.

• Springfield has been a leader in the ecological movement, and has the following **conservation** areas in the city: Schneelock Brook between Allen Street and the East Longmeadow line; White Cedar Bog, a 24-acre remnant of the ice age with a rare wealth of plant life, including the northernmost stand of coastal white cedars, off Bay Street; Duggan Leatherleague bogs off Walsh Street; three small kettlehole ponds scooped out and flooded by receding glaciers from 8,000 years ago; Grayson Drive Kettle area, a 16-acre wetland wildlife sanctuary fed by two streams between Boston Road and the Mill River; Mill pond access on Gourley Road, north of South Branch Parkway, a three-acre wetland; Garvey Drive promontory on Lake Massasoit, a five-acre woodland and peninsula of white pines and black oak; Indian Orchard Kame on Goodwine Street, a glacial formation that offers a natural setting for geology and a spectacular view of the Connecticut Valley; Entry Dingle, a 20-acre wooded ravine entered at Valentina Park off White Street; Seymour Dingle conservation area on Aberdeen, Plum, and Seymour Streets, 15 acres of stream valley, wooded slopes, sedge meadows, and swamp; Delta Hills preserve, bounded by Prince and Stanley Streets and the Chicopee line, 55 acres of brooks, prairie, rugged ravine, dense woodland, and swamp; and the Venture Pond conservation area on Collingwood Drive off Wilbraham Road, three acres of field and shrubs giving access to a seven-acre pond for fishing, boating and ice skating. The city maintains an Environmental Education Center. Telephone: 413/732-2181.

• **Court Square's Municipal Group** consists of three impressive structures: administrative offices of City Hall, the Campanile, and Symphony Hall; together, they made up the city's Bicentennial symbol.

The Municipal Group was built in 1909 after a nationwide architectural competition won by New York architects Pell and Corbett. The complex consists of two side-by-side limestone buildings with classic Corinthian columns, separated by the 300-foot campanile. This group, which has been recognized as one of the most beautiful municipal complexes in the nation, overlooks historic Court Square.

In addition to their utilitarian aspects, the buildings are also of great interest to the student of history and architecture. They were built at the turn of the century at a cost of two million dollars, which included furnishings. The construction of all three buildings is steel and reinforced concrete, faced with Indiana limestone and 27 different types of marble from all parts of the world. The various wooden pieces and ceilings were all crafted with great care, yet throughout, utilitarianism was the watchword. Of particular note are the bronze doors on all three buildings, executed by sculptress Gail Sherman Corbett, which depict scenes from Springfield's past, the city and state coats of arms, plus the symbols of justice and the beehive for a successful community, surrounded by the laurel of peace. President William H. Taft was the featured speaker at the Municipal Group's dedication ceremonies in 1913.

• At **City Hall** the mayor (**Richard E. Neal**) works, licenses are issued, and the various other components of Springfield city life are carried on. Open Monday through Friday, 9:00 a.m. to 5:00 p.m. Telephone: 413/787-6000.

• The **Campanile** rises 300 feet in the air to a bell tower with 12 carillon bells, which are played electrically on a regular schedule. Tours are available to the tower's observation deck free of charge, weekdays 2:30 p.m. to 3:45 p.m., with children under 18 accompanied by an adult. The surrounding area for some 30 miles is visible on clear days, and the tower's clock can be seen from three miles away.

• A building that since 1912 was called Municipal Auditorium has recently been renamed **Symphony Hall** because of its outstanding acoustics. That change also signals recognition of the Springfield Symphony Orchestra, a fully professional metropolitan orchestra of 75 instruments with **Raymond Harvey** as music director.

A number of other groups also play in the hall, including string quartets and quintets, and the Western Massachusetts Young People's Orchestra, comprised of youngsters from 12 to 21 years of age. The classic Greek building has been host to many famous performers, including the Boston Symphony, Cleveland Orchestra, Lily Pons, Arthur Fiedler, Yehudi Menuhin, Jascha Heifetz, Jose Iturbi, Van Cliburn, Eugene Ormandy, Kirsten Flagstad, Patrice Munsell, Roberta Peters, Rise Stevens, Paul Robeson, Ezio Pinza, Robert Merrill, etc. Of Symphony Hall Ignace Paderewski said, "I struck a chord and waited...and the hall just sang to me." Serge Koussevitzky commented that he "knew of no auditorium of its size in the world which could compare with it." The hall contains seating for 2,600 and has a lovely mahogany room on the second floor. The Springfield Symphony Orchestra (SSO) concert season includes Great Performances, classical concerts, pops concerts, and staged operas with internationally famed guest artists. There is an active Women's Symphony League that sponsors an annual ball each spring, plus many other events throughout the year. Telephone: 413/733-2291.

• First Church of Christ, Congregational, better known as **Old First Church** at Court Square was the fourteenth church founded in the Massachusetts Bay Colony, the first church established in the area. Formal worship began with Pynchon and the early settlers, with Reverend George Moxon the first minister in 1637. It began at first in homes, then in various meeting houses, and eventually this church was built in 1819. Designed by builder-architect Isaac Damon, the building style is early Greek Revival; its cost was $15,000.00. Dr. Samuel Osgood, the minister at the time, served the church 45 years. Through the church are many valuable items that have been donated by members: an Honor Roll of World War II veterans, Rembrandt Bible, antique communion table, hymn boards, a clock bequeathed by Edward Pynchon, the original oil lamp used by the minister on his pulpit, etc. Of note outside is the rooster on the church steeple, made in London, which measures four feet from tail to beak and weighs 60 pounds; it has perched there since 1768. The church bell was cast in 1826. Many famous people have been associated with Old First Church: the body of former President John Quincy Adams lay in state in the sanctuary in 1848 on its way back to Boston from Washington; Jenny Lind, the famous Swedish soprano, sang there in 1851;

John Brown of Harper's Ferry fame attended church there, as did Daniel Webster on several occasions; and Deacon Samuel Chapin (*The Puritan*) was a church deacon. The church was declared a Massachusetts Historic Landmark in October of 1971. Old First Church welcomes the public to its Sunday services at 11:00 a.m. and is open by appointment for tours. Telephone: 413/737-1411.

• The downtown's oldest commercial building, the **Byers Block,** is located in Court Square. It contained many law offices, and dates to 1835 when much of Elm Street was occupied by commercial buildings constructed for postmaster James Byers. Among the practicing lawyers was George Ashmun, best remembered for nominating Abraham Lincoln for the presidency at the 1880 convention.

• The **Court Square Building** now has a parking garage occupying what was once the entrance to the famous Court Square Theatre where Helen Hayes made her debut, *Ben Hur* and its cast of 400 performed, and such notables as Jack Benny, W. C. Fields, Katherine Cornell, and Sarah Bernhardt all played.

• **Hampden County Courthouse** was designed in 1871 by Henry Hobson Richardson, although remodeling in 1906 destroyed many of the Richardsonian elements. Monson granite was used in the structure, modeled after the Palazzo Vecchio in Italy. The Superior Court Building has served as the seat of justice for Hampden County for the last century, but has recently been replaced by the new Hall of Justice (1976). Other important new structures in Springfield's downtown area include the Bank of Boston Building (1982) at 1350 Main Street, Center Square (1982) at 1441 Main Street, the Federal Building (1982) at 550 Main Street, and Monarch Place (1987) at 331 Main Street.

• **Court Square's green** encapsulates much of Springfield's history. Stone markers near Elm Street designate the site of the First Meeting House (1645) and Parsons Tavern, visited in 1775 by George Washington.

Springfield bills itself as a city of **Firsts:**

• The first successful commercially sold automobile was constructed in the U. S. in 1892-3 by the Duryea brothers of Springfield.

• The first American-made automobile, actually a steam carriage, was built in Springfield by Thomas Blanchard.

• The first railroad sleeping car made in the country was built for George Pullman by T. W. Wason and Company in Springfield in 1850.

• The first U. S. musket (Model 1795) was made in the Springfield Armory, and the Springfield (1903) and Garand (1937) rifles also originated there.

• A number of firsts are cited in the field of education: adult education in 1851, general-science/music-appreciation course (1896-1905), YMCA college training (1880), and agricultural extension course (1913).

• The Seymour Planetarium, first projection planetarium constructed in the nation, was devised and constructed by the Springfielid Science Museum's Director, Frank Korkosz.

• The game of basketball was invented in Springfield in 1891 by Dr. James Naismith.

• Friction matches were patented in Springfield in 1836 by Alonzo D. Phillips.

• The first U. S. Government postal cards were manufactured in Springfield in 1873.

• The meat-packing industry was started in Springfield in the 17th century by the son of the city's founder, John Pynchon.

• The first retail sale of frozen foods were made in Springfield in 1930.

• The first Junior Achievement program was started in Springfield in 1919 by Horace A. Moses to teach high school youth the American free-enterprise system.

• The first commercial radio station, Westinghouse's WBZ, went on the air from Springfield's Hotel Kimball in September of 1921

• The Springfield City Library was the first library in the U. S. to circulate recordings.

• The first monkey wrench was introduced in 1860 by Amos Call of Springfield.

• The first wading pool to be built in a public park was installed at Springfield's Forest Park in 1899.

• The first dog show in the country was held in Springfield in April, 1875.

• The world's first Air Mail Courier Service was performed with the services of a Springfield Indian Motocycle, which was the first cycle manufactured in America.

• The first parking meter in the U. S. (the red ball meter) was fashioned by Charley Martin of Springfield; it was widely used in the 1950s.

• Located right in the heart of Springfield, with access from Route 5 in Longmeadow or from Sumner Avenue in **Forest Park,** 750 acres offering year-round recreational facilities. Included are picnic areas, tennis courts, baseball fields, lakes, gardens, nature trails, refreshment spots, paddle boats, pony rides, a hockey rink, swimming pools, the James P. Heady Kiddieland Zoo and Ecology Center, lawn bowling, shuffleboard, and band concerts. The park is free and open daily 6:30 a.m. to 9:00 p.m. during summer; shorter (posted) hours in winter and early spring. Kiddieland Zoo charges a fee of $.25 for children under five, $.50 ages six and up; paddle boats accommodate four and the fee is $5.00; the train ride is $.75 per person. Hours for these special facilities are approximately 10:00 a.m. to 4:00 p.m. or dusk. Free concerts are Saturday or Sunday at the amphitheatre; watch the newspaper for details. Telephone: 413/787-6434 (Zoo Society 733-2251).

• Springfield offers two public **golf courses:** Franconia on Dwight Road, (telephone: 413/739-8548) and Veterans on South Branch Parkway (telephone: 783-7102).

• When Springfield celebrated the 125th anniversary of its incorporation as a city on June 5, 1977, its outdoor pancake breakfast table, 1,500 feet long, earned it a place in the *Guiness Book of World Records* as the longest breakfast table in the world. That statistic has developed into quite a rivalry with Grand Rapids, Michigan, so Springfield bested itself with the city's 350th birthday celebration in 1986 by feeding pancakes to 24,000 people on a 2,500-foot long table. The challenge continues...

• **Harambee Holiday** (from a Swahili word meaning celebration), dedicated to the celebration of Black culture, is an annual summertime event that takes place in Winchester Square.

• Springfield's **Historical Commission,** which

operates from City Hall (telephone: 413/736-2711) has been actively trying to preserve much of the city's outstanding architectural heritage. Historic areas that are part of the federal government's listing on the National Register of Historic Places include: Quadrangle/Mattoon, McKnight, Maple-Union Corners, South Congregational Church, Ames Hill/Crescent Hill, Court Square, Armory Square, Memorial Square, and the State Armory on Howard Street. Historic Districts of the city include: 1. Forest Park Heights; 2. Maple Street Hill; 3. Lower Maple Street; 4. Memorial Square; 5. Main Street; 6. Court Square; 7. Quadrangle/Mattoon Historic District; 8. Springfield Armory; and 9. McKnight District. The commission has listings of particular interesting places. **Historical American Buildings** in Springfield include:

1. Alexander House
2. Boston Road Stone, a carved marker dating to 1763, erected by Joseph Wait, located on the grounds of the Springfield Armory.
3. Church of the Unity at 207 State Street, a Gothic Revival church built in 1867 by architect Henry Hobson Richardson, destroyed in the 1950s.

• The **"Springfield Indians,"** a locally owned and managed hockey team affiliated with the American Hockey League, have provided professional hockey excitement to the fans of Western Massachusetts for over 50 years. The Indians play all of their home games in the Springfield Civic Center, 58 Dwight Street. Telephone: 413/736-4546. The first professional hockey game in the area was played on Wednesday, December 1, 1926 at the Eastern States Coliseum, with the Springfield Indians facing off against the Boston Tigers; since that event, Springfield has had many loyal hockey fans. The name most associated with the Indians is that of Eddie Shore, who started with the team in 1939, winning with them three straight league and Calder Cup championships 1959-62.

• **Indian Motocycle Museum and Hall of Fame** is located in the very last building owned by the Indian Motocycle Company. It is a living museum that pays tribute to Carl Oscar Hedstrom the inventor and George M. Hendee who was America's amateur High Wheeler Bicycle Champion for five years for distances of 1 to 20 miles. These two gentlemen were the cofounders of this famous firm and in 1901 introduced a single cylinder one and three quarter-horsepower motorcycle that weighed 98 lbs., thus becoming the first gasoline powered motorcycle to be marketed in America. Displayed are some of the many products they made, such as the granddaddy of all snowmobiles, cars, airplane engines, outboard motors, sidecar street sweepers, sidecar taxi cabs, sidecar fire engines, etc. Various models of Indian Motocycles covering the years 1901-53 are shown. The company ceased manufacturing in 1953. Enhancing the display are other all-American made motorcycles; everything is in running condition. The photo gallery is extensive, and showcases are filled with related memorabilia. The toy motorcycle collection is fabulous. It is rare indeed that a museum of this kind can be put together which is historically and educationally important not only to Springfield history, but also to the country. The museum was founded in 1973 by Charles Manthos, President and Director. It is open daily Monday through Sunday, 1:00 p.m. to 5:00 p.m., summers 10:00 a.m. to 5:00 p.m., closed Thanksgiving, Christmas, and New Year's. Admission is $2.00 for adults, $1.00 for children. Telephone: 413/737-2624.

• A healthy diversity of **industry** is found in Springfield, where 18,700 persons are employed by over 35 manufacturing firms with annual multimillion dollar payrolls. Its chief industries include chemicals, fabricated metal products, machinery, printing and publishing, apparel and other finished goods, and paper and allied products. Some of its products known the world over include American Saw, Breck hair preparations, Buxton billfolds, Columbia bikes, Digital computers, Friendly Ice Cream, James River Graphics, Merriam Webster dictionaries, Milton Bradley games and toys, Monsanto plastics, Package Machines, Smith and Wesson revolvers, Spalding sporting goods, Tampax, Titeflex hoses, and U. S. envelopes. Its businesses include headquarters for several large insurance companies, and it is the home of the original Taylor Rental Company. Many of these companies are open by appointment for group tours, but be sure to call first.

• The **Jewish Community Center** at 1160 Dickinson

Street provides a wide variety of events throughout the year that are open to the public. Telephone: 413/739-4715.

- There are several outstanding and symbolic **landmarks** throughout Springfield, including:

   1. The Springfield cemetery off of Maple Street on Cemetery Avenue, which contains a bronze relief by Saint-Gaudens representing J. G. Holland, author and first editor of the *Springfield Republic* newspaper.

   2. Merrick Park, at the corner of State and Maple Streets, where Saint-Gaudens' *The Puritan* statue stands.

   3. Site of King Philip's Stockade, the vantage point from which Indian King Philip is said to have directed and observed the burning of Springfield in 1675.

Where have you found excellence for nearly a century?
THE MACDUFFIE SCHOOL
Now accepting applications for September
Girls, grades 7-12
For information, please call Admissions **734-4971**

- **MacDuffie School for Girls** on Ames Hill Drive is a boarding and day school for girls, grades 7 to 12. Founded in 1890, the school has 60 boarders and 120 day students and offers a six-week summer program. Twelve states and eleven foreign countries are represented at this strictly college preparatory school with strong college placement. It has regional accreditation and is a member of the New England Association of Schools and Colleges. Telephone: 413/734-4971.

- Named for farmer/owner William F. Mattoon who decided to sell some of his land in 1870 for rowhouses, **Mattoon Street** today symbolizes Springfield's historic preservation at its finest. Composed largely of mansard-style residences, it is Springfield's most complete street of townhouses, being restored to its former Victorian splendor. Located on the "brow of the hill," Mattoon Street parallels the Quadrangle complex off Chestnut Street. Some of its more famous residents have included builder B. F. Farrar; Lieutenant Governor William H. Haile; Margaret Calhoun, wife of Springfield politician William B. Calhoun; jeweler Henry W. Hallet; author Mason Green; and landscape painter George Newell Bowers. On the eastern end of the street is the **Grace Baptist Church** (formerly North Congregational Church), dating back to 1873. It is the only church left in Springfield designed by architect Henry Hobson Richardson. It was built at a cost of $120,000.00 with local brownstone used to enhance its Romanesque style; Tiffany glass windows were added in 1913. The church is not open to the public for specific tours, but services are held there each Sunday at 10:30 a.m. and 7:00 p.m. Mattoon Street itself is at all times available for viewing by citizens interested in seeing what neighborhood cooperation can do for inner-city rebirth. Each year the Mattoon Street Association sponsors the Mattoon Street Arts Festival the weekend after Labor Day, an open house in May, and an antique show in June. In addition, it holds celebrations for the 4th of July and Halloween, as well as a caroling party the Sunday before Christmas.

- The city's largest employer is Baystate **Medical Center,** located at 759 Chestnut Street. A multifaceted hospital, it provides comprehensive medical services including: community health education, nursing education programs, emergency psychiatric care, outpatient and inpatient psychiatric care, maternal health services, blood banks, community clinics, social services, emergency room treatment, outpatient and inpatient medical services, and volunteer recruitment, training, and supervision. Telephone: 413/787-2500.

- One of the nation's oldest and most honored **newspapers,** the *Springfield Republican* was founded in 1824 by Samuel Bowles, and became almost a national institution under the liberal editorship of Dr. Josiah G. Holland. An amusing announcement by Samuel Bowles appeared in the November 1825 issue of the *Springfield Republican:* "We shall publish no marriage unless the writing is accompanied by a piece of the wedding cake, and a little wine, if convenient—but we are not particular as to that." The paper stayed in the Bowles family for several generations and today is part of the Newhouse group. There are three publications: *The Sunday Republican* (circulation 145,000); *The Morning Union* (circulation 75,000); and the *Springfield Daily News* (circulation 79,000). Each of the newspapers is editorially independent, but all are housed in a spacious new highly-automated plant at 1860 Main Street, where full-color capacity presses can print, cut, fold, and count more than 2,000 newspapers a minute. It is one of the largest and most technologically advanced plants in the U. S. Free tours of the facility for groups of 15 to 35 members are available weekdays from 9:00 a.m. to 2:30 p.m. by appointment only. All aspects of the newspaper are discussed in the one and a half-hour tour. Morning is the suggested time for the tours, and appointments should be made several weeks in advance by calling the Personnel Department. Telephone: 413/785-1000.

- The Springfield **Police** Department is headquartered at 130 Pearl Street; it allows tours of its facilities to interested citizen groups. It is noteworthy that the first policewomen in Springfield were appointed in 1918. Telephone: 413/787-6350.
- Springfield was named in 1640 for the hometown of its founder **William Pynchon** (1590?-1662). A shareholder in the Massachusetts Bay Colony, Pynchon sailed from Southampton with Governor John Winthrop and his family in 1630 to colonize in North America. Pynchon was an early leader in the forming of Springfield until he published a theological tract in 1650 called "The Meritorious Price of Our Redemption," which caused the church authorities to denounce him and his fellow settlers to badger him for heretical views. However, Pynchon's son John (1626?-1703) was to make an indelible mark of contribution for the family name on its settlement in Springfield. John held important elective and appointive offices in the city and state, continued to run his father's businesses, built the first brick house in the Connecticut valley, and fought in King Philip's War. The towns of Northampton, Deerfield, and Hadley were built on lands owned by the Pynchon family. The William Pynchon Memorial Building of the Quadrangle, built in 1927, commemorates Springfield's founder as a foremost colonizer, merchant, and politician in his era.

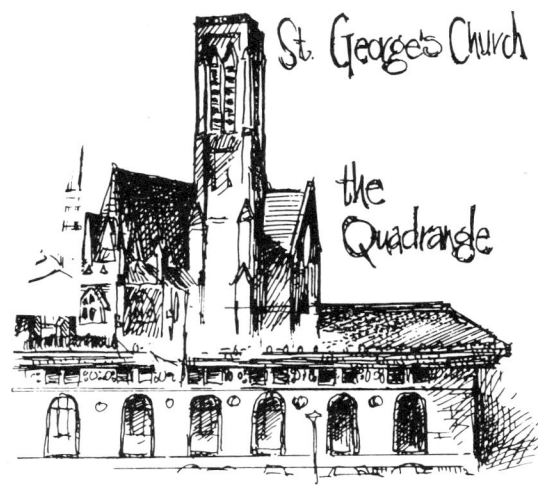

- A unique cultural center, **The Quadrangle** is found in the heart of Springfield's downtown area. Located near State and Chestnut Streets, in the form of a quadrangle, the unique cultural complex was organized in 1857. **The Springfield Library and Museums Association** is headed by a 30-member Board of Trustees, including the Mayor of Springfield, the Vice Chairman of the School Committee, and the President of the City Council as ex-officio members. Its operating costs of $8,000,000.00 per year are covered by city, state, and federal funds; endowments and gifts; grants; and membership fees of "Friends of the Quadrangle." The Quadrangle is made up of the main building of the City Library system, the Connecticut Valley Historical Museum, the Museum of Fine Arts, the Springfield Science Museum, and the George Walter Vincent Smith Art Museum. Eight branch libraries, located throughout the city, are also part of this dynamic, private, non-profit association. The four museums are open Tuesday through Sunday, 12:00 p.m. to 5:00 p.m., closed Monday. Admission to all museums and libraries is free, and there is parking available at the Quadrangle at the association's parking lots on Edwards and State Streets. For additional information, contact the Springfield Library and Museums Association, 220 State Street. Telephone: 413/739-3871.

- The **Puritan** statue, sculpted in bronze in 1877 by Augustus St. Gaudens, stands at the entrance to the Quadrangle on the rise of Merrick Park. A symbol of Springfield's history, the statue is of Deacon Samuel Chapin (1598-1675), who served on Springfield's first Board of Selectmen in 1644. The site marks the spot where Chapin stood to let his Puritan beliefs about the New World be known. The monument is said to represent a composite of the Chapin family type and was sculpted for the deacon's descendant, Chester W. Chapin, president of the Boston and Albany Railroad.

The Statue of the Puritan in Merrick Park

With sober foot unswerving, lip severe,
   And lid that droops to shield the inner sight;
   Dark-browned, stern-willed, a shadow in the light
Of alien times, and yet no alien here;
Revered and dreaded, loved, but yet with fear;
   He moves, the somber shade of that old night
   Whence grew our morn, the ghost of that grim might
That nursed to strength the Nation's youth austere
   Mark the grave thought that lines the hollow cheek,
The hardy hand that guards the sacred book,
   The sinewy limb, and what the tin lips speak
Of iron will to mould the era—look
   In reverence, and as ye mutely scan
The heroic figure, see, rough-limned, a man!
                        —Whitmore, 1852

- The services of the **Springfield City Library** are available free of charge to all Massachusetts residents. The system contains over 650,000 volumes and lends records, videocassettes, compact discs, films, and pamphlets. In addition, large print books and talking books are available for the handicapped.

The library offers the services of a comprehensive Reference Department, an extensive Art and Music

Department, a Periodical Reading Room, Genealogy and Local History Room, and a Children's room. Programming is also an important part of service to the community—a great variety of programs for adults and children, exhibits, demonstrations, movies, book discussions, arts and crafts, and much more are planned every month in the branch libraries.

The Springfield City Library is comprised of the Central Library at 220 State Street (telephone: 413/739-3871) and these branches:

Brightwood, 220 Birnie Avenue	737-4765
East Springfield, 21 Osborne Terrace	733-6731
Forest Park, 380 Belmont Avenue	733-7019
Indian Orchard, 44 Oak Street	543-3918
Liberty, 773 Liberty Street	732-1033
Pine Point, 204 Boston Road	782-2335
Sixteen Acres, 1187 Parker Street	783-2161
Winchester Square, 765 State Street	732-6294
Bookmobile Headquarters, 765 State Street	733-2414

The first unit of the Springfield Library and Museums Association, the City Library was organized in 1857. The present Central Library building was constructed in 1912 from a design by architect Edward Tilton in the style of the Italian Renaissance. The project was funded by local citizenry and a generous donation from Andrew Carnegie. The Springfield Library was the first library in the nation to circulate recordings.

Winter hours for the Central Library are: Monday through Thursday 9:00 a.m. to 9:00 p.m.; Friday through Saturday, 9:00 a.m. to 5:00 p.m.; Sunday 1:00 p.m. to 5:00 p.m.; summer hours are: Monday through Thursday, 9:00 a.m. to 8:00 p.m.; Friday, 9:00 a.m. to 5:00 p.m., closed Saturday and Sunday.

• Named in honor of the founder of Springfield, the William Pynchon Memorial Building houses the **Connecticut Valley Historical Museum.** It is widely known for its collection of Connecticut Valley decorative arts and 17th century documents of the Pynchon family. The newest unit of the Springfield Library and Museums Association, the Georgian Colonial building was erected in 1927 and contains exhibit galleries and period rooms. Included are a kitchen dating back to about 1700, a commons room and bed chamber from a tavern built in nearby Chicopee in 1785, and a Federal period dining room. The galleries display the museum's collection of furniture, art, silver, pewter, and glass made and used in the Connecticut Valley. Of special interest are paintings by Joseph Whiting Stock and James Sanford Ellsworth; furniture by William Lloyd and other area cabinetmakers; portraits of early Springfield residents; and a collection of paintings and prints of the Connecticut Valley. Accredited in 1973 by the American Association of Museums, the Connecticut Valley Historical Museum is known nationally to scholars of this country's early history. Hours are Tuesday through Sunday, 1:00 p.m. to 5:00 p.m. Telephone: 413/732-3080.

• Since its opening in 1933, the **Springfield Museum of Fine Arts** has contained one of the country's leading collections of European, Far Eastern, and American paintings and sculpture. A center for all the arts, an art history museum covering the period from 3,000 B. C. to contemporary times, the museum's main thrusts have been acquisition, education, exhibition, and cooperation with community agencies. It is located at 49 Chestnut Street on the Quadrangle in a building of simple limestone exterior whose architectural grace extends to the interior. The visitor enters a magnificent interior court where the museum's best American paintings are exhibited, including the huge *Historical Monument of the American Republic* by Erastus Salisbury Field. Marble staircases lead to eleven galleries on the second floor. There can be found art from the Gothic period of the 14th century, the Renaissance, the Baroque period, 18th century and 19th century France, 17th century Holland, and 18th century England and two galleries for special exhibitions. The first floor contains two Oriental galleries displaying artifacts spanning 4,000 years of Far Eastern culture. Other features are a gallery of 18th century and early 19th century American paintings and furniture and two galleries of 20th century art. There is also a museum shop where gifts may be purchased and a Sales and Rental Gallery. The galleries are arranged by period and countries to portray the influence each has had on the other. Many of the great masters are represented throughout: Tiepolo, Chardin, Sargent, Monet, Erastus Salisbury Field, Edwin Dickinson, Lyonel Feininger, Picasso, Copley, etc. The museum is dedicated to community participation in its programs, and offers frequent gallery talks, tours, and guest lectures, all of which are either free to the public or charge a small admission fee. Hours are Tuesday through Sunday, 12:00 p.m. to 5:00 p.m. Telephone: 413/732-6092.

• Natural history and physical exhibits are displayed at the **Springfield Science Museum.** The museum offers both permanent and changing exhibits of interest to all ages, including: dioramas with numerous mounted animals and birds; the spectacular two-level R. E. Phelon African Hall, depicting the wildlife and cultures of Africa; Dinosaur Hall with a 20-foot tall replica of Tyrannosaurus rex; shell hall; an aquarium; a 100-seat planetarium; a display on early aviation in Springfield with a 1937 Zeta airplane; a Woodland Indian stone bowl workshop and numerous archeological specimens; a life-sized transparent anatomical woman; and a large new participatory area for families. Museum shop public hours are Tuesday through Sunday, 12:00 p.m. to 5:00 p.m., with school group programs in the morning by advance reservation. Public planetarium shows are given eight times weekly on Tuesday, Thursday, Saturday, and Sunday; small fee for planetarium tickets. Telephone: 413/733-1194.

• One man's extensive collection of decorative arts of the major civilizations of the world, especially China and Japan, can be found at the **George Walter Vincent Smith Art Museum** (GWVS) at the Quadrangle. Housed in an Italianate yellow brick and terra cotta structure designed in the manner of a Florentine palace, the art museum dates to 1895, when Smith brought together his pieces representing crafted accomplishments of world artisans. Included in the galleries are exhibits of jade, cloisonne, porcelains, tapestries, and armor. The museum's nationally recognized 19th century Italian paintings, together with its 19th century American paintings, forms one of the most comprehensive collections assembled from the studios of the actual artists at the time. Worldwide interest has been focused on the collection of Japanese armor and the weaponry from Europe, the Near East, and the Orient. One of the earliest public museums in America, the GWVS maintains its traditional collections of the late George Walter Vincent and Belle Townsley Smith and also has frequently changing exhibits. Class instruction for children and adults in drawing, painting, art history, and handcrafts is available to residents in Western Massachusetts. Hours are Tuesday through Sunday, 12:00 p.m. to 5:00 p.m. Telephone: 513/733-4214.

• The catchword in Springfield is **revitalization,** revising and renewing present properties rather than destroying them and starting anew. **Springfield Central, Inc.,** at 338 Worthington Street (telephone: 413/732-7467) operates programs to stimulate the economy of the city through various activities and projects, which result in attracting tourists, new business, and industry and in expansion and modernization. Urban growth and renewal services are also provided to clear, renew, and/or rehabilitate old housing in downtown Springfield. The **Pioneer Valley Convention and Visitors Bureau** at 56 Dwight Street (telephone: 787-1548) was established for

the promotion of tourism, businesses, and industries. Its program is designed to provide stimulation to the economy of given communities by various activities and projects, which result in attracting large numbers of tourists, new business and industry. Further, the **Mayor's Office for Community Affairs** (MOCA) at 1250 Main Street (telephone: 787-6622) offers a variety of arts services and programs to the general community, including consultation and technical assistance to individuals and groups; amateur and professional artists workshops; and Telefun, a clearinghouse for community activities and special events, such as the Big 4th Festival, Summer Sounds, Sundays in the Park, and First Night. The next area for revitalization in Springfield is its riverfront area.

• At one point, Springfield was a center for **sporting events** for all of New England and the northeastern part of the nation, and still today sports play a large role in its lifestyle. Its YMCA, located at 275 Chestnut Street, was one of the first in the nation; basketball was invented here in 1891; the Morgan Horse originated with a Springfieldite named Justin Morgan; the Springfield Bicycle Club was known worldwide for its famous tournaments of the 1880s; the universally favorite Indian Motocycle was manufactured in Springfield at the turn of the century; the Duryea car, the first gasoline-powered one made for sale, won the first automobile race in 1895; Springfield baseball greats have included Roger Connor and Tom Burns; Harvard-Yale football games were played in Springfield's neutral ground from 1889-1894; great football names include Jim Thorpe and Amos Alonzo Stagg; Dr. J. McCurdy brought lawn hockey to Springfield in 1896; Springfield's hockey team, the Indians, have been a home team since 1926; Everett H. Barney of Springfield invented a method of clamping skates to shoes in 1864, and soon patented and produced the device into a financial success; roller polo took place in Springfield in 1898 at Andrew Whitney's rink; the Springfield Golf Club was organized in 1897, the Rod and Gun Club in 1874, and the first tennis club was formed in the early 1800s on Dale Street; the Connecticut River has long been used for rowing regattas and general pleasure cruising; and Springfield track stars have included "Pooch" Donovan and "Cuckoo" Collins. Its recent sports heroes are Olympic gymnast Tim Daggett and tennis star Tim Mayotte.

And some sports trivia: Jack Stone, better known as "Cyclone Stone," set a flagpole-sitting record of 52 days, 21 hours, and 40 minutes in the summer of 1930. Everett McGowen roller-skated for 146 consecutive hours in a rink off Boston Road in the 1930s. Springfield native George Hendee was amateur bicycle champion of America. The Greater Springfield Sports Club is located at PO Box 1888, Springfield (01100); Telephone: 413/732-8531.

The **Springfield Department of Parks and Recreation,** with offices at Forest Park, conducts summer art and music programs, and has many recreational offerings. In addition to the municipal golf courses, it has parks at Forest Park on Sumner Avenue, Van Horn Park on Armory Street, Blunt Park between Bay Street and Roosevelt Avenue, Riverfront Park at the foot of State Street, North Branch Park between Breckwood Boulevard, and Parker Sreet, and Greenleaf at Parker Street. Swimming is available at Forest Park, Lake Lorraine, and Five-Mile Pond. The department also sponsors and manages the Springfield Golden Age Club at 1277 Main Street. Telephone: 413/736-0284.

Springfield Heritage State Park on Main Street includes downtown's Court Square, a new urban common dominated by the Municipal Group of City Hall, Symphony Hall, and the 300-foot Campanile, and Riverfront Park, where an outdoor stage hosts concerts, theatre, and dance performances. Telephone: 413/737-6099.

• A song that the school children of Springfield learn goes like this:
S-P-R-I-N-G-F-I-E-L-D
There's a Springfield in most every state
From the coast of Maine to the Golden Gate.
All of them are lovely, and show a lot of class
But if you please, the greatest of these is Springfield, Mass!

• Since 1935 the **Springfield Adult Education Council** has provided an informative, educational lecture series free to the public. Over the years it has sponsored lectures by Richard Nixon, Hubert Humphrey, Arthur Schlesinger, Jr., Walt Kelly, Agnes DeMille, Lewis Mumford, Everett Dirksen, Betty Friedan, Ralph Nader, Dick Gregory, Bruno Bettleheim, Dr. Mary Calderone, Walter Kerr, Clive Barnes, Thomas Hoving, William Colby, Alex Haley, Kurt Waldheim, Abba Eban, Charles Kuralt, Red Auerbach, Liv Ullmann, etc. In celebration of its 50th anniversary in 1985, the program included free lectures by Henry Kissinger, Beverly Sills, Jean-Michael Cousteau, and John Kenneth Galbraith. Telephone 413/781-0337.

• **Springfield College,** at 263 Alden Street, is a private, nonsectarian coeducational liberal arts and professional college. Emphasis for the approximately 2,200 undergraduate men and women is placed on professional preparation programs with the Division of Health, Physical Education, and Recreation and the Division of Continuing Education. There are nearly 400 students enrolled in the graduate program, and the college offers a Ph.D. program in physical education. It is accredited by the New England Association of Schools and Colleges, the Board of Collegiate Authority of the Commonwealth of Massachusetts, and the National Council for Accreditation of Teacher Education. Telephone: 413/787-2100.

• Founded in 1967, **Springfield Technical Community College** (STCC) is the most comprehensive institution in the Massachusetts community college system, the largest one in the commonwealth, and the only one located on a National Historic site. Approximately 8,000 men and women are enrolled in over 60 associate degree or certificate programs in health/human services, engineering technologies, business administration, liberal arts and sciences, and engineering/science transfer. STCC's Division of Continuing Education offers summer and evening classes, including special interest courses and workshops designed for allied health professionals and for the business community through the Center for Business/Industry Development. Situated on the Springfield Armory National Historic site, STCC shares the 55-acre ground with the National Park Service. It has a "Self-Guided Walking Tour" brochure available. Telephone: 413/781-7822.

- **Television stations** in Greater Springfield include: ABC—WGGB (40), 1300 Liberty Street, Springfield. Telephone: 413/785-1911. CBS—WFSB (3), 3 Constitution Plaza, Hartford, Connecticut. Telephone: 203/728-3333. NBC—WWLP (22): Telephone: 413/786-2200. PBS—WGBY (57): 44 Hampden Street. Telephone: 781-2801

Most of the area colleges maintain radio stations; commercial ones include WAQY 525-4141, WHYN 781-1101, WIXY 525-4141, WMAS 737-1414, and WSPR 732-4182.

- Ever since the days when the divine Sarah Bernhardt performed at Court Square in Springfield, the city has taken a great interest in **theatre**. Today, in addition to its professional repertory group at Stage/West, there is a branch of the American National Theatre and Academy (Springfield ANTA), a resident theatre company based at Springfield College, and many local colleges and communities have performing arts groups.

Springfield's resident professional theatre, **Stage/West** is located at One Columbus Center, directly off I-91. A theatre group of the first rank, it annually presents a variety of plays, ranging from the classics to current comedies. Stage/West opened its first season in 1967, and since then has gained national recognition, especially for such performances as *Count Dracula, The Miracle Worker, The Glass Menagerie, Arms And The Man, Guys And Dolls, The Crucible, Happy Days,* and various Shakespearean plays. The Box Office is open Monday 10:00 a.m. to 5:00 p.m.; Tuesday through Friday, 10:00 a.m. to curtain; Saturday and Sunday 12:00 p.m. to curtain. Telephone: 413/781-2340. Prices range from $12.00 to $23.00: student and group discounts available.

- Until the adoption of standard **time** in 1883, Springfield had its own time zone, which was five minutes later than that adopted by Boston.

- With its location on the east bank of the Connecticut River, midway between major cities of the Northeast, **transportation** has always played a major role in Springfield's history. Originally, the river was invaluable for fur and other trading ventures, and was the reason the government decided to establish the armory there. Thomas Blanchard, whose lathe invention can be seen at the Armory Museum, was also responsible for a successful steam wagon in 1826. The first railroad train came in 1839, and West Springfield became headquarters for the Boston and Albany Railroad. Thomas and Charles Wason's car works built many of the railroad cars, some of the first horse cars, many of the trolleys used by the Springfield Street Railway Company, and the first steam fire engines designed for quick transport by horse. Streetcars, which stimulated the development of Springfield's outer neighborhoods in the 1870s, were carrying 14,000,000 passengers over 68 miles of line by the turn of the century. Goodyear rubber was manufactured in Springfield, as were Westfield's Columbia bicycles, Indian Motocycles, and the Duryea and Knox cars. The first gasoline car made for sale was built in Springfield in 1892 by Frank Duryea. Rolls-Royce cars were assembled in a Springfield plant from 1921-3. The grandeur of the architecture at Union Station on Lyman Street signifies the importance of the railroad here in days gone by. Springfield was also at one point a famous aerial center, with many ballooning flights made there. Airplanes have also been a part of Springfield's history, with the "Gee Bee" model airplane constructed by the Granville brothers in 1929. Today, Springfield is located near Bradley International Airport, and is involved in working on plans to best deal with mass transportation.

- **Western New England College,** at 1215 Wilbraham Road, is a fully accredited private coeducational institution seeking to combine professional with liberal education in an atmosphere of personal concern for each student. The College serves more than 6,000 full-time and part-time students with undergraduate and graduate programs in its Schools of Arts and Sciences, Business, Continuing Higher Education, Engineering, and Law. The School of Law is the only law school in the commonwealth outside of the Boston area. The 120-acre campus, lcoated in a suburban section of the city about three miles from downtown, houses a 16-building complex of Georgian colonial and contemporary architecture. Lectures, art exhibits, sports events, and a host of other special events are open to the public during the academic year. Telephone: 413/782-3111.

- Organized in 1884, the **Springfield Women's Club** at 49 Chestnut Street has greatly contributed to the civic and cultural enrichment of the city for more than a century.

TOLLAND, Massachusetts
Population: 268 Zip Code: 01034

Named for a town in Wales, Tolland is a small rural community with nearly two-thirds of its acreage under controlled forest development. Located in the extreme southwest corner of Hampden County, Tolland has the smallest population in the municipality.

Trips and trivia:
- The **Burt Hill** section of town, south of Route 57, is the highest point between the Farmington River and the Rhode Island border. It is a marvelously scenic route, extremely mountainous.
- Events in town include an annual major **horse show,** sponsored by the Tolland Equestrian Association, held the last weekend in August, plus the Firemen's Craft sale held 4th of July weekend.
- **Lair Mountain** in North Tolland has a fire tower that affords a spectacular view of Mt. Greylock to the north and Talcott Mountain in Hartford, Connecticut to the south. It is reached via Schoolhouse Road heading north, left onto Beldon Road.
- An early colonial **saltbox** on Clubhouse Road in Tolland Center was moved there from Cape Cod. Other buildings of interest to the architectural student include: the Georgian Colonial (1765) at the corner of Clubhouse Road and Route 57, the Greek Revival town hall and church, classic gable-to-street Greek Revival dwelling on Route 57, and structures around the town center.
- The **Tolland-Otis State Forest** on East Otis Reservoir at Route 8 and Route 23 offers boating, cross-country skiing, fishing, horseback riding, hunting, picnicking, snowmobiling, and swimming on its 2,940 acres. **Tolland State Forest** has 3,000 acres for camping and general recreation. A small entry fee is charged.
- The private **Tunxis Club** is located around Noyes Pond.
- The Tolland **Volunteer Fire Department** annually holds a 4th of July celebration at the center of town featuring antiques, food, and handicrafts.

WALES, Massachusetts
Population: 1,062 Zip Code: 01081

This small rural town, located in the eastern part of Hampden County, was named for James Lawrence Wales, a town benefactor who acknowledged a $2,000.00 legacy in 1826.

Trips and trivia:
- The first **fabric dryer** was invented in the mid-19th century in Wales by local blacksmith Warren Shaw. A working model is in the Wales Library on Route 19 at the corner of Church Street.
- There is local speculation that traces of **gold** available for panning still exist in a collectible quantity in the town, as gold has been discovered there at various times.
- **Lake George,** also called Wales Pond, is a popular summer recreation area for swimming, boating, fishing, hunting, and picnicking. At 917 feet, it is reputed to be the highest spring-fed lake in the Commonwealth.
- the Baptist Society's **Meeting House** (1803), at the corner of Union Road and Route 19 overlooking Lake George, is maintained to this day by the third oldest existing Baptist Society in the country. It was originally built by many church denominations in the town.
- The oldest **mill** in the town, built in the early 19th century for the manufacture of wool and satinet, still stands on Main Street. Other interesting structures around Wales include Howard Fountain at the corner of Main Street and Haynes Hill Road and Cyrus Munger House on Monson Road which, dating from the early 1700s, is thought to be the town's oldest standing home.

TUPPER HILL
NORCROSS WILDLIFE SANCTUARY
WALES, MASS.

- Tupper Hill **Norcross Wildlife Sanctuary** is located on Peck Road in Wales, but the mailing address is RD No. 2 in Monson. It is a 3,000-acre wildlife sanctuary of wooded hills, lakes, and streams and features a variety of rare wildflowers, ferns, and trees native to the Eastern Seaboard (from the Carolinas to Canada), plus free wildlife indigenous to the area. In addition to self-guiding walking trails, there is a museum of natural history where programs are offered on insects, plants, and animals. The sanctuary was established in 1939 by Arthur D. Norcross and is maintained by the Norcross Wildlife Foundation, Inc., whose purpose is "the conservation of wildlife and the active practice of conservation for the benefit of the public. This includes the collection and propagation of wild plants, the preservation of birds and all forms of animal wildlife and the conservation of land and water." Situated on the Monson-Wales road, the sanctuary can be reached eastward from Route 32 or west from Route 19 onto Peck Road. A sign indicates free parking near the museum. Admission is also free to the sanctuary, open year-round, Monday through Saturday, 8:00 a.m. to 4:00 p.m. Special tours can be arranged. Telephone: 413/267-9654.
- **Veineke Brook,** south of town, is named for a local story about a Hessian (German soldier for hire) who established a village in the area where he was taken prisoner in 1777. Today only scattered cellar holes of that community remain.
- The **Wales County Fair,** an annual event each August, is held on Main Street, with livestock exhibits, contests, a midway, and handicrafts. Telephone: 413/245-9376.

WESTFIELD, Massachusetts

Population: 31,433   Zip Code: 01085

As an old fishing and hunting area and the chief village of the Warranoke Indians, Westfield was known as Streamfield, then *Woronoco* (meaning winding land), The Pure Food Town for an old crusade, and The Whip City for its predominant industry of the 19th century. Today it is a highly urbanized city.

Trips and trivia:

• The largest city-owned airfield in the area is to be found at **Barnes Airport.** Open 24 hours a day, it is the third largest airport in New England, with runways large enough to handle the biggest commercial carrier equipment. It is open for tours.

• The first **bicycle factory** in the country was established in Westfield in 1877. Pioneer in the effort was Albert A. Pope, known as the Founder of the American Bicycle Industry, who made the first Columbia bike. The Columbia Manufacturing Company is still in Westfield, on Clyde Street, open by appointment for tours. Telephone: 413/562-3664.

• **Concerts on the Green** is a presentation of the Westfield Center for Early Keyboard Studies, whose activities are supported by the Massachusetts Council on the Arts and Humanities. Its 1986-7 season featured fortepianist Malcolm Bilson. Located at One Cottage Street, it is open weekdays, except Wednesday, 9:00 a.m. to 11:00 a.m. and 2:00 p.m. to 4:00 p.m. Telephone: 413/527-7664.

• **Historic American Buildings** in Westfield include:
1. Arnold House at 140 Franklin Street, built 1800
2. Albert Fowler Tobacco Barn on South Street, built 1855

In addition, there are a number of historic places worth noting: Clapp Tavern (1730) at 53 Court Street; the 1735 House, also called the **Dewey House** (1735) at 87 South Maple Street, the first authentically restored colonial house open to the public—maintained by the Western Hampden Historical Society (telephone: 413/562-3657 or 568-8539); the Henry Stiles House on West Silver Street, also dating to 1735; Fowler Tavern at Main and Exchange streets; Western Avenue's Steven Sackett Tavern (1760), with the Connecticut Valley doorway; the 1817 Fowler-Gillett House on Court Street that serves today as a library; the Westfield Municipal Building on Court Street; the octagon house at 28 King Street; and the Victorian railroad station on North Elm Street that today is a furniture store. There are many interesting structures to be seen throughout the city, particularly on Main Street, Court Street, Franklin Street, Broad Street, and West Silver Street.

• The Department of Environmental Management runs **Hampton Ponds State Park,** (telephone: 413/532-3985) on Route 202, which has 35 acres of swimming, fishing, boating, and picnicking recreation. There is a fee of $2.00, or a season pass for $15.00, with a quarter charged for walk-ins. If swimming pools are your preferences, try Camp Shephard on North West Road.

• Westfield is the site of **Colonel Henry Knox's** stopover on his famous Ticonderoga-Boston Cannon Trek.

• In the Green in the center of Westfield is a **monument** to one of the city's famous soldier-sons: General William, a miltary hero against Shay's Rebellion of 1787.

• One of New England's most outstanding parks, **Stanley Park** is near Route 20 off Western Avenue, with entrances on Western Avenue and Kensington Avenue. It has been in existence since 1949, honoring Frank Stanley Beveridge. Approximately 200 acres, the park contains many flower gardens, picnic areas, a dining pavilion, woodland trails, a meeting house that can be reserved by groups, and the famous Carillon Tower. The vast floral gardens include a rose garden with over 50 varieties of roses, serving as a test garden for the All-American Rose Selections, Inc. Adding to the beauty of the park are a waterwheel, a covered bridge, a blacksmith shop, the International Bridge of Understanding, a replica of a New England meeting house, and a recently included Japanese Garden. The fountain located in the center of a five-acre arboretum is illuminated each night by varicolored lights. Also, the Rotary Club's Eternal Light for Peace, the first light to be dedicated in a movement that will encircle the globe, burns at all times in the park. There is a 30 foot by 32 foot map of the U. S. and Canada inlaid with slate in front of the Carillon Tower which, at 96 feet high, is the focal point of the park. The tower contains 25 English and 61 Flemish bells, an organ, stained glass windows, and sculptured bronze doors. Summer concerts with the carillon take place Thursday and Saturday nights and Sunday afternoons at the park, free to the public. Also, free weekly Sunday evening concerts are held in the pavilion, along with many other special events. Telephone: 413/568-9312. Other attractions include dinosaur tracks, the enchanted oak, lily ponds with swans, and the prayer boulder. The Stanley Park of Westfield is open from 8:00 a.m. to dusk from mid-May to mid-October.

• The city's library, containing 100,000 volumes, is called the **Westfield Athenaeum.** Located at the corner of Elm Street and Court Street on the Green, it is also the home of two oustanding museums:

1. The Jasper Rand Art Museum has regularly changing exhibits of well-known American artists. It is open weekdays, except Wednesday, 9:00 a.m. to 9:00 p.m.; Saturday, 9:00 a.m. to 5:00 p.m. (except summers). Telephone: 413/568-7833.

2. The Edwin Smith Historical Museum features a colonial kitchen and a typical late 18th century New England living room in addition to other antique furniture, old costumes, Indian artifacts, and holiday exhibits. It is open Monday, Wednesday, Friday, and Saturday 1:00 p.m. to 5:00 p.m.; Friday 7:00 p.m. to 9:00 p.m.; closed Saturday during the summer.

• The **Westfield Fair,** an annual livestock show, is held each third full weekend of August on the fairgrounds at Russellville Road. Held since 1927, the fair features livestock and decoration exhibits, oxen and horse drawings, a midway, etc. Telephone: 413/562-3526.

• **Westfield State College** (WSC) located on Western Avenue, is a state-supported liberal arts college with a broad range of career-oriented majors, minors, and fields of concentration. Among these are criminal justice, business administration, computer science, and elementary and secondary education. Founded in 1838, WSC began as the nation's first public coeducational teachers college and will be celebrating its sesquicentennial with a series of special events. The college moved to its 227-acre campus in 1956 and currently enrolls 3,000 undergraduate men and women, with 1,870 students in the graduate and continuing studies division. It is accredited by the New England Association of Schools and Colleges and the National Council for Accreditation of Teacher Education. Facilities for meetings and conferences are available. Telephone: 413/568-3311.

• The **Westfield White Water Canoe Races** on the Westfield River is an annual event each April; events are planned for canoes and covered boats in novice, intermediate, expert, and marathon classes. For more information, contact the **Westfield Chamber of Commerce** at 166 Elm Street. Telephone: 413/568-8731.

WEST SPRINGFIELD, Massachusetts
Population:

Once part of Springfield and now a residential and industrial suburb, West Springfield's original settlement was on "Chicuppe Plains" in 1655, now the town's north end.

Trips and Trivia:
• West Springfield's town *common* was the campsite of armies under Generals Amherst, Burgoyne, and Riedsel; and the drill group of Captain Luke Day's insurgents of Shay's Rebellion.

• What is believed to be the only dated saltbox house in the country can be found at 70 Park Street in West Springfield's Historical Museum, **The Josiah Day House.** Built in 1754 when the town was part of Springfield under the rule of George the Third of England over the Massachusetts Bay Colony, the house is maintained today by the private Ramapogue Historical Society. It is furnished with early period antiques. There are a number of exhibits throughout the house which, because of its small size, can allow only a limited group in at a time; tours must be limited to 30 people. Children must be supervised. The house, occupied by the descendants of Josiah Day until 1902, is open year-round to the public, Saturday and Sunday 1:00 p.m. to 5:00 p.m., otherwise by appointement. (Telephone: 413/734-8322.) There is a modest admission charge, with group rates available. The museum can be reached via Route 20 over the North End Bridge to Park Street, where the Josiah Day House faces the eastern end of the town common. It was placed on the National Register of Historic Places in 1975.

• "The Big E"—one of the biggest and most colorful fairs in the country—takes place each year mid-September at the **Eastern States Exposition** grounds. It lights up the town of West Springfield for 12 days and nights, always including the third week of September in its run. The Big E is the largest livestock show in the East,

featuring judging of many types of animals, a gold star A-rated horse show, crafts, exhibits, its own colonial village, and the unique Avenue of States with large buildings that are replicas of the six New England state capitols. Funland, the Better Living Center (a 123,000 square foot commercial building), Farm-a-rama, the Coliseum, and the New England Center are only a few of the other areas that help to draw over a million fairgoers annually. The 175-acre fairgrounds have 52 permanent buildings, some used throughout the year for off-season events. Entertainment at The Big E includes top names such as Louise Mandrell, The Judds, Johnny Cash, etc. Two outdoor bandshells house continuous entertainment for all ages. The fairgrounds are open 8:00 a.m. to 10:00 p.m. Parking, for which a fee is charged, is available on the grounds and in nearby lots across from the fair. There is an admission charge, with special discount days. For current information, contact The Big E at 1305 Memorial Avenue. Telephone: 413/737-BIGE.

• **Historic American Buildings** of West Springfield are all located at Storrowton Village, but many other interesting structures exist in the town, including the Ely House on Main Street, designed in 1850 by Richard Upjohn, one of the finest examples of the Italian Villa style in the region; First Congregational Church (c. 1802), on Elm Street, now a Masonic Temple; houses on Dewey Street at Sibley Avenue, Piper Road at Birnie Avenue, and 1872 Westfield Street; two brick Federal homes on Route 5; the Levi Brooks House on Cayenne Street; the Hale House on Park Street, a unique Greek Revival design with Victorian embellishments; the factory complex in the Mittineague section; the Baltimore truss railroad bridge (1905) over the Connecticut River; the Memorial Bridge of 1922; and West Springfield's first historic district in the region. The Broadway Historic District, established in 1972.

• **Storrowton Village** is a restored Early American village of buildings of New England that were dismantled and reassembled to recreate a typical town green. Located on the grounds of the Eastern States Exposition, the village is operated by the Exposition, with staffing for activities provided by members of the Storrowton Volunteer Service. Emphasis is on "the development of an understanding of the 19th century way of life," with interpreters describing the lifestyle of the people who might have lived and worked in the buildings. The village was donated to the Exposition in 1929 by Mrs. James Storrow of Boston. She bought all of the buildings, had them dismantled and moved to Storrowton Village, and then reconstructed there, board by board, nail by nail. The buildings include:

The John Atkinston Tavern, built during the late 18th century, moved from Prescott, Massachusetts. It is now a gracious dining place and features an Early American menu.

The granite Chesterfield Blacksmith Shop, from New Hampshire, built during the early or mid-19th century (Historic American Building). It is still operated as a forge at special events throughout the year.

Zacharish Eddy Law Office (1810), moved from Eddyville in the town of Middleborough, Massachusetts, where Eddy practiced law from 1806-1860 (Historic American Building).

Levi and Peletiah Gilbert Homestead (1794), once a farmhouse in West Brookfield, Massachusetts, now a living museum (Historic American Building).

The Little Red Schoolhouse, built in 1810, which was attended by five generations of children in the town of Whately, where it was built of locally made brick. Milton Bradley used the schoolhouse as a symbol of their 100th anniversary in 1960. It is operated as a 19th century school for children during the year.

Phillips House, the oldest of the buildings, was built in 1767 in Taunton, Massachusetts. It houses museum offices and special exhibits of The Institute of Early American Education.

Captain John Potter Mansion is a historical museum, built in 1775 by Captain Potter, who was with George Washington at White Plains and Valley Forge. Potter himself made all the nails, latches, and hinges, and cut out all the elaborate ornamentation in wood for the house (Historic American Building).

New Hampshire's Salisbury Meeting House, built in 1834, was taken down timber by timber and reconstructed at Storrowton in 1929 (Historic American Building).

Town House (1822), formerly a Baptist meeting house in Southwick, Massachusetts. It is now a part of Storrowton Tavern.

In addition, Storrowton maintains a village store, featuring the finest in handcrafted items, antique reproductions, cookbooks, foods, and herbal specialties. The village potter, candlemaker, and blacksmith keep them well supplied with materials such as church warden pipes, porcelain pie birds, mochaware items, wrought iron pot hooks, candle holders, and scented hand-dipped candles. Storrowton's tree-shaded green of restored homes, one of the oldest in the country, represents a true New England town of the late 18th century and early 19th century. The village is open to the public daily, except Mondays, May 1 through Labor Day, 1:00 p.m. to 5:00 p.m. One and a half-hour group tours can be arranged. Telephone: 413/781-0136.

WILBRAHAM, Massachusetts
Population: 11,984

Set aside in 1741 as the Fourth Precinct of Springfield, Wilbraham became incorporated as its own township in 1763. Although it wasn't necessarily named for Wilbraham, England, the town's schoolchildren have established a pen-pal correspondence with many British students their same ages. It is mostly known as the home of **Friendly Ice Cream.**

Trips and trivia:
- "New England's Finest White Holland Turkeys" can be found at **Bennett's Turkey Farm** at 599 Main Street near Tinkham Road. Established in 1923, the family turkey business has existed for three generations of Bennetts. It is the second largest turkey farm in the state, raising 30,000 White Holland Turkeys annually. The Bennetts are happy to arrange free group tours. Telephone: 413/596-3135. Each year on Thanksgiving Day the Bennetts donate a turkey to the first man and first woman to win the five-mile "Turkey Trot" race up Wilbraham Mountain.
- The Wilbraham Museum **A Child's Place** at 678 Main Street is a child's fantasy come true: it offers playgroups, workshops, party places, music, art, dance, games, etc. Staffed by volunteers, the museum is open Sunday 1:00 p.m. to 4:00 p.m.; Tuesday 9:30 to 12:00 p.m.; Thursday, 3:30 p.m. to 5:00 p.m.
- **Community Gardens** at Thayer Brook off Bennett Road is a project of the Wilbraham Conservation Commission, allowing 25 foot by 50 foot plots to all town residents. There are 166 acres of open woodland.
- The first lending **library** in the Connecticut Valley was a private one, dating to 1882 with shares in it sold to subscribers as early as 1782, which was located in a house razed to make room for the present Mile Tree School playground on Main Street. Wilbraham's current library at Crane Park in the center of town has over 40,000 volumes and changing exhibits.
- Built in 1905, **The Little Red Schoolhouse** on Springfield Street near the town center was used as such until the late 1970s; today it houses the Wilbraham Counseling Center.
- **Main Street** seems to typify a classic New England one. There are many interesting structures, running from Boston Road (Route 20 the Old Post Road) to the town of Hampden, including: the **Methodist Meeting House** (1794) at 450 Old Post Road that the town has purchased to house Wilbraham memorabilia, the oldest Methodist Meeting House in New England; Crane Park in the center of town with a statue commemorating local Civil War heroes; the Academy; Foskit Memorial Grange Hall (1901); The Sausage House (c. 1850) at No. 499; the Trepp-restored (previously Yellow Cat Tavern) at No. 515; an early Federal at No. 568 (c. 1810); Merrick Homestead at No. 651, an unusual Stone House built in 1832, etc. The Wilbraham Women's Club recently put out a cookbook titled *Main Street a la Carte* that features key Main Street homes. Other interesting places around town include a saltbox on Three Rivers Road, two early Georgian Colonials on Mountain Road (No. 182, built in 1748 and No. 218, 1769), plus Red Bridge Power Station in the northeast corner of town, a brick Victorian industrial building constructed over an inlet from the Chicopee River. In addition, the cemeteries at East Wilbraham, Glendale, Woodland Dell, and Tinkham Road (Adams Cemetery) contain a history in epitaphs that make for fun and unusual grave rubbings. The Glendale Methodist Church at the corner of Glendale and Monson Roads, built in 1868, is the oldest standing church building in the town still used as a house of worship.
- A famous legend in Wilbraham, that of the **Pesky Sarpent** immortalized in the song "On Springfield Mountain" concerns "Timothy, son of Thomas Mirick and Mary Mirick, (who) was Bit by a Ratel Snake one August the 7th, 1761, and Dyed within about 2 or 3 ours he being 22 years 2 months and 3 days old and vary near the point of marriage." Timothy's gravestone may be seen in the

Adams Cemetery, and his relatives still live in town (Charles Merrick considered by many to be the town historian.) The site of the Pesky Sarpent tragedy, on what is presently Oakland Street, has been commemorated with a historical marker.

• In honor of the Bicentennial, many town residents cooperated to put together **Wilbraham Quilt, 1976,** a 30-octagon representation of the town's history and highlights. The quilt, which has been donated to the Wilbraham Historical Commission and which hangs in the Meeting House, won First Prize in its category at the 1977 Eastern States Exposition contest.

• There is an active **recreation** program in Wilbraham, including programs under the auspices of the Playground and Recreation Committee; Spec Pond on Boston Road, where there is a summer camp and facilities for swimming, skating, fishing, and picnicking at the pavilion; Nine-Mile Pond also on Boston Road has swimming and boating; 75 acres at Twelve-Mile Brook on Crane Hill Road for hiking and trout fishing; and Bruuer Pond on Main Street for ice-skating and bird-watching. Besides the Wilbraham Arts Council, there are also over 40 town organizations, including the Atheneum Society, church and PTA groups, Civil Air Patrol, community theatre, Indian Guides, Junior Chamber of Commerce, the Grange, Homeowners, La Leche League, Lions, League of Women Voters, Newcomers, scouts, sports groups, Rotary International, Unico, women's clubs, and Young at Heart. The Biannual Wilbraham Town Fair is held alternate springs, and the Wilbraham Peach Festival's Labor Day weekend parade is fast becoming an area attraction. The Wilbraham Country Club on Stony Hill Road is a town-owned property popular for golf in the summer and sledding and cross-country skiing in the winter. Telephone: 413/596-8887.

• **Wilbraham and Monson Academy** on Main Street is a college preparatory boarding and day school for grades 9 to 12, and a day school for grades 7 and 8. Founded in 1804, the Academy has an enrollment of approximately 240 boarding and 230 day students. It is accredited by the New England Association of Schools and Colleges and holds membershp in NAIS, ISAM, and Cum Laude. Also on the campus is the Academy Hill Day School for Gifted Children, grades K to 6. Telephone: 413/596-6811.

• The **Wilbraham Mountains** offer a spectacular view of the Connecticut River Valley, and on winter evenings one can easily see the skiing lights at faraway Mt. Tom contrasting with the bright bustle of Springfield's city center. On a clear day, Mt. Toby to the north is visible, while to the south one can see the trap ridge of Connecticut.

Hampshire County

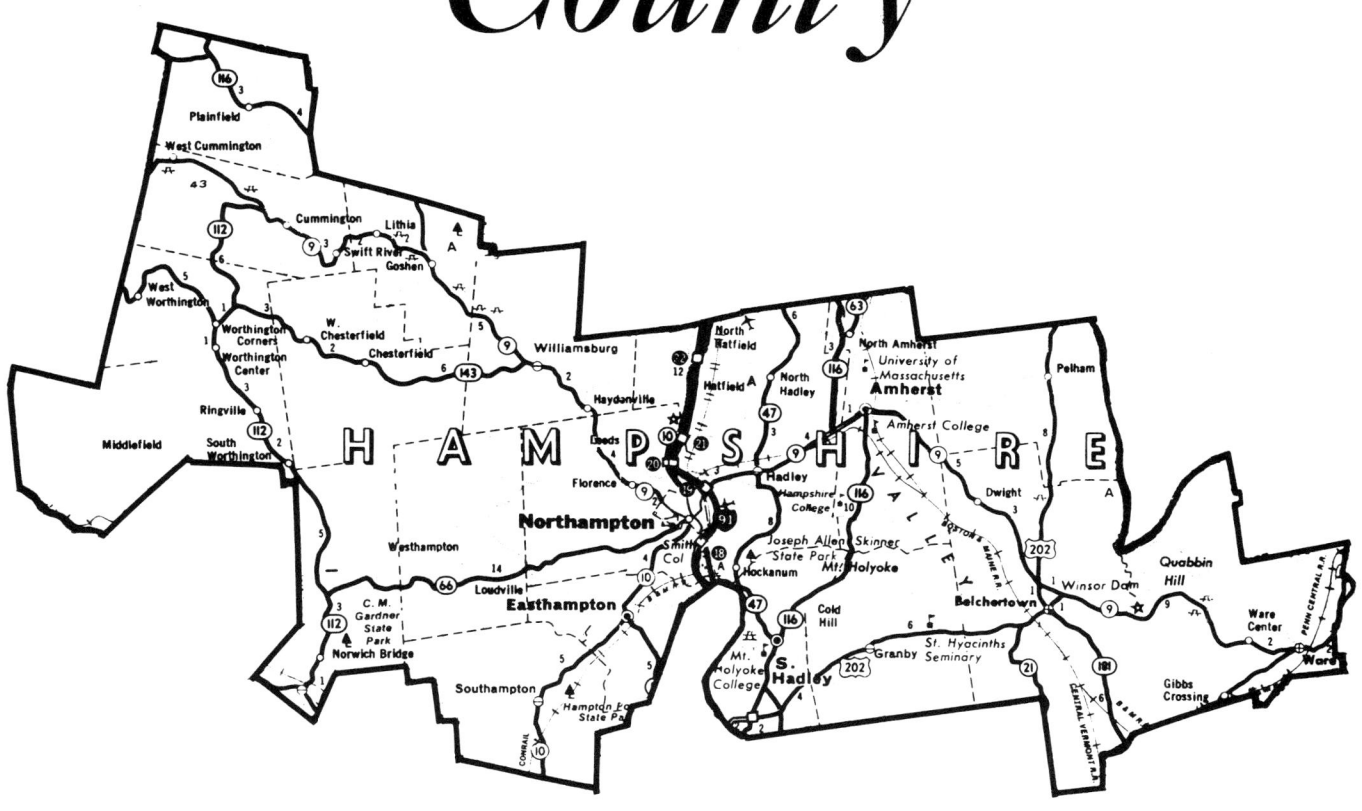

Hampshire County

AMHERST, Massachusetts
Population: 26,331   Zip Code: 01002

Founded in 1759, named for Lord Jeffrey Amherst, the "Town of Amherst gracefully combines the tradition and heritage of its colonial past with...its distinction as one of New England's major centers of education." It is located in the middle of the Pioneer Valley and has some of the most interesting shops and specialty stores in the area.

Amherst, Massachusetts
Center of Distinction

Trips and trivia:

• The **Amherst Chamber of Commerce** is located at 11 Spring Street, in the basement of the Lord Jeffrey Inn, and is open Monday through Friday, 9:00 a.m. to 3:00 p.m. Telephone: 413/253-9666. The Chamber maintains an information booth from May until mid-October, daily from 10:00 a.m. to 4:00 p.m. on the Town Commons.

• **Amherst College** is an independent liberal arts college for a student body of approximately 1,500 men and women working toward B. A. or Ph.D. Degrees in a five-college cooperative arrangement. Founded in 1921 by, among others, Noah Webster (the lexicographer) and Samual Fowler Dickinson (poet Emily's grandfather), the school sits on nearly 1,000 acres adjacent to the center of Amherst. It was the first college in the country to adopt the concept of student government. Among its many facilities are: Alumni Gymnasium and Alumni House; Robert Frost Library, containing 650,000 volumes, and 2,100 periodicals; Mead Art Building open Monday through Friday, 10:00 a.m. to 4:30 p.m., Saturday and Sunday, 1:00 p.m. to 5:00 p.m. (telephone: 413/542-2335); Merrill Science Center, containing departments of astronomy, chemistry, and physics; and Pratt Museum of Natural History, featuring archaeology and ethnography of the American Indian, open Monday through Saturday, 9:00 a.m. to 4:00 p.m.; Sunday 1:00 p.m. to 4:00 p.m. during the academic year. Telephone: 542-2233. Be sure to check out the Hitchcock Collection of Fossil Footprints and the Anthropological Center; the kids'll love it! Also at Amherst are the Bassett Planetarium, Buckley Recital Hall, Computer Center, Kirby Theatre, Music Building, Observatory, War Memorial, and Wildlife Sanctuary. Main telephone: 413/542-2000.

• Located at the Nehemiah Strong House Museum (1744) at 67 Amity Street, PO Box 739, is the **Amherst Historical Society.** Founded in 1899, its purpose then and now is "to promote educational, historical, antiquarian, literary, and artistic activities related to the Town of Amherst, Massachusetts. For information on its hours, check under museums in the yellow pages.

• Year-round on Saturday mornings at 10:00 a.m. **antique auctions** are held at the Amherst Auction Galleries at the junction of Routes 116 and 63 in North Amherst. Previews are held Friday 6:00 p.m. to 9:00 p.m.; Saturday, 8:00 a.m. to 10:00 a.m. In addition, booksales are held bi-monthly on Sundays at 10:00 a.m.

• **Conservation areas** in the town include: Mill River, Mount Castor Marsh, Fort River, Lawrence Swamp, Holyoke Range, and Podick. The active Amherst Conservation Commission, under the auspices of the Kestral Trust, has published a booklet called, "Around and About Amherst: An Outdoor Guide To The Region Around Amherst, Massachusetts" available from PO Box 426.

• The **Dickinson Homestead** at 280 Main Street marks the birthplace and residence of poet Emily Dickinson, Amherst's most famous native. Registered with the U. S. Department of the Interior as a National Historic Landmark, the house is owned by Amherst College and is a college residence. Part of the homestead is open to the public by appointment, including the living room and the

poet's bedroom, where she wrote much of her poetry. Appointments can be made through the Public Affairs Office at Amherst College. Telephone: 413/542-2321. Tours Tuesday and Friday, year-round at 3:00 p.m., 3:45 p.m., and 4:30 p.m. There is an admission fee of $3.00 per adult; children under 12 free. Tours are guided by volunteers, and the income derived from admission fees is used solely for purposes of maintaining the homestead. The Mansion was built in 1813 by Samuel Fowler Dickinson, Emily's grandfather, who was a founder of Amherst College. Of the house, Emily once wrote, "Sweet hours have perished here./This is a timid room—/Within its precincts hopes have played/Now fallow in the tomb."

• Amherst is popular as a fishing, hunting, and outdoor sports town. **Groff Park** off Mill Lane just east of the Grist Mill on Fort River, is a town recreation area offering picnic and some game facilities. The **Holyoke Range Forest** on Route 116 allows hiking, horseback, riding, hunting, and cross-country skiing. Telephone: 413/253-2883.

• **Hampshire College,** founded in 1965, is a private liberal arts college that sees itself as an experimenting educational institution testing new ideas in the curriculum. Students are encouraged to undertake independent work as part of their study, and students progress through a series of divisions loosely modeled on graduate committees, receiving narrative evaluations in lieu of grades. Approximately 1,000 undergraduates study humanities and arts, communications and cognitive science, natural science, and social sciences. The college is located on a 550-acre campus and is accredited by the State of Massachusetts and the New England Association of Schools and Colleges. Telephone: 413/549-4600.

• The **Hitchcock Center for the Environment,** 525 South Pleasant Street, is open for environmental education and natural history programs for school children and adults; during the winter months, it is open to the public for snowshoeing and cross-country skiing. A seasonal schedule of its events is available through the Center or the Chamber. Hitchcock is located on Route 116, one mile south of Amherst Center.

• The town's public library at 43 Amity Street, **The Jones Library** has been described as one of the most attractive small public libraries in the country. Endowed by Chicago lumber merchant Samuel Minot Jones, the beautiful building opened in 1928. Aside from a circulating collection of some 90,000 contemporary volumes, the library maintains special collections, which include materials on Sidney Waugh, Ray Stannard Baker, Harlan Fiske Stone, Helen Hunt Jackson, Clifton Johnson, and Amherst authors. The special collections also have memorial rooms that house extensive Emily Dickinson and Robert Frost materials and the Boltwood Collection of local history and genealogy. The library sponsors monthly art exhibits in its Gallery; exhibits from its own historical collections; and frequent film showings, poetry readings, and concerts. All persons are eligible for library cards; just bring identification and proof of your current mailing address. The Jones Library Office and special collections are open weekdays, 9:00 a.m. to 5:00 p.m. The circulating collection is open Monday and Friday 9:00 a.m. to 5:30 p.m.; Tuesday, Wednesday, Thursday until 9:30 p.m.; Saturday 10:00 a.m. to 5:30 p.m. Appointments for group tours can be requested. Telephone: 413/256-0246. There are branch libraries at 8 Montague Road in North Amherst and at the Munson Memorial Building in South Amherst.

• A prospector's trench, the **Leverett Lead Mine** in North Amherst contains two open trenches of barite, galena, chalcopyrite, and sphalerite. It is located off Route 63.

• **Lord Jeffrey Amherst** (1717-1797), for whom the town was named, was a British general famous for his role in the French and Indian War. His military feats included commanding the British army against the French fortress of Louisburg in 1758, being commander-in-chief in North America for the captures of Ticonderoga and Crown Point, an attack on Montreal in 1760, and the appointment as governor general of British North America.

• The proud possessor of many beautiful trees, Amherst has an **Ornamental Tree Association** founded in 1857, which features many rare imported specimens. Through the years, Amherst has cooperated with the agricultural college at Sapporo, Japan, on the island of Hokkaido, and many different seeds have been planted successfully in the town. One example is the Katsura tree, *Cercidiphyllum Japonicum,* located at 50 Fairview Way.

• Amherst has had many famous **residents,** including:

1. Ray Stannard Baker (1870-1946), American journalist and author who lived at 118 Sunset Avenue in a house dating to 1916. Writing under the pen name of David Grayson, he was the authorized biographer of Woodrow Wilson.

2. Ithamar Conkey of 664 Main Street (1840) was Judge of Probate from 1834-58 for Hampshire County.

3. Eugene Field (1850-1895), American poet and journalist, editor of a column called "Sharps and Flats" in the *Chicago Record* (then called *Morning News*). He was best known as a poet of childhood, including such pieces as *Wynken, Blynken, and Nod* and *Little Boy Blue*. His 1839 house is at 219 Amity Street.

4. The father of sculptor Daniel Chester French (see Chesterwood) was the president of the University of Massachusetts from 1864-6.

5. Robert Lee Frost (1874-1963), American poet, was a professor of English at Amherst College intermittently from 1916-38, living in the 1875 house at 43 Sunset Avenue. Frost was awarded Pulitzer Prizes in the years 1923, 1930, 1936, and 1942. He is considered by many to be America's poet laureate.

6. Geologist Edward Hitchcock served as president of Amherst College while in residence at the 1828 home at 271 South Pleasant Street. His son Edward (1828-1911) was professor of hygiene and physical education at the college, the first such position at an American college.

7. Helen Hunt Jackson, the author, lived at 249 South Pleasant Street in a home dated c. 1830.

8. Samuel Minot Jones, benefactor of the town library.

9. General Mattoon of Revolutionary War fame, the town's first member of Congress. Mary Mattoon, wife of Ebeneezer, has local streets and the Amherst Chapter of the Daughters of the American Revolution named in her honor.

10. Mary Heaton Vorse (1881-1966), American writer.

11. Sidney Biehler Waugh (1904-1963), noted for his monumental and architectural sculpture. He worked on many facades and groups of public buildings in Washington, D. C.; designed for Steuben glass; created President Truman's gift to the newly-married Princess Elizabeth and the Duke of Edinburgh in 1947; did medalist work for the U. S. and private mints; and authored several important studies of glass, design, and sculpture.

12. Noah Webster (1758-1843), lexicographer and author who moved to Amherst in 1812, was a Hampshire County Representative, a trustee and then president of Amherst Academy, and a founder of Amherst College. Webster was the publisher of the two-volume *An American Dictionary of the English Language* in 1828.

13. Professor George Whicher, distinguished teacher at Amherst College and biographer of Emily Dickinson.

• The Amherst Historical Society owns and maintains the Nehemiah **Strong House Museum** at 67 Amity Street, and the Amherst Garden Club maintains a period garden there. The 1744 home, containing collections of china, costumes, glass, and furniture, is open 2:00 p.m. to 5:00 p.m. during the summer; a contribution is expected.

Another interesting structure around Amherst is Stockbridge House, on the university campus, the oldest house in town. Built in 1728 by Samuel Boltwood, it is located behind the Merrill Science Center next to The Homestead (1762). Montague House (Mark's Meadow) of 1844 vintage is farther up North Pleasant Street, in the School of Education complex. Dickinson-Boggs Tavern at 6 South East Street, built c. 1770, has a huge ballroom on the second floor, and Kellogg House at 76 North East Street (1758) was the first post office in town.

There are a number of fascinating early colonial homes throughout the town, including the Solomon Boltwood House (1745) at 243 Amity Street, Azarish Dickinson House (also 1745) at 207 Leverett Road, and the Georgian-style Simeon Clark House on South Pleasant Street and the Martin Kellogg House on Mill Lake.

North Amherst Congregational Church and the South Congregational Church are evidence of the Federal period of building in the town, while other interesting church buildings include: the Unitarian Church (1892-4) with stained-glass windows by Louis C. Tiffany and John LaFarge; Saint Bridgid's Church of 1923-4 vintage at 132 North Pleasant Street, designed after a church in Verona, Italy; 79 South Pleasant Street's First Baptist Church (c. 1837), now the Town and Country Building; Grace

Episcopal Church at 18 Boltwood Avenue, dating to 1965-6; and the First Congregational Church (1867) at 165 Main Street.

Many of the buildings at Amherst College—including the Octagon across from the president's house, Converse Hall (1917), and the First Congregational Meeting House (1828-9)/College Hall—show influences of varying architectural styles.

Other places around town that should be mentioned are the Grist Mill on West Street; Old Row at Amherst College; Austin Dickinson (1856) home at 214 Main Street and Noah Dickinson's 1754 house at 743 Main Street; the Leonard M. Hills House (1860) at 35 Triangle Street, now owned by the Amherst Women's Club; a dwelling at 576 Main Street; West Cemetery (1730) on Triangle Street; the Dickinson Grave Site; Phoenix Row/Cook's Block (1838-9) at 1-12 Main Street; Todd House at 90 Spring Street, the first house in town in the Queen Anne Style (1886-7); the Henry Hills House (1862-3) at Main Street, renovated for use by the Amherst Boys' Club; the Amherst Town Hall at Main and Boltwood Streets; the Amherst Central Post Office; the Jones and Morgan Libraries; Fisher House (1830) at 227 South Pleasant Street, where the Nelson sisters taught school for many years; nearby Merchants' Row (1881); the Joseph Smith Place (1789) at 522 South Pleasant Street; and then, just for contrast, the Murray Lincoln Center at the University of Massachusetts. Walks through Cushman Village and around Fiddlers Green in South Amherst are very interesting also.

• **The University of Massachusetts** at Amherst is the principal campus of the commonwealth's system of public higher education and the largest university, public or private, in New England. Founded in 1863 as a land grant college under the Morrill Act, it has grown from a small agricultural college into a major research university with more than 100 disciplines offered in ten schools, colleges, and faculties: Arts and Sciences, Humanities and Fine Arts, Natural Sciences and Mathematics, Social and Behavioral Sciences, Education, Engineering, Food and Natural Resources, Health Sciences, Management, and Physical Education. Special academic programs include: The Five College Interchange Program (with Smith, Mount Holyoke, Amherst, and Hampshire Colleges, telephone: 413/545-2191); Foreign Area Studies (545-3427); Honors Program (545-2483); W. E. B. DuBois Department of Afro-American Studies (545-2751); Department of Legal Studies (545-2000); Medical Technology Program (545-0019); Social Thought and Political Economy (545-2191); Women's Studies (545-1922); Stockbridge School of Agriculture (545-2222); and Center on Aging (545-1306). The Division of Continuing Education (545-2414) offers credit courses and noncredit programs to full- and part-time students and to members of the community. The University also offers a Bachelor's Degree with Individual Concentration (telephone: 545/0736) and a University Without Walls Program (telephone: 545-1378).

Services offered to the commonwealth and community include: the Math/Science/Technology Education Project, a model teacher recruitment and education program; the Massachusetts Institute for Social and Economic Research, providing data collection and analysis for the public and private sectors; the Social and Demographic Institute, providing research on social science and policy issues; the Small Business Development Center, offering services to small businesses throughout the state; and the Labor Relations and Research Center.

The 1,200-acre campus has 150 buildings, including 41 dormitories housing 12,000 students; five libraries containing more than two million volumes (The Tower billed as the tallest library in the world); the Fine Arts Center, which attracts national and international dance, theatre, and musical productions; and the Lederle Graduate Research Center, which houses classrooms, laboratories, and computers and received half of the University's annual $40 million in sponsored research.

With an enrollment of approximately 20,000 undergraduate and 7,000 graduate students, the University will award 3,800 bachelor's degrees, 900 master's degrees, and 300 doctorate degrees in 1987. Seventy-four percent of the students are Massachusetts residents; 21% are from other states, and 5% are foreign students. The campus community includes 1,500 faculty, 900 professional staff, and 2,500 classified staff.

The University of Massachusetts at Amherst is accredited by the New England Association of Colleges and Secondary Schools. The main phone number is 413/545-0111.

BELCHERTOWN, Massachusetts

Population: 5,936   Zip Code: 01007

Named for Colonial Governor Jonathan Belcher (1682-1757), a principal landowner and co-founder of Princeton College, Belchertown is the second largest town in land area in the commonwealth.

Trips and trivia:
- The annual **Belchertown Fair,** held in early October at the Old Town Hall, features handwork exhibits, horse draws, and an old-fashioned church supper.

- The town is well known for **Belchertown State School,** one of seven mental retardation facilities of the Department of Mental Health. Located on Route 202, Belchertown State School employs a workforce of 1,550 persons providing quality care to its 367 residents on the 843-acre campus.

- **Clapp Memorial Library** on South Main Street is a local landmark. John Francis Clapp was born and raised in Belchertown but moved to Brooklyn, New York, at the age of 16, where he was a prominent business man for nearly 60 years. In his will, which was probated in 1882, he entrusted his brothers Everett, Edward, and Dwight Clapp with the sum of $40,000 to construct and furnish a free public library. Construction was started in the summer of 1883, and the Richardsonian Romanesque building was completed and dedicated on June 20, 1887. It was built with Longmeadow brownstone in the form of a Latin cross, and has two interesting stained-glass memorial windows. The architect was H. F. Kilburn of New York, who designed all of the Clapp houses on Main Street. Telephone: 413/323-6224.
- Native son **Josiah Gilbert Holland** (1819-1881) is remembered by Belchertown's Holland Glen on Route 109. Holland was an editor and writer, best known for his work on the *Springfield Republican* newspaper, *Scribner's Monthly,* Titcomb's letters (a pseudonym), and his *History of Western Massachusetts,* written in 1855.
- The largest municipality in area in the region (60 acres) quite naturally has many **interesting houses** that reflect its history. Drive around and check out Lincoln House on North Main Street (Route 202), reputed to be the site of the first town meeting. Other noteworthy Main Street dwellings include: Crystal Spring Farm (1799); Parsons House of 1771, whose roof was used as a signal tower during the Revolutionary War; two Federals of the 1825-30 era; Ephraim Montague House (1840) on South Main Street; and the two Clapp houses, one known as the Witt House, where local historian Mark Doolittle lived. The home of Elijam C. Bridgman, early missionary to China, is a late 18th century home on Bay Road not far from Stebbins Street. The Bay Road, the original road from Northampton and Hadley to Boston, makes for a nice sightseeing architectural tour. Also note the late 18th century Georgian Colonial at the junction of Warren Wright and Orchard Street, said to be architecturally the finest in Belchertown.
- Two natural ponds owned by the state and well-stocked for fishing are **Lake Metacomet** and **Lake Arcadia,** both in the northern part of town. In addition, there are facilities for picnicking, swimming, and boating.
- Representing the latest in modern equipment and engineering know-how, the **Charles L. McLaughlin Fish Hatchery** on Route 9 is one of the largest trout-rearing facilities in the East. Owned and operated by the commonwealth, it produces over one million fish a year, which are used to stock public waters throughout the state. Visitors can see the hatchery building's 22 concrete nursery tanks with fiberglass hatching troughs, plus two display tanks in front of the modern headquarters building. The hatchery is part of the 1,000-acre Swift River Wildlife Management Area, under the Division of Fisheries and Wildlife, supported by sportsmen through their purchase of licenses. It is the largest trout hatchery east of the Mississippi. To reach the hatchery, take Route 9 from the center of town one mile past Quabbin Reservoir. It is open daily 9:00 a.m. to 4:00 p.m., including holidays. Admission is free, and tours can be arranged by appointment. Telephone: 413/323-7671.
- There are three remaining **milestones** in the town: on Federal Street's Route 9 toward Amherst is one marking the mileage to Boston and Northampton, said to have been erected per order of Benjamin Franklin during his term as postmaster; in the center of town, at the junction of Routes 202, 21, and 181; and in front of South Cemetery near Cold Spring Road. The spring, for which the town was first named, is marked by a historic marker and is now on the property of the University Horticultural

Research Center, located at the Thomas Sabin Farm that dates to 1871.

• Sprawling over 128 square miles, **Quabbin Reservoir** (meaning many waters) is a man-made lake that stores 412 billion gallons of water. Run by the Metropolitan Water District Commission to service nearly two million inhabitants, Quabbin is the largest man-made body of water in the world designed exclusively for drinking. When it was constructed in the 1930s, the towns of Dana, Enfield, Greenwich, and Prescott were buried and lost. Quabbin is an animal and bird refuge center, an environment enjoyed by fishermen, hikers, and picnickers. There are picnic tables; parking; public rest rooms; Quabbin Park Cemetery; hiking trails; an observation tower on Quabbin Mountain, which provides an extensive panorama in all directions; Windsor Dam, and Goodnough Dike. Boat rentals are available from April through October, with fishing permitted under certain restrictions. Fishing licenses for the season or the week are available at Lawrence Memorial Hall on the southern end of Belchertown's common. Quabbin is open daily to the public at no cost. From the center of town, drive a few miles east on Route 9.

the Stone House Museum

• The **Stone House Museum** on Maple Street is furnished in part as a house and in part as a museum, with displays of furniture, Bennington ware, china, pewter, needlework and other handwork, war relics, portraits, and many household and farm implements. One of few early stone homes in the region, the Stone House was built in 1827 and deeded to the Belchertown Historical Association in 1922. It is especially known for its large collection of Rogers Group Sculpture; in addition, the museum maintains a library with many early Belchertown Church records. Next to this fieldstone building is the **Ford Annex Carriage House,** named for donor Henry Ford, displaying many of the period carriages that made Belchertown famous in the mid-1800s. The museum complex is open from May 15 through October 15, Wednesday and Saturday, 2:00 p.m. to 5:00 p.m. There is a small admission charge. Telephone: 413/323-7502 or 323-7891.

• Belchertown's five-acre **Town Common,** where local residents were mustered and drilled for various wars, contains memorials to its veterans amidst the 1865 Romanesque Revival Old Town Hall, now used as a community center; War House (1802); and three interesting churches: The Congregational Church (1789), Green Revival-style St. Francis Church of 1836, and the 1823 Methodist Chuch that was built in Springfield, taken down, and moved to Belchertown in 1872.

CHESTERFIELD, Massachusetts
Population: 704   Zip Code: 01012

Believed to be named for the 4th Earl of Chesterfield, Philip Dormer Stanhope (1694-1773), English statesman and man of letters, Chesterfield has been known for the manufacturing of wood products since the 19th century. It likes to think of itself as "The Friendly Town," drawing in many summer residents.

Trips and trivia:
• **Chesterfield Gorge,** located off Route 143 just west of the West Chesterfield Bridge, is a grooved chasm 30 feet deep, created by the passage of the Westfield River through a narrow chasm. Owned and maintained by the Trustees of Reservations, this 60-acre area has facilities for picnicking, hiking, and swimming. There is a slight parking fee. Follow signs off of Route 143 to River Road indicating the gorge. **East Branch State Forest** on River Road offers canoeing, fishing, hiking, and hunting. Telephone: 413/532-3985.

• At one point Chesterfield was best known for its average family size of ten **children** per family!

• The Chesterfield Historical Society maintains the **Edwards Memorial Museum,** located in the center of town near the library. Telephone: 413/296-4735. The Museum displays local historical items, and is free to the public Wednesday, 2:00 p.m. to 5:00 p.m. from July 4th to Labor Day.

• The annual Chesterfield barbecue, parade, and sports events take place each year over **4th of July** weekend.

• There are a number of interesting buildings in the **town center,** including the First Congregational Church of 1835 and the Town Hall that was built in 1848 as a Greek Revival Methodist Church. Also, don't miss the Starkweather House on Main Road, an 1822 Federal, or the Luce House cape (c. 1765) on Sugar Hill Road and the Benjamin Pierce Tavern on Roberts Meadow Road, a 1797 Georgian Colonial.

CUMMINGTON, Massachusetts
Population: 562   Zip Code: 01026

Named for Colonel Cummings, purchaser of the land, Cummington has been called the archetype of New England villages.

Trips and trivia:
• The town is rich in its **architecture.** In addition to the Bryant Homestead and Kingman Tavern, it has the Gothic Revival 1839 Congregational Church in West Cummington, the 1845 Greek Revival Church, Thanatopsis House (c. 1801) on Luther Shaw Road, Shingle-style Tod Morden House of 1900 off Stage Road, and an 1839 Congregational Church in Cummington Village. Warner Farm has recently been accepted as a national landmark.

• An annual **Berkshire Balloonfest,** where amateur pilots from throughout the East compete for top awards, has become quite an event at Cummington Farm on South Road on the third weekend in August. Over 10,000 spectators arrive by 7:00 a.m. Saturday to watch the competition. The farm, over 700 acres of fields and trails, is a popular ski-touring center.

- The **William Cullen Bryant Homestead** on Route 112, where the famous American poet and newspaper editor was born, is both a national and a state historic landmark. The three-story home is furnished mostly with Bryant's own belongings and memorabilia of his world travels; nothing has been added to the collection. It was here in 1812 that the 14-year old poet wrote his most famous poem, *Thanatopsis* (meaning a view of death). The house is really two houses in one: Bryant's grandfather originally built a one and a half-story saltbox that was expanded and elevated in 1865-6, with a new lower floor added at that time. The house is owned by the Trustees of Reservations (TOR), open from the last weekend in June through Labor Day; Friday, Saturday, Sunday, and holidays 1:00 p.m. to 5:00 p.m., Labor Day through Columbus Day Saturday, Sunday, and holidays 1:00 p.m. to 5:00 p.m. Admission is $3.00 per adult, $1.50 children 6-16; groups can arrange special appointments. Telephone: 413/634-2244. The Bryant Homestead can be reached off Route 9 onto 112 South to the reservation sign.
- Summer *concerts* are given Saturday evenings by the Greenwood Music Camp and on Sundays by the Cummington School for the Arts. The **Cummington Fairgounds** off Route 9 have held an annual summer celebration of agricultural exhibits and entertainment for nearly 100 years.
- **Deerfield Reservation,** state-owned property of 260 acres on Route 9, is available for wildlife preservation and limited recreational use such as picnicking and horseback riding.
- **Kingman Tavern Historical Museum** off of Route 9 in Cummington Village on Main Street is a town-owned and operated museum open to the public free of charge. Dating back to 1800, the structure was the town's first post office, and at varous times in Cummington's history served as a store, tavern, and meeting hall. Today it serves as a museum of the town's history, containing a number of exhibits, a barn, carriage shed, and cider mill. It is a memorial to native son Worcester Reed Warner (1846-1929), American telescope-maker and founder of Warner and Swasey Company of Cleveland, Ohio, manufacturers of machines and tools for the study of astronomy. Kingman Tavern is open Saturday afternoons from 2:00 p.m. to 5:00 p.m. during July and August, otherwise by appointment. It is completely staffed by volunteers. Many local historical items have been catalogued by the Cummington Historical Society.
- The poet laureate of the United States was just recently announced: poet/professor **Richard Wilbur,** Cummington resident. A former Smith College professor, Wilbur has won the Pulitzer Prize for his poetry, the applause of theatregoers for his lyrics to the musical *Candide,* and the praise of scholars for his translations of Moliere.
- **Windsor State Forest,** on a branch of the Westfield River, comes into West Cummington at Routes 91 and 116, offering facilities for swimming, picnicking, fishing, hiking, and winter sports.

EASTHAMPTON, Massachusetts
Population: 15,080   Zip Code: 01027

Its strategic location at the Oxbow of the Connecticut River accounts for the fact that Easthampton has been an active industrial town since the 1780s.

Trips and trivia:
- **Arcadia Nature Center and Wildlife Sanctuary,** owned and operated by the Massachusetts Audubon

Society, is located in both Easthampton and Northampton on the banks of the famous Oxbow. It contains over 500 acres of natural and managed habitat for songbirds, waterfowl, and mammals. Five miles of interpreted trails are maintained for walking, snowshoeing, and tour skiing. It sponsors guided field trips, day camps, nature and environmental classes, camp-outs, a nursery school, and an annual nature conference, "Focus: Outdoors." Special programs for school classes can be arranged. Arcadia features the Cornelia Mendenhall Native Garden and an observation tower overlooking a large marsh. Trails are open year-round, six days a week, closed Mondays. There is a charge for use of the trails: $2.00 for adults; $1.00 for children 6-16 and seniors. Free to members of Massachusetts Audubon. Take exit 18 off I-91, right onto Route 5, south one mile, right onto East Street another mile, then right on Fort Hill Road. Telephone: 413/584-3009.

• The town's many **cemeteries** tell much of its history. Check them out: East Street, St. Brigid's, Main Street, Brookside, and St. Stanislaus. Old East Burying Ground has a particularly interesting memorial fence and gates.

• **Fishing** is a popular pastime in Easthampton, with abundant trout, shad, and other fresh-water fish. The Connecticut River is also a good source for sailing and water skiing. There is a state-owned boat ramp on the Oxbow at Route 5. There is swimming at the Easthampton Park and Recreation Commission's Nonotuck Park, plus facilities for picnics and tents. Other spots include Brakey's Pond off Glendale Road, Clear Falls Pond, and Nashawannuck Pond Town Beach.

• The town's many **landmarks** include: Pioneer Cemetery marker on Clapp Street; Old Canal Bed off Northampton Street near O'Neil; and the downtown area's Town Hall (1868), Memorial Hall (1863), library, and various churches. Many of the old brick factory buildings along the Nashawannuck River are still in evidence, and there are many lovely antique homes throughout the area. There is an access to Mount Tom State Reservation, the range named for Springfield pioneeer Rowland Thomas, in the Holyoke-Easthampton Road on route 141.

• **Pascommuck Boulder,** also called First Settlers Monument, marks the town's first settlement in 1664. Located off East Street on Fort Hill Road, it commemorates the site of a 1704 Indian massacre in what is now the village of Mount Tom.

• The first successful use of **vulcanized rubber** in woven goods was established in Easthampton, as was the first elastic web mill in the country, both in the mid-1800s.

• **The Williston Northampton School** on Payson Avenue is a coeducational college preparatory school of 500+ boarding and day students in grades 7 to 12. The school was established in 1971 through the merger of two schools that had shared common activities for many years. Williston Academy was founded in 1841 by Samuel Williston, the son of a minister, who in 1806 had to walk 100 miles to Andover to find a secondary education. When he and his wife Emily had amassed a small fortune through their button manufacturing business, they determined to make a school available for area students. The Northampton School for Girls was founded in 1924 by Miss Sarah B. Whitaker and Miss Dorothy M. Bement to

fill the need for preparatory education for girls in the Smith College and Mount Holyoke College area. Williston Northampton has a strong academic program with great emphasis on the processes and techniques of learning, plus an active extra-curricular and athletic program on its 155-acre campus. Telephone: 413/527-1520.

GOSHEN, Massachusetts
Population: 483   Zip Code: 01032

According to local legend, this Biblical town gets its name because "as Goshen of old was the best part of Egypt, the title seemed appropriate for what was claimed to be the best part of Chesterfield."

Trips and trivia:

• **Annual events** in the town include a Gala Fun Weekend held the third weekend in July, featuring a flea market, block dance, chicken barbeque, and special events for the children—sponsored by the Goshen Recreation Association. In August, on the second Saturday of the month, the Ladies' Benevolent Association of the Goshen Congregational Church sponsors an annual flower show, fair, and church supper at its Main Street location.

• **DAR State Forest,** the first one in the U.S., is located on Route 9. The 1,020-acre tract offers facilities for swimming, boating, camping, hiking, fishing, and picnicking. Telephone: 413/268-7098. Camping is popular around Goshen's **Highland and Upper Lakes.** Hikers enjoy collecting wild blueberries around the area. The watershed of the Westfield and Mill Rivers is a favorite of trout fishermen.

• Local **landmarks** include Devil's Den at Roger's Brook, the morass at Lily Pond, the John Williams Tavern (1779) off Cape Street, the Goshen Cemetery with tombstones dating to 1774, the 1783 Goshen Congregational Church on Route 9 at the town center, and the Town Hall (c. 1910).

• The tiny village of **Lithia** in Goshen is named for the

huge beds of lithium-based silicates that used to be mined there. Rock hunters are particularly interested in the deposits of spodumene and tourmaline found in the area.

• **Moore's Hill,** the highest point in town, has a state fire observation tower.

GRANBY, Massachusetts
Population: 5,473   Zip Code: 01033

Granby, which occupies land where dinosaurs once roamed and the Nipmuck Indians once occupied, is today a peaceful residential village. It was named for John Manners (1721-1770), Marquis of Granby (England), commander-in-chief of the British in Germany during the Seven Years War and a popular leader in the Colonies.

Trips and trivia:
• **Aldrich Lake** houses the oldest waterwheel and grist mill in the state, the old mill (c. 1837) being probably the finest surviving example of its kind in the region. It has a large over-shot waterwheel that was used for the town's many old industries, providing auxiliary power used to pull trolley cars over the South Hadley "Notch" to Amherst. The Pioneer Valley Boy Scout Camp is situated on Aldrich Lake.

• There are gravestones in the **cemeteries** on Bachelor and Kellogg Streets that date back to the 1760s.

• At an altitude of 380 feet, **Cold Hill** on Upper High Street offers a great view of the Connecticut Valley. Fishing and boating are available at **Forge Pond,** with an entrance off East State Street or Route 202.

• **Dinosaurs** have been associated with Granby since 1968, when Rouville Gingras discovered some footprints in his yard. The 200 million year discovery was verified by well-known paleontologists, and they were believed to be the largest footprints discovered in the U. S.; one recently uncovered print is that of a theropod carnivorous dinosaur, 50 feet from head to tail. The quarry is now state-owned.

• At the base of Mount Norowottuck are the **Horse-Sheds,** weathered sandstone shelters said to be a hiding place for Daniel Shays and his fellow rebels.

• **St. Hyacinth College and Seminary** at 66 School Street is a Roman Catholic liberal arts college for men supported by the Conventual Franciscan Friars, which educates approximately 60 undergraduates. The student body is comprised of lay students, religious brothers, and candidates for the priesthood. Established in 1927, the school grants a bachelor's degree in philosophy and offers a pre-theological program. It is accredited by the New England Association of Schools and Colleges. Telephone: 413/467-7191.

• Granby's **village green** features classic New England architecture in its 1821 Federal-style Church of Christ at 1841 Chapel, Town House (1822), and early 19th century Pitchawam House, the town's last tavern. Nearby is the Alpheus Ferry Tavern (1816) at 16 Parish Hill Road, and farther out is the Josiah Montague House (c. 1760) at 202 West Street and the Ferry Homestead saltbox (c. 1700) at 64 Ferry Hill Road.

HADLEY, Massachusetts
Population: 3,750   Zip Code: 01035

Named for Hadleigh, England, former home of some of its founders, religious dissidents from Connecticut, the town of Hadley was settled in 1659. Its Indian name, Norowottuck, means "the town in the midst of the river."

Trips and trivia:
• The **"Angle of Hadley,"** also known in F. A. Chapman's oil painting as *The Perils of Our Forefathers,* tells the legend of the Regicide, General Goffe, who was hidden in Parson Russell's home for many years. During that time, he saved local residents from an Indian attack in 1675. His strange appearance and disappearance have been shrouded in mystery.

• Late in 1977, 17 public and private buildings comprising the **Center of Hadley** were listed on the National Register of Historic Places. Located at the intersection of Routes 9 and 47 (Russell and Middle Streets), they include: the Greek Revival Hadley Town Hall of 1841; the First Congregational Church with its Christopher Wren-type spire (1804), moved to this location in 1841; the Goodwin Memorial Library; Hadley Farm Museum; Hook and Russell Schools; St. John's Church; the Hadley Branch of the Amherst Savings bank; and nine private homes on South Middle Street. Also of note around town are the home of Clarence Hawkes, Hadley's blind author, on West Street; Ben Smith Tavern on Middle Street (1774), noted as an example of a Colonial inn with exterior changes; and the Samuel Porter House on West Street, now known as the McQueston House which, dating from 1713, is the oldest house in town. Its witches' crosses on the typical Connecticut Valley doorway make it one of the most photographed houses around.

• The town library is named in honor of one of Hadley's greatest benefactors, William Goodwin, the trustee responsible for bringing the Hopkins' legacy to the town. On the second floor of the **Goodwin Memorial Library** is the Historical Museum, headquarters for the Hadley Historical Society. There is a branch library at North Hadley.

• At the junction of Routes 9 and 47 is the **Hadley Farm Museum,** which houses antique implements used by local farmers: "A practical picture of the lives of those who had settled in Hadley and its environs more than 300 years ago." The collection is in a 1782 barn that was part of the historic Porter-Phelps-Hunting estate, moved to its current location in the center of town in 1930. The first broom-making machine can be found there along with many other fascinating tools such as butter churns,

cobblers' benches, plows, spinning wheels, a 15-seat stagecoach, oxcart, hay tedders, peddler's wagon, beehives, a complete smithy, and a model scale barn from 1934. Our favorite was the "three-tined dung fork"! Run by the Hadley Farm Museum Association, the museum operates free of charge, but donations are appreciated. It is open from May 1 through October 15, Tuesday through Saturday, 10:00 a.m. to 4:30 p.m.; Sunday 1:30 p.m. to 4:30 p.m. Children must be accompanied by adults.

• The town contains quite a number of **historic markers,** such as the one at Route 9 marking its entrance to the Hadley-Northampton line: "Indian land called Norowottuck. Settled in 1630 by families from Hartford. The Regicides, Generals Coffee and Whalley were concealed for 15 years in the Pastor's House." Also:

1. Site of the First Meeting House on West Street Common.
2. Site of the home of Rev. John Russell, sanctuary of the Regicides, also on West Street.
3. "Fighting" Joe Hooker, a major general in the Civil War, commemorated at his birthplace with a Daughters of the American Revolution stone on West Street.
4. Site of Hopkins Academy, incorporated in 1813, on Russell Street.
5. West Street's Site of the Ferry to Northampton.
6. Site of the Hopkins Grist Mill, which was burned by the Indians in 1675, on Route 47 in North Hadley.
7. Also in North Hadley, the site of an Indian fort where Indian skeletons were discovered early in this century.
8. Old Hadley Cemetery of Cemetery Road off West Street, used since the founding of the town.

• The name **Hadley** has been linked to the Hadley chest and the Hadley rose. Roses, gardenias, carnations, and chrysanthemums are specialties at local greenhouses. The Hadley rose, the Talisman rose, and the Hadley gardenia were all developed in the town.

• The **Hopkins Fund,** the oldest continuous charitable trust in the country, came into existence in 1657 at the death of Edward Hopkins of England, an early governor of Connecticut. Hopkins Academy, now Hadley's public high school, was established by this fund in 1664-5, and continues to benefit from it. Hopkins Academy is the oldest educational institution in Western Massachusetts and the seventh oldest in the U. S.

• Hadley started out as a farming town in 1659; raising beef cattle was an early **industry.** Broom corn later became the chief crop and the manufacture of brooms and broom tools the chief occupation. Hadley remains a largely rural community, known for raising potatoes, asparagus, cucumbers, squash, and other vegetables, as well as for producing tobacco and dairy products. Residential and commercial growth is replacing agriculture in a few sections.

FORTY ACRES

PORTER–PHELPS–HUNTINGTON HOUSE
HADLEY, MASSACHUSETTS
01035

• Forty Acres, the **Porter-Phelps-Huntington House,** is known as the most important house in Hadley and its greatest attraction. Located two miles north of the junction of Routes 9 and 47, toward Sunderland, this 1752 family homestead contains the furnishings and belongings of six generations of one family.

Frederick Dan Huntington, first bishop of the Episcopal Diocese of New York, used the house as a summer residence up until the time of his death in 1904; after that, it became jointly owned by his six children. Dr. and Mrs. James Lincoln Huntington gathered the support to turn the homestead into a foundation, and helped donate the house and its contents to the Porter-Phelps-Huntington Foundation, Inc., in 1955. The house was built by Moses Porter on a tract of Hadley land called "Forty Acres and its Skirts," the first house outside the stockade. It was eventually enlarged and beautified under the direction of Charles Phelps, but since 1799 the house has seen no structural change. The house is open to the public from May 15 through October 15, Saturday to Wednesday (closed Thursday and Friday) from 1:00 to 4:30 p.m. Telephone: 413/584-4699. Admission is $2.00 for adults; $.75 for children under 12. The Porter-Phelps-Huntington House is listed on the National Register of Historic Places.

• Local folklore includes the story of **Mary (Molly) Webster** who was blamed by the townspeople for all that went wrong, and accused of witchcraft. In 1683 she was judged not guilty of the crime at a trial in Boston, but following her acquittal she was again accused of bewitching and causing the death of a prominent Hadley citizen, Deacon Philip Smith. She was "hung till nearly died," then buried in the snow by local young men—but she survived the ordeal to live many years thereafter!

• Hadley's mile-long **West Street Common** and the 59 houses that surround it are located on the spot where the original town was laid out in 1659. The picturesque common has existed since that early time. In addition, there are many lovely structures to be found in North Hadley, such as the 1834 Second Congregational Church and the Village Hall building (1864-1871), which today is used as a fire station, library, and community center. The southern end, called the Hockanum area, is situated between the Connecticut River and the Holyoke Range. Of note are two former taverns, now privates homes: the Enos Lyman saltbox of 1743 on Barstow Lane off Hockanum Road and the White Horse Tavern on Route 47, built by Ebeneezer Pomeroy in 1747. Also on Route 47 is the last of the town's brick one-room schoolhouse, dating to 1840.

HATFIELD, Massachusetts
Population: 2,825   Zip Code: 01038

A town over 300 years old, Hatfield was named after an English town. It is famous as the residence of many well-known educators.

Trips and trivia:

• The **Baracca Gallery** at 197 Pantry Road in Northfield is open by appointment only. Telephone: 413/247-5262. It features sculpture and fountains for interior and exterior, from small and intimate to large scale site-specific.

• **First Congregational Church** (United Church of Christ) celebrated its 300th anniversary in 1970. It is the fourth oldest in the Valley, preceded only by the Old First Church of Springfield, the First Church of Northampton, and the First Church of Hadley, its mother church. The church "had its beginning in 1688 when the first settler on the west side of the river decided it was too hazardous to cross the river and started proceedings to get a church on the west side, which finally materialized in 1670 by the establishing of the Town of Hatfield."

• The town has a number of **Historic American Buildings:**
  1. Cornelia Billings House, built early 19th century.
  2. Lieutenant David Billings House at 77 Main Street, a Georgian Colonial built in 1783.
  3. Cotton (Morton) Partridge House at the corner of Bridge Lane and lower Main Street, built before 1727.

Other interesting structures include: the 1865 mansard-style home at 26 Main Street; the John Dickinson House at South Street and Bridge Lane, an early Colonial saltbox with an unusually designed and beautifully detailed Georgian doorway; another saltbox, the Roswell Billings House (1760), with a choice Connecticut Valley doorway; the 1849 Greek Revival Church; 1750 Third Meeting House; Smith Academy (1871) in Victorian brick, a mansard residence at 86 Main Street; St. Joseph's Church (1892); Italian Villa at 89 Main Street; Greek Revival home at 40 School Street; a rare brick Federal residence at 17 Maple Street; the Hatfield Barn, formerly the Jonathan Graves House, an impressive Victorian Gothic on Elm Street; and an early 19th century mill building at the Mill River on Bridge Street, now known as the "gun shop."

• Many **Hatfieldites** have distinguished themselves in history:
  1. Reverend Jonathan Dickinson (1688-1747), a leading defender of Presbyterianism, who obtained the charter and served as the first president of what became Princeton University.
  2. Colonel Oliver Patridge, one of the "River Gods" who came out of the French and Indian conflicts.
  3. Oliver Smith, a philanthropist whose bequests founded the Smith Vocational High School and the Smith Charities in Northampton.
  4. Elisha Williams (1694-1755), a Congregational clergyman and educator who was rector of Yale College.
  5. Ephraim Williams (1714-55), captain of the Massachusetts militia in 1745, who bequeathed a substantial portion of his estate to the founding of a free school that was to become Williams College in 1793.
  6. Israel Williams (1709-88), another "River God," half-brother of Elisha Williams, who was responsible for actually implementing Ephraim Williams' bequest toward the establishment of Williams College.

• A bassviol that was used to accompany singing in the church in the 18th century is in the **Memorial Hall Museum** on Main Street, which was the property of Samuel Patridge. Also to be found there is the charter granted by William and Mary.

• A curious order from the town selectmen in 1672 claimed that "all **racing** in the meadows and highways should be stopped because of the damage done to the fields and crops. In addition to the danger of being hurt, many children and servants spend too much time in watching the sport." Today's **recreational opportunities** include fishing at both Running Gutter Brook in the western part of the town and Great Pond in the center, plus gliding at Pilgrim Airport.

• A significant historic structure is the **Sophia Smith Homestead** at 75 Main Street, the birthplace and home of the founder of Smith College in 1875. Sophia (1796-1870) inherited a fortune from her brother Austin and, on the advice of pastor John Morton Greene, decided to establish the women's college. Her 1700 home was purchased in 1915 by the Smith College Alumnae Association and was refurbished and refurnished by the Class of 1896.

HUNTINGTON, Massachusetts
Population: 1,593   Zip Code: 01050

A popular resort and recreation area, Huntington was originally called Murrayfield, then Norwich, but changed its name in 1855 for the Honorable Charles P. Huntington of Northampton.

Trips and trivia:

• **Boulder Park,** named for an enormous rock by the roadside, can be found in the Chester-Blandford State Forest. **Charles M. Gardner State Park** on Worthington Road (Route 112) has facilities for picnicking, horseback riding, swimming, fishing, and hiking.

Telephone: 413/532-3985. **Huntington State Forest** off Route 66 on Samson Road is also open to the public, and **Norwich Lake** off Route 66 on Pisgah Road is the site of many summer homes and camps; it is a very popular swimming and boating area.

• The town's **earliest buildings** include a late 18th century gambrel on Country Road near a Georgian Colonial saltbox; a Federal house on Fish Avenue at Cook Hill Road; the 1841 First Congregational Church of Greek Revival architecture on Searle Road in the Norwich Hill section of town; two Greek Revival homes on Route 20; the Romanesque Revival-style Highland Grange Hall on the town green (c. 1862); and a former schoolhouse at Route 112 and Bromley Road.

• Historian Richard Garvey adds more information in his *Springfield Daily News* article about the background to **Huntington's name change:** "Norwich was named for the Connecticut town from which the settlers came, but when parts of Chester and Blandford were added to form a larger township, the newcomers wanted a new name. At that point, Attorney Charles Phelps Huntington submitted his bill for the complicated land swapping, and the townspeople had a brilliant idea. They would name the town for him, and he would mark the bill paid. Huntington was so pleased, he added $100.00 as his gift to start a library, and a grateful town still remembers him."

• **Knightville Dam** on Route 112, built for flood control, is the scene each year for the start of the annual Westfield River whitewater canoe races held in April. The first dual facility dam in New England was the **Littlefield Dam** off Route 112, built at a cost of seven million dollars to provide flood control for Westfield and a future supplemental water supply for Springfield.

• **Murrayfield Grammar School** on Worthington Road contains a historic bell stolen by Union soldiers from New Orleans during the Civil War.

• The first **power loom** for making flannel and Marseilles bedspreads was introduced in Huntington.

• Also, it was the first town in Hampshire County to have **railroad service,** and the Western Railroad (later called the Boston and Albany) turned it into a busy manufacturing center for some time.

MIDDLEFIELD, Massachusetts
Population: 4,044   Zip Code: 01243

Once part of the ancient ground of the Mohican Indians, Middlefield today is primarily a rural and summer resort area located in the extreme southeast corner.

Trips and trivia:
• The former **Blossom Tavern** (c. 1780), located at the corner of Arthur Pease and Main Roads, has two virtually identical front facades and a springboard floor on the second floor. Other interesting structures include the house on Town Hill Road that has a gambrel roof in front and a saltbox roofline at the rear; the church in the center of town, combined from two separate buildings; Greek Revival residences along Main Road; and the Italianate-style house at the corner of Main and Town Hill Roads.

• **Drumlins,** tear-shaped hills that are the rsult of glacial drift, can be found at the eastern corner of town.

• From the summit of **Garnet Hill,** five different states can be seen.

• **Glendale Falls,** located at the Trustees of Reservations Park off Clark Wright Road in the southeastern part of town, attracts summer tourists.

• The Highland Agricultural Society has held its annual fair and cattle show at the **Middlefield Fair Grounds** since 1857. The event usually takes place the second weekend in August.

NORTHAMPTON, Massachusetts
Population: 29,664   Zip Code: 01060

Historical markers along Route 109 at the Northampton-Williamsburg line and Route 5 at the Northampton-Easthampton line proclaim: "Indian land called Nonotuck, bought in 1653, the home of Jonathan Edwards, Joseph Hawley, and Timothy Dwight. Seat of Smith College." Called "Meadow City" and "The Paradise of America," Northampton was one of the first settlements in Western Massachusetts, and one of the first county seats.

Trips and trivia:
• Throughout the city traces of **anvil stones,** water-worn glacial stones resembling blacksmiths' tools, remind residents and visitors alike of Northampton's long history.

• **Child's Park** on Route 9's Elm Street near upper Prospect Street, has a 22-acre expanse of gardens and pathways. The rose section is especially noteworthy. There is no admission charge, and the park is open until dusk during the spring, summer, and fall. The Tea House can be rented for weddings and receptions.

• The **Clarke School for the Deaf** on Round Hill Road was established in 1867 as the first permanent, oral, residential school for the deaf in the U. S. It was the first school in the country to prepare the profoundly deaf for useful lives, to train teachers in the oral method, to carry on a continuing research program, to use compression-type hearing aids, and to offer a Master of Education of the Deaf degree (in cooperation with Smith College). Approximately 120 students ages 4 to 17 are enrolled in a full academic program for preparation for graduation at the ninth grade level. Clarke was one of the first schools to use television and computers as important tools in the education of the deaf. Captioning news programs, which has become a national trend, is an idea that originated at Clarke.

Alexander Graham Bell spent 51 years of his life associated with Clarke as a teacher, researcher, and member of the School's Board of Trustees. Other famous Americans associated with Clarke include President and Mrs. Calvin Coolidge, Clarence W. Barron, and President John F. Kennedy.

From its humble beginnings, Clarke has grown into one of the most comprehensive centers for oral education in the country today. Clarke currently boasts eight service centers designed to meet the needs of hearing-impaired individuals and their families at every stage of life. These service modules, which include the Center for Audiological Services, the Center for Early Intervention, the Mainstream Center, Summer Programs, the Research Center, Teacher Training Program, and the Assistive Devices Center help over 3,000 hearing-impaired people and their families each year. Telephone: 413/584-3450.

• One of Northampton's most famous residents was **Calvin Coolidge** (1872-1933), the 30th President of the U. S. Although born in Plymouth, Vermont, Coolidge went to Amherst College and settled in Northampton to practice law and serve as its mayor from 1910-1. He was a member of the Massachusetts State Senate from 1912-5, lieutenant governor of the state from 1916-8, then governor 1919-20, gaining national attention for his stance on the Boston police strike of 1919. Coolidge served as Vice President under President Warren G. Harding, assuming that office at Harding's death in 1923. Then he was elected President in his own right in 1924, serving a full term until 1929. The city has many places that commemorate Coolidge, including:

1. Coolidge's first Northampton House at 21 Massasoit Street, where he lived with his bride, Grace Goodhue Coolidge, in 1905 while she was a teacher at the Clarke School for the Deaf. Later, the Coolidges moved to The Beeches after their Washington days.
2. Calvin Coolidge's Law Offices, the Masonic Temple.
3. Forbes Library's Calvin Coolidge Memorial Room.

• The *Daily Hampshire Gazette,* one of the oldest daily newspapers in continuous publication in the country, is published in Northampton. It was founded in 1786 by William Butler in an effort to combat discontent over Shay's Rebellion.

• Another famous Northamptonite was the 18th century Puritan divine **Jonathan Edwards** (1703-58), leader of the revivalist Great Awakening of 1740, the first such religious movement in the country. Accepting the Calvinistic doctrine of absolute divine sovereignty and the right to bestow eternal salvation or damnation and being a powerful speaker and leader, Edwards made both converts and enemies. His 1737 work, *A Faithful Narrative of the Surprising Work of God in the Conversion of Many Hundred Souls in Northampton, and the Neighboring Towns and Villages* had a great effect on George Whitefield's founding of Calvinistic Methodism. A dispute with the Northampton congregation on the terms of admission into the church led to his dismissal, and in 1751 he went to Stockbridge, Massachusetts, as a missionary to the Indians, where he wrote his great philosophical treatise on the *Freedom of the Will* in 1754. Edwards served as president of the College of New Jersey (Princeton University) 1757-8, and was elected to the American Hall of Fame in 1900.

• One of the largest and best resource centers of its type in New England, **Forbes Library** is a sub-regional reference and inter-library local center for small libraries throughout Western Massachusetts, part of the Western Regional Library system. Built in 1894 in the Richardsonian Romanesque style and founded under the will of judge Charles E. Forbes, the library at 20 West Street contains 280,000 volumes and changing exhibits of the photographs and paintings of area artists. Its most famous component is the Calvin Coolidge Memorial Room, containing manuscripts and memorabilia of the 30th President of the U. S. A collection of souvenirs, scrapbooks, and gifts dealing with Coolidge are contained in the room, many of them having been contributed by the President and his wife. His 5,000-volume personal library, family memorabilia, and portrait by Howard Chander Christie are all there. The library is open Monday through Saturday, 9:00 a.m. to 5:00 p.m.; Sunday, 1:00 p.m. to 5:00 p.m.; closed Memorial Day, 4th of July, Thanksgiving and Christmas. Telephone: 413/584-8550. Two other local libraries of interest are the Lilly Library in Florence and the Hampshire County Law Library, open 9:00 a.m. to 5:00 p.m. daily at the Court House Annex.

• There are a number of interesting **galleries** around Northampton, particularly around Green Street and the town center. It also has a wealth of **historic buildings,** such as:

1. Griffin House (1700); Bridge Street Cemetery (1661); houses of the Northampton Historical Society; Lathrop-Butler House (1848)
2. Gaylord-Bassett Villa (1850) and Montgomery House (1840) on Pomeroy Terrace
3. 94 Hawley Street's Federal-style House (1823)
4. Dr. Sylvester Graham's House at 111 Pleasant Street
5. A house by architect Thomas Pratt at 83 North Street (1812)
6. Smith Charities (1848), Hampshire County Court House (1886), First Church of Christ (1876), the 1849 Northampton City Hall, Memorial Hall (1873), Academy of Music (1890), and the 1856 Gas Works Building on Main Street
7. The 1761 Colonial house, Noah Parsons House (1755), and Hunt-Brewster House (c. 1870) on Old South Street
8. Conz Street's Seth Strong House (1819) and the Seth Strong Round House (1829), said to be the first of six round houses built in New England
9. On South Street view the preserved Bartlett House, Theodore Bartlett House (1820), Drury Homestead (c. 1713), Colonel Elisah Strong Home (1800), Daughters of the American Revolution 1713 Clapp House, Ferry House (a 1704 garrison), and Eleazer Strong House of 1797
10. Elm Street features Grecourt Gates (1924), commemorating the Smith Relief Unit of World War I, St. Mary's Church (1885), Mary Ellen Chase House of 1810, the 1827 Dewey House on the campus, plus the Elizabeth Drew House (1780) and Maltby House (c. 1700), Merritt Clark House (1841), Jewett Homestead, 1828 Clarke House, Hankins House (1730), and Hammond House (1891)
11. Churchill House (1760) at 38 Franklin Street
12. Rogers Hill Road has three interesting houses

belonging to the Clarke School for the Deaf: Rogers Hall (1823), the 1840 Queen Anne Cottage, and The Gables (1845)

13. Prospect Hill has The Manse, the Solomon Stoddard House (1684), and Smith College's Capan House (1825)

14. Other historic spots to check out include Paradise Pond, Mill River, the Florence Congregational Church, and the mills at Bay State and Leeds

- Along with its many other city services, Northampton also maintains three well-known **hospitals:** Cooley-Dickinson, which offers a Tel-Med tape service on health and medical issues at 413/586-5800, Monday through Friday, 10:00 a.m. to 8:00 p.m.; Northampton State Hospital; and the U. S. Veterans Hospital.

- **Hotel Northampton,** which opened in April of 1927, contains a notable collection of Currier and Ives prints, brass and pewter, and Rogers groups. In the rear is Wiggins Tavern, reconstructed from a 125-year old building, with a country store built in 1820.

- It was Swedish soprano **Jenny Lind** (1820-1887), known as "The Swedish Nightingale," who coined the phrase "The Paradise of America" for Northampton and for which Paradise Pond is named. An unrivaled master of coloratura, Lind came to the city for her honeymoon while on concert tour in 1852. Mementoes of her visit are contained in the Isaac Damon House.

- **Look Memorial Park,** located at 300 North Main Street on Route 9 of the Berkshire Trail in the Florence section of Northampton, consists of 150 acres of recreational pleasure. Facilities include the Frank E. Dow Pavilion and many other picnicking areas, a wading pool and full-sized swimming pool, pedal boats and canoes, the C. P. Hunting steam train, Longwoods Zoo (featuring native deer, peacocks, pheasants and raccoons), a playground and game equipment, fishing in Mill River, the Pines Outdoor Theatre, tennis courts, softball fields, and refreshment areas. There is a $1.00 per vehicle entry charge for admission to the park, with season passes available. Some of the services call for reservations and/or a modest fee. Telephone: 413/584-5457. The park is open year-round, dawn to sunset, with the swimming pool, train, boats, and food service units open 11:00 a.m. to 7:00 p.m. Memorial Day to Labor Day. A gift to the city in 1928 by Mrs. Fannie Burr Look, the park is city-owned, receives no tax dollars for support, and is administered by a Board of Trustees with the mayor as an ex-officio member. It is named in honor of Frank Newhall Look, chief executive of the Prophylactic Brush Company in Florence 1877-1911.

- "Home of Friendly Flying," **Northampton Airport** on Old Ferry Road is the site of skydiving and ultralights in the town. Formerly called Lafleur Airport, it celebrated its 50th anniversary in 1979. Telephone: 413/584-1860.

- The Greater **Northampton Chamber of Commerce,** committed to "an extensive program of public service," is located at 62 State Street. It maintains a tourist information booth at the corner of King Street and Merrick Lane daily from 10:00 a.m. to 6:00 p.m., May through October. Telephone: 413/584-1900.

- The **Northampton Historical Society,** headquartered in the 1813 Isaac Damon House, is an active organization preserving the heritage of its city. It owns and maintains an architectural complex on Bridge Street of the Isaac Damon House (1813), Parsons House (c. 1728), Shepherd House (c. 1798), and the Shepherd Barn (c. 1825). It also preserves and exhibits notable collections of furniture, paintings, ceramics, and costumes. The Society had its beginning in 1884 as the Northampton City Library and Museum in Memorial Hall on Main Street and was formally organized and incorporated in 1905. It has just completed the Damon Education Center, an addition to the Damon House, where after-school programs for children, lectures for adults, workshops, seminars, and special events for all ages are held. Recent projects include the publication of a new history on Northampton, an ongoing series of booklets based on the collections, and a slide/audio production on the history of the city.

The home of the famous architect **Isaac Damon** at 46 Bridge Street has been preserved by the Northampton Historical society. It was built by Damon himself for his own use. Isaac Damon is well represented throughout New England by the churches, bridges, and many public buildings he designed. The house is now used for the Society's offices, workrooms, library, and archives. Nine rooms house a study collection of 18th century, 19th century, and 20th century dresses, uniforms, bonnets, and accessories of men's and women's clothing.

The **Parsons House** is located at 58 Bridge Street. Built c. 1728, it contains a typical 1840s parlor furnished with distinctive antiques and historical material set up to represent the time when the Wright family lived in the house. Also exhibited is the 1930s bedroom of Anna Catherine Bliss, a Parsons descendant and donor of the house to the Society. Other rooms have changing exhibits such as the Prospect House on Mt. Holyoke and Northampton and the Constitution.

At 66 Bridge Street is the **Shepherd House,** built c. 1798 by Asahel Pomeroy, son of the famous native soldier General Seth Pomeroy of Northampton. The house, owned by Pomeroy descendants and later by the Shepherd family, contains many family artifacts.

The **Shepherd Barn** in back of the house at 66 Bridge Street was built c. 1825. It contains displays of farm implements, sleighs, Northampton weathervanes and signs, water pipes, tubs, early hand pumps, and an exhibit of the Connecticut Valley Indians, the area's first inhabitants.

Guided tours of the Parsons and Shepherd Houses and Shepherd Barn are conducted on Wednesday, Saturday, and Sunday, 2:00 p.m. to 4:30 p.m. There is a $2.00 admission charge to the complex to view all exhibits; group rates and special programs are available. The office is open for researchers (by appointment) 9:00 a.m. to 5:00 p.m., Tuesday through Friday. Telephone: 413/584-6011.

• **Pulaski Park,** a monument to Casimir Pulaski who helped his country during the Revolutionary War, is open to the public year-round. It is located on Main Street in the center of the city.

• The oldest state-aided public day vocational school in the country, **Smith's Agricultural and Vocational High School** was founded as an agricultural school for young men and women with a bequest from philanthropist Oliver Smith, and has been in operation since 1908. The current areas of vocational study include auto body repair and automotive maintenance, carpentry, an electrical department, drafting, painting and decorating, home economics, and practical nursing.

• **Smith College,** one of the "Seven Sisters," is the largest privately endowed liberal arts college for women in the U. S. It has an undergraduate enrollment of 2,600 students, confers the bachelor of arts degree on some 600 women each year and has about 46,500 living alumnae. Founded in 1871, the school today sits on a 125-acre campus, and welcomes the public to the Smith College Museum of Art Tuesday through Saturday, 12:00 p.m. to 5:00 p.m.; Sunday, 2:00 p.m. to 5:00 p.m. Telephone: 413/584-2700, extension 2760. The college's Lyman Plant House, open to the public daily from 8:00 a.m. to 4:15 p.m., presents a chrysanthemum show each fall and bulb show each spring. Other college buildings of interest are the Clark Science Center, the Library with its 980,000-volume collection, and the Mendenhall Center for the Performing Arts, which presents several major productions each year. Although Smith College has many distinguished alumnae, three of the most famous include First Lady Nancy Reagan and women's rights activists Betty Friedan and Gloria Steinem. The campus is located at the top of Northampton's Main Street at the Grecourt Gates. Tours can be arranged at the Admissions Office, and maps and information are available in the Office of Public Relations, Pierce Hall. Note that it has its own Zip Code: 01063. Telephone: 413/584-2700.

• The **Smith College Campus School,** under the auspices of the Smith College Department of Education and Child Study, is a coeducational day school for ages 3 to 12 years. There are 156 boys and 153 girls. In addition, the school also provides an Infant Care Center for babies one and a half to twelve months old. The school actively participates in the Smith-Northampton summer program, offering classes in science, physical education, literature, and mathematics for all children in the community in grades 3 to 12. Telephone: 584-2700, extension 3260.

• The oldest fair in continuous existence in the nation, Northampton's **Three-County Fair,** is an annual September event taking place from the Friday before Labor Day through the following Saturday, featuring: pari-mutual racing Monday through Saturday, ox and horse drawings, agricultural exhibits, 4-H judging contests, Kiddies' Days, grange exhibits, rides, shows, and games week-long on the Midway, polka bands, and fun for all. In addition, the New England Morgan Horse Show, the largest single-breed horse show in the U. S. takes place on the fairgrounds each year the last week in July. The fairgrounds have been located on Route 9's Bridge Street since 1818.

PELHAM, Massachusetts
Population: 937　　　　　　　　　　Zip Code: 01002

Settled by Scotch Presbyterians in 1738, Pelham is thought to be named for Henry Pelham (1695?-1754), who was the leading minister in the British government in 1743. Bordering on Quabbin Reservoir on the east, it is located at the northeastern corner of the county.

Trips and trivia:
• **Charcoal Kilns** at Pelham Hollow, built by David Shores in 1862 but later demolished by the Quabbin Reservoir floods, have been designated Historic American Buildings. They were brick, with a circular barrel vault and dome. Note also the interesting tombstone inscriptions at **Knight's Corner Cemetery** on the south side of Packardville Road near the intersection of Route 202.

• Pelham claims the oldest meetinghouse in continuous use in the country. Dating back to 1743, the **Pelham Meeting House** has been designated a national historic landmark.

• **Mount Lincoln,** at an elevation of 1,238 feet according to the U. S. Geological Survey, has granite bedrock and a tower with an impressive view of the surrounding Triassic area. The easiest way to reach it is by Packardville Road; Lincoln Tower Road joins it on the north side, near a cemetery.

• The **Pelham Historical Society, Inc.,** operates a museum in the former 1839 Congregational church located on Pelham Hill at 374 Amherst Road. The museum, which is open Sundays, 1:00 p.m. to 4:00 p.m., May to September and by appointment, is part of the Pelham Town Hall Complex. This is a Massachusetts Historic Landmark that also includes the **Pelham Town Hall** (1743), the oldest town hall in continuous use in New England, and the old

burial grounds. The museum contains the original stone lintel from over the fireplace in Conkey's Tavern (now under the Quabbin Reservoir) where Daniel Shays presumably planned his rebellion. It also contains old photographs of various houses and locations in the town, the sort of tools Pelham residents worked with in the 18th century and 19th century, maps, an organ, a newly-updated Archives Collection, and other material. Telephone: 413/253-2739.

• The famed **Poison Oyster Stone** is from Pelham. Originally in Knight's Cemetery (replaced there by a replica), it is now in the town museum, and reads as follows:
Warren Gibbs
Died by arsenic poison
March 23, 1860 Aged 36 years
5 months and 23 days
Think my friends when this you see
How my wife hath dealt by me
She in some oysters did prepare
Some poison for my lot and share
Then of the same I did partake
And nature yielded to its fate
Before she my wife became
Mary Felton was her name
Erected by his brother
Wm Gibbs

• Other noteworthy **structures** around town include: Old Cook Tavern on Enfield Road; Harkness Road's Orient Farm (c. 1750) and "Lilac Land" (c. 1800); the United Church of Pelham (c. 1840) on Amherst Road; and an early mill structure that was at one point used as a fishing rod factory and today houses Human Resource Development Press and The Carkhuff Institute of Human Technology.

• It was from Pelham in 1787 that **Daniel Shays** found his following of 1,100 to stage the Shays' Rebellion against the Springfield Armory in protest over high taxes and mortgage foreclosures, and it was here where he retreated in defeat. Shay's Encampment Site is marked in the eastern part of town. Route 202 is called Daniel Shays Highway after the town's most celebrated resident.

PLAINFIELD, Massachusetts
Population: 287   Zip Code: 01070

A small farming community in the northwestern corner of the county, Plainfield is well known for its wild blueberries and is popular as a spot for antiquers and rock hunters. It has the lowest population in Hampshire County.

Trips and trivia:
• **Berkshire Green Acres** off Route 116 is a recreation spot featuring picnicking, swimming, fishing, hiking trails, and camping. **Plainfield Pond** is a popular fishing spot, and there are several trout streams throughout the town.
• The town's most interesting buildings are clustered around **Plainfield Center,** including the Plainfield Congregational Church of 1846, the Plainfield Town Hall (1847), and nearby houses. Also located in the town center, at the corner of Main and Central Streets, is the **Shaw-Hudson House** (1833), built by Samuel Shaw. The house contains the office of a doctor who was married to William Cullen Bryant's sister; Dr. Shaw's 19th century office has been preserved intact, complete with antique furnishings. Left in trust to the Plainfield Congregational Church, the house operates as a museum that is open to the public May through October at a slight admission fee.
• The **Town Library** was previously the Moses Hallock School, named for the town's first pastor who kept the school in his home. Educated there were such famous students as poet William Cullen Bryant and radical abolitionist John Brown.

• Plainfield commemorates the birthplace of author **Charles Dudley Warner** on Union Street. Warner's *On Being a Boy* captures his Plainfield youth, and his poem *The Mountain Miller* deals with the ruins of the mill of Joseph Beals.

SOUTH HADLEY, Massachusetts
Population: 17,033   Zip Code: 01075

Settled in 1659, South Hadley combines a history of urban industry and educational opportunities in both its architecture and lifeblood. It is best known as the home of the first women's college in the United States.

Trips and trivia:
• Various **buildings** represent the town's activities. In South Hadley Falls is the remnant of the old canal, the Squire Bowdoin House at 38 Carew Street, United Methodist Church, and the old fire station on North Main Street. The village contains many interesting dwellings, including: the Georgian Colonial (1742) at 7 Silver Street, the saltbox on Morgan Road, two gambrels on Woodbridge Street that have been designated Historic American Buildings—The Sycamores (1788) and the Rawson House (1733/1788), Wright House at 96 College Street, and the late Victorian and early 20th century structures at the college.
• The first **canal** in the country was built in 1794 in South Hadley Falls, a navigable waterway constructed around the river falls by the "Proprietors of Locks and Canals on the Connecticut River." One unique feature of this first canal system was its "inclined plane" for drawing boats from the lower canal to the upper basin through a six-wheeled, chain-drawn car or wagon.
• **Devil's Football,** a 300-ton magnetic boulder, goes with a legend that it was kicked by Satan from the Devil's Garden at Amherst Notch.

• The World's Largest Dinosaur Footprint Quarry, Nash's **Dinosaurland** on Amherst Road, is maintained by

Carlton S. Nash, who in 1933 discovered a stony ledge in South Hadley which contained "some imprints" left by the ponderous prehistoric dinosaurs that dominated life on this planet over a million years ago. Seven years later, the young geologist completed his studies at Amherst College and purchased the small area containing his secret find. Since then, Nash has operated the museum and sold the footprints for use as unique and practical gifts such as for garden walks, door steps, fireplaces, collections, and plaques. Open daily April 1st to Christmas. Telephone: 413/467-9566.

• **Mount Holyoke College** is the oldest continuing institution of higher education for women in the country. In 1971, it reaffirmed its decision to remain a college for women. Founded by Mary Lyon in 1837, it is located on an 800-acre campus with two lakes, two museums, an indoor observatory, arboretum, 18-hole championshp golf course, 19 tennis courts, and a riding facility with indoor heated ring and extensive riding trails. The college's Willits-Hallowell center is a conference facility as well as a center for faculty, students, and alumnae. A full program of lectures, plays, concerts, and art exhibits is open to the public, often without charge. The Mount Holyoke College Summer Theatre operates from late June through mid-August, and is a popular area attraction. Sights of particular interest to visitors are: The Library (the vaulted ceiling of the main reading room is a copy of Westminster in London); the Skinner Museum; the Mount Holyoke College Art Museum; the Observatory, built in 1881 and containing two telescopes, a 90-year old eight-inch Alvan Clark reflector and a new 24-inch reflector; Talcott Arboretum, containing a jungle room; and the monument marking Mary Lyon's grave. All of these are free of charge, open to the public at specific hours or by appointment. Telephone: 413/538-2000.

Highly competitive in admissions, with a 520,000-volume library, new facilities in the sciences, studio art and theatre departments, Mount Holyoke has 1,950 students; it has Phi Beta Kappa and Sigma Xi Chapters on its campus. Prominent graduates include Frances Perkins, the first woman to serve in a presidential cabinet, Ella Grasso, former governor of Connecticut, and alumna Elizabeth T. Kennan, President of the College.

• At an elevation of 878 feet, **Mount Holyoke,** named for Springfield pioneer Elizur Holyoke, offers a spectacular view of the Connecticut Valley and its river from the summit house. The pre-Civil War hotel, no longer in operation except for sight-seeing, entertained many famous visitors in its day, such as Charles Dickens, Nathaniel Hawthorne, Abraham Lincoln, Jenny Lind, and Senator Charles Sumner. From its intersection with Route 116, drive northwest on Route 47 for two miles to the Skinner State Park, then one-half mile to the parking lot. Bring a picnic lunch, since this is a great spot for a hike. The Mount Holyoke Summit House is in the town of Hadley, although located in Skinner State Park.

• A narrow rock-bound passage through the base of Mount Holyoke called **Pass of Thermopylae** is said to have been constructed by early settlers who poured water on the rock in winter and then raked away the frozen gravel that slid off.

• The **Jospeh Skinner Museum** is located in a former church at 35 Woodbridge Street and contains collections of decorative arts, furniture, woodworking and agricultural implements, geological specimens, fossils, shells, historical memorabilia, and Indian artifacts. A second building on the grounds, a former schoolhouse, contains a New England bird collection. The museum was established in 1933 by Joseph Allen Skinner, who traveled around the world gathering items that are now in the museum. The main building was constructed in 1846 as the First Congregational Church for the town of Prescott. When that town was flooded by the Quabbin Reservoir, Skinner purchased the building and moved it to its present site in South Hadley. The museum is open free of charge May through October, Wednesday to Sunday, 2:00 p.m. to 5:00 p.m. Telephone: 413/538-2085.

• Another influence of the Skinner family is the **Joseph Allen Skinner State Park** on Route 47, at the summit of Mount Holyoke. Open 10:00 a.m. to 8:00 p.m., it is reached by going as far as you can along the park's steep round, the reward being arrival at the top of one of the highest peaks in the entire Pioneer Valley. There are picnic, horseback, hiking, and snowmobile trails available, all at no charge. On the way to the Skinner State Park you pass by **Titan's Piazza,** a volcanic formation of overhanging rock columns that has been classified as one of the world's major natural phenomena.

• **Waterskiers** of the Pioneer Valley Ski Club have their headquarters at Brunelle's Marina at 1 Alvord Street.

The marina is open year-round, with a boat dock and launch facilities, snowmobiles for hire, and picnic tables for swimmers and/or ice fishermen.

SOUTHAMPTON, Massachusetts
Population: 3,069 Zip Code: 01073

Named for Southampton, England, this lovely rural town lies in the valley of the Manhan River between Mount Pomeroy and Mount Tom. Southampton, settled in 1732, is located in the southwestern corner of Hampshire County.

Trips and trivia:
- **Cedarhurst Pond,** a "picnic and recreation park," off of Route 10, $1.00 admission for adults. **Parsons Memorial Forest** on East Street, off Route 10, has facilities for fishing, picnicking, and trails.
- The Southampton Historical Society is headquartered in the **Clark-Chapman House** (1827) on Main Street in the center of town. Historical exhibits are housed there for viewing by appointment with Mrs. Theodore L. Hendrick, 52 Cold Spring Road. Telephone: 413/527-3933.
- Old **Edwards House** on Maple Street behind the church marks the spot where townspeople took refuge during the French and Indian War raids. Other buildings of interest in the town include: the Eleazar Hannum Homestead (c. 1734) on Pomeroy Meadow Road and another saltbox, the Ebenezar Kingsley Homestead on Route 10; the Jonathan Judd House; Ichabod Strong House (1768) on Route 10; Israel Sheldon House (1768) on Crooked Ledge Road; Woodbridge Hall (1793) on East Street; Mill buildings on the Manhan River; and the granite quarry off Crooked Ledge Road, lead mines off Lead Mine Road, and the copper mine at Wolf Hill.
- A **monument** to the 104th infantry of the 26th (Yankee) Division that was reruited in Southampton in 1917, located in the center cemetery, bears a bas-relief showing the presentation of the regiment's citation in France for bravery in 1918.
- The **Old Southampton Church** on Route 10, dedicated in 1788, is one of the oldest churches in the region still in use. Originally constructed as a meeting house, its steeple was added in 1822. The Southampton Conservation Commission put out a revised edition of its **Points of Interest** map in 1976, including: caves on Mt. Breakneck and nearby beaver dams; scenic areas; cemeteries; dams; quarries; and mill sites; reservoirs; horse trails; pine and evergreen forests; ponds; a lead mine on Little Mountain; Manhan Meadows Sanctuary; the site of the Kennedy plane crash; remains of the old New Haven-Northampton Canal of the 1830s; and the Lyman Conservation Area.
- The **Sheldon English and Classical School,** founded in 1829 in Southampton, was at one point considered one of the first and best preparatory schools in the East.

WARE, Massachusetts
Population: 8,679 Zip Code: 01082

A sign along Route 9 welcomes the visitor to Ware as "The Town That Can't Be Licked," in honor of its recovery from the Great Depression of the 1930s. This strong industrial community spreads along both sides of the Ware River.

Trips and trivia:
- A **covered bridge** spanning the Ware River at Gilbertville in Worcester County joins the two counties.
- I Ware Center, the **Congregational Meeting House,** believed to date from 1799, is a particularly interesting structure by Isaac Damon. Others there include: the adjacent cemetery, three colonial houses nearby, Babcock-Bould and Paige Taverns, and in the downtown area, the pre-Victorian Town Hall, the Storrs Block of 1887 (which has since burned down) across Main Street, the structure that used to be the Unitarian Church, and the Young Men's Library Association at East Main and Church Streets. Also of note are the stone mill building on East Main Street that is still in industrial use, a Georgian Colonial on Doane Road, and many structures built to house the town's working population.
- **Grenville Park** near Main Street in the town center is a well-maintained nature area with facilities for picnicking, tennis, and little league baseball; there is no fee.
- There are a number of **mill outlet stores,** Ware Industries, east of the downtown area, with products ranging from textiles to shoes to machines—all at very reasonable prices.
- **Quabbin Park Cemetery,** established in 1938 to consolidate the cemeteries of the towns that were lost to Quabbin Reservoir, is located on Route 9 in Ware at the entrance to the Quabbin Dike.
- The earliest white settlers (c. 1717) called Ware "The Manour of Peace," but the **town's name** was later changed to the Indian "Nemameseck," meaning fishing baskets or weirs (pronounced ware). The **town seal** represents an Indian standing, spear in hand, above a roughly constructed weir.

WESTHAMPTON, Massachusetts
Population: 1,040

Called "Long Division" when it was a part of Northampton, Westhampton became incorporated as a township in 1778. It has seven hills over 1,000 feet high: Breakneck Hill, Canada Mountain, Cub Hill, Hanging Mountain, Mt. Pisgah, Spruce Hill, and Tob Hill.

Trips and trivia:
- **Hampshire Regional School** in Westhampton serves the students of that town plus Chesterfield, Goshen, Southampton, and Williamsburg.

Maple Sugar Time

- The first recorded industry in the town was **maple syrup making,** and that tradition is still carried on today. During the March through April season, visitors are welcome at the Leo Aloisi farm on North Road, Runnymeade, the Charles M. Norris farm on South Road, and the Parsons farm on Easthampton Road.
- Westhampton has associated with it a number of famous **people:**
  1. Ethan Allen (1738-89) of American Revolution fame, commander of the Green Mountain Boys, was part owner of a lead mine in the town that helped supply bullets during the war.
  2. Sylvester Judd (1813-53), American Unitarian clergyman and author, first town clerk and publisher of the Hampshire Gazette, recorded the entire history of the Connecticut Valley.
  3. Reverend Enoch Hale (1753-1837), brother of patriot Nathan Hale ("I only regret that I have but one life to lose for my country.") served as the town's minister for 57 years and helped prevent the townspeople from participating in Shays' Rebellion. He was also the author of a spelling book for children.
- There are many opportunities for **recreation** in Westhampton: horseback riding along woodland trails at Fuller's Horse Farm; Pine Island Lake swimming for summer residents; and camping, picnicking, and swimming at Windy Acres on South Road.
- The town's typical **village center** "remains one of the few unspoiled in Western Massachusetts," according to its Board of Selectmen. Most notable is the Congregational Church (1829) standing sentinel on Tob Hill, plus the nearby Town Hall, the late 18th century Captain Jared Hunt House on North Road, 1810 Sylvester Judd House (now used as the church parsonage), Phelps House (1801) on Stage Road, and the Loud House (1816) on South Road. Other interesting structures outside the center include the Georgian Colonial on Southampton Road featuring a classic nine-window facade; the 1768 saltbox on Route 66, which is thought to be the oldest surviving building in the town; Samuel Kingsley III House; the former brick schoolhouse on Southampton Road; South Road's 1816 Enoch Hale House and a 1794 house built by Judd; and the early 19th century Parsons Sawmill on Easthampton Road. Although none of the houses are open for public tours, they make for fascinating viewing for the motorist.
- The **White Reservoir** provides water for the city of Holyoke.

WILLIAMSBURG, Massachusetts
Population: 2,342   Zip Code: 01096

Once called "Hatfield Woods," Williamsburg was named for the Williams family of Hatfield. The township is made up of two villages: Haydenville on the south, and Williamsburg center in the north. Both villages have developed along the Mill River.

Trips and trivia:
- **Devil's Den Brook** is a rocky gorge off Old Goshen Road.
- The first area of the town to be settled was Haydenville, where cloth-covered buttons are believed to have been first manufactured by machines. It was named by industrialist Lieutenant Governor Hayden (1863-1906), whose 1800 home on Main Street is now in private use. The cluster of buildings and homes around the old brass works is listed on the National Register of Historic Places. There are many interesting architectural structures interspersed throughout the town. In Haydenville, note the century-old industrial building on Route 9 that was used as a brass works, the Greek Revival houses nearby, Haydenville Congregational Church, and houses for mill workers on Fort Hill Road. Williamsburg itself features another Congregational Church, the Williamsburg Blacksmith Shoppe (1840), Williams House (c. 1812) that was for a long time used as an inn, the former Town Hall, and the c. 1810 Wells/Packard House. Other notable places include Clary House (1812) on Hyde Hill Road and Ely House on Old Goshen Road.
- **Meekins Library** was donated to the town by sheep-raiser Stephen Meekins; it is uniquely styled of stone. Telephone: 413/268-7472.
- The **Mill River** supplied water power that helped many industries in town—buttons, cotton, hardware, ironware, leather, silk, and woolens—until a disastrous dam burst on May 16, 1874, wiping out in one hour the entire industrial area and killing 85 people. Most of the mills were not rebuilt.
- Williamsburg's first settler was **John Miller** of Northampton who, in 1735, built himself a cabin there and lived and hunted in solitude for 17 years.
- **Petticoat Hill,** named for a family of seven daughters who all washed their five petticoats on the same day each week and hung the 35 on a hilltop so that they billowed over the area, is a 60-acre property owned by the Trustees of Reservations. There are picnic and trail facilities open to the public. On Route 9 turn west at the sign by Williams House, where a steep climb through the forest leads to the 1,185-foot summit. It is open year-round, free to the public.
- The **Williamsburg Historical Society, Inc.,** maintains a museum at its headquarters on Main Street along Route 9. Featured there are ancient farm implements and tools, quilts, and photographs and memorabilia of the Great Flood of 1874 that wiped out much of the Mill River Valley. The exhibits are in the 1841 Town Hall, available free to the public Sunday afternoons 2:00 p.m. to 5:00 p.m. Telephone: 413/268-7332. The **Williamsburg Grange** holds an annual Grange Fair and Flower Show each year in September. Telephone: 413/268-3386.

WORTHINGTON, Massachusetts
Population: 910   Zip Code: 01098

Named for one of its original proprietors, John Worthington of Springfield, this agricultural and recreational town was settled in 1764. It is located in the westernmost section of the county in 33½ acres, centered on a high plateau with an elevation of about 1,500 feet. Worthington welcomes visitors by a sign commemorating its "over 200 years of gracious living."

Trips and trivia:
- **Berkshire Park,** located at the junction of Routes

112 and 143, is a campground with fishing, picnicking, swimming, and hiking trails open to the public. Telephone: 413/238-5918. Worthington is a very popular summer and winter resort, offering many fishing streams, a public golf club, picnicking, horseback, and snow trails, plus blueberry-picking in season. It can be reached from two branches of the Berkshire Trail: Route 112 from Cummington or Route 143 from Chesterfield and Williamsburg.

• South Worthington marks the site of the birthplace of **Reverend Russell H. Conwell,** the first president of Temple University. The main building was constructed c. 1800, with other additions made later.

• Newcomers to the town are told of its many attractive **features:** the Golf Club, organized in 1904; water system, installed in 1910; volunteer fire department, founded in 1946; Health Center, organized in 1950; summer concerts in the historic South Worthington Academy Building by the "Sevenars," the Robert Schrade Family of concert pianists; swim and tennis, rod and gun clubs; Grange Chapter; Thursday morning coffee for the women; and the Town Library, staffed by volunteers and student aides. On Tuesday nights during the sumer there are auctions at the Sena Barn on Buffington Hill Road. Telephone: 413/228-5302.

• **Indian Oven,** an oval-shaped, three-foot hole in a boulder, is a local interest point. It can be found in the woods to the left of Indian Oven Road off Route 112.

• The town's main industry is **potato farming.** For a view of the process, stop by Alber Farms on Huntington Road, one of the largest potato growers in New England.

• At opposite ends of town are **waterfalls** that have been described as true natural wonders:

1. Bradley Falls, or the South Worthington Cascade in the Little River off Route 112 below the bridge, a gentle 50-foot drop.

2. West Worthington Falls on River Road off Route 143 in the middle branch of the Westfield River, a 75-foot plunge into a gorge. Local legend has it that an Indian brave and his sweetheart leapt to their deaths there.

• While there are many interesting structures in this rural New England town, the majority are to be found at **Worthington Corners.** They include: the 1806 Jonathan Woodbridge House, an early Georgian Colonial on Old North Road, and a Greek Revival with Ionic portico that was raised from the original one and a half story height on Old Buffington Hill Road. Elsewhere, check out another Georgian Colonial on Clark Road, a 1769 early Colonial on West Street, Buffington House (1806) on Buffington Hill Road at Ridge Road, the Gothic Revival on Route 112 at Radiker Road, plus Worthington Town Hall (1855), South Worthington Church (1847) and the Congregational Society's Church (1888), plus the Conwell Academy (1894) in South Worthington.

Extra Ordinaries

Extra Ordinaries

Airports
According to Bill Callahan of the Federal Aviation Administration's Department of Transportation, there are 83 airports in the commonwealth, 141 counting seaplane bases and helistops. The Massachusetts Aeronautics Commission, located at Boston-Logan Airport in East Boston (telephone: 617/727-5350) lists these airports and their phone numbers in Western Massachusetts:
1. Agawam 413/786-1646
2. Great Barrington 528-1010
3. Hatfield 665-8700
4. North Adams 663-9653
5. Northampton 584-1860
6. Orange 617/544-6911
7. Palmer 413/283-7531
8. Pittsfield 499-0213
9. Turners Falls 863-9391
10. Westfield 568-8517

In addition, there is a seaplane base located out of Agawam-Springfield on the Connecticut River. Telephone: 413/734-0955.

These specified landing areas have all been approved by the Massachusetts Aeronautics Commission for public use. All the airports provide service during their published hours of operation, and current field conditions can be obtained by the commission, any barracks of the State Police, or from Boston and Worcester FAA Flight Service Stations.

The Appalachian National Scenic Trail
For 83 miles the Appalachian Mountain National Scenic Trails go through the state of Massachusetts, entering south of Mt. Everett and leaving north of Mt. Williams, crossing Mt. Greylock en route. This famous 5,000-mile footpath starts at Mt. Katahdin in Maine, winds through the Berkshire Mountains where at one point it follows the old Mohawk Trail along the Hoosic River and eventually leads to the state of Georgia. Where it touches the commonwealth, the state has cooperated greatly in its preservation.

Perhaps you'd like to join the Appalachian Mountain Club, which is located at 5 Joy Street on Beacon Hill in Boston 02108. Telephone: 617/523-0636. The oldest club of its kind in the country, AMC today has a membership of over 20,000 worldwide, although centered in New England and New York. Its purpose since 1876 has been "to explore the mountains of New England and adjacent regions, both for scientific and artistic purposes, and in general to cultivate an interest in geographical studies." The club building in Boston, open to the public Monday through Friday, 9:00 a.m. to 5:00 p.m.; Saturday, 10:00 a.m. to 4:00 p.m., houses one of the largest libraries on mountaineering in the country and numerous maps and photographic collections. There are chapters in Berkshire County and in Springfield, offering publications and programs.

Apple Orchards of Western Massachusetts
"Johnny Appleseed" (John Chapman, 1774-1845) was born in nearby Leominster, Massachusetts, and New England and New York have long been called McIntosh Country. The apple orchards in Western Massachusetts that are part of the New York and New England Apple Institute, Box 833 in Westfield, Massachusetts 01085. (Telephone: 413/568-2331) are listed here:
1. Apex Orchards, Peckville Road (off of Route 2), Shelburne—413/625-2744
2. Atkins Farm, Corner Bay Road and Route 116, S. Amherst—253-3243
3. Bluebird Acres, 714 Parker Street (off of Route 21), East Longmeadow—525-6012
4. Cheney Orchards, Inc., Apple Road (off of Routes 148 and 20), Brimfield—436-7688
5. Clarkdale Fruit Farms, Upper Road off of Route 2A), W. Deerfield—772-6797
6. Cook's Farm, Haynes Hill (off of Route 20), Brimfield—245-4321
7. Green Acres Fruit Farm, 868 Main Street (south of Route 20), Wilbraham—596-3016
8. Mohawk Orchards, Inc., Colrain-Shelburne Road (off Route 2), Shelburne—625-2874
9. Rice Fruit Farm, 757 Main Street (south of Route 20), Wilbraham—596-4002

Most of these orchards feature apples and other seasonal fruits and vegetables. You can pick your own apples at Atkins, Bluebird Acres, Clarkdale, and Cook's. All are open daily seasonally, inluding Sundays, with Atkins, Bluebird Acres and Mohawk Orchards, open year-round.

Bed and Breakfasts in Western Massachusetts
(Note: all telephone numbers are in the 413/ exchange unless otherwise noted. Zip codes are listed after the town's name.)
1. **Berkshire County** (Berkshire Bed and Breakfast, 268-7244)
Adams (01220):
  Avery's Butternut Inn, Six East Street 743-9493
Beckett (01223):
  Canterbury Farm, Fred Snow Road, 623-8765
Dalton (01226):
  Dalton House, 955 Main Street, 413/684-3854
Great Barrington:
  Elling's Guest House, 250 Maple Avenue,

528-4103 (01230)
Littlejohn Manor, Newboy Monument Lane, 528-2882
Seekonk Pines, 142 Seekonk Cross Road, 528-4192
Thornewood Inn, 453 Stockbridge Road, 528-3828
The Turning Point Inn, RFD #2, 528-4777
Lee (01238): 1777 Greylock House, 243-1717
The Donahoes, Fairview Street, 243-1496
Haus Andreas, Stockbridge Road, 243-3298
Jirak's Guest House, 60 Laurel Lane, 243-3201
Ramsey House, 203 West Park Street, 243-1598
Lenox (01240): 25 Clifford Inn, 25 Clifford Street, 637-3330
Amity House, 15 Cliffwood Street, 637-0005
Birchwood Inn, 7 Hubbard Street, 637-2600
Brook Farm Inn, 15 Hawthorne Street, 637-3013
Cornell House, 197 Pittsfield Road, 637-0562
The Quincy Lodge, 19 Stockbridge Road, 637-9750
Underledge Inn, 76 Clifford Street, 637-0236
Walker House, 74 Walker Street, 637-1271
Whistler's Inn, 5 Greenwood Street, 637-0975
Peru (01235):
 Chalet d'Alicia B&B, East Windsor Road, 655-8292
Pittsfield (01201):
 Greer B&B, 193 Wendell Avenue, 443-3669
 White Horse Inn, 378 South Street, 443-0961
Richmond (01254):
 Middlerise B&B, Route 41, 698-2687
 Westgate, Route 295, 698-2657
Sandisfield (01255):
 New Boston Inn, Routes 57 and 8, 258-4477
Sheffield (01257):
 Centuryhurst Antiques, Main Street, 229-8131
 Colonel Ashley Inn, Bow Wow Road, 229-2929
 Oak Lodge B&B, South Main Street, 229-8531
 Staveleigh House, South Main Street, 229-2129
 Unique B&B, Upper Mountain Road, 229-3363
South Lee (01260):
 Federal House, Route 102, 243-1824
 Historic Merrell Tavern Inn, Route 102, 243-1794
Stockbridge (01262):
 The Inn at Stockbridge, Route 7 North, 298-3337
 Stirling Moffat Guest House, Box 1295, 298-5539
Tyringham (01254):
 The Golden Goose, Main Road, 243-3008
Williamstown: (01267)
 River Bend Farm, 643 Simonds Road, 458-5504
 Steep Acres Farm, 520 White Oaks Road, 458-3774
 Upland Meadow House, 1249 Northwest Hill Road, 458-3990

Franklin County
 (In the Country Bed and Breakfast, 628-3382)
Ashfield (01330):
 Apple Inn, Main Street, 628-4729
 Ashfield Inn, Main Street, 628-4571
 Bullfrog B&B, Box 210, 628-4493
 Gold Leaf Inn, Main Street, 628-3392
 Hidden Hills B&B, Baptist Corner Road, 628-2574
Bernardston (01337):
 Bernardston Inn, Routes 5 and 10, 648-9282
Buckland (01328):
 1797 House, Charlemont Road, 625-2975
 The Scott House, Hawley Road, 625-6624
Charlemont (01339):
 Forest Way Farm, Route 8A (Heath), 337-8321
Colrain (01340):
 Grandmother's House, Box 37, 624-3771
Conway (01341):
 Hilltop B&B, Truce Road, 369-4928
 Poundsworth, Old Cricket Hill Road, 369-4420
Northfield (01360):
 Centennial House B&B, 94 Main Street, 498-5921
 Northfield Country House, School Street, 498-2692
Shelburne Falls (01370):
 Country Comfort, 15 Masonic Avenue, 625-9877
 Fiske Farm, Zerah Fiske Road, 625-6375
 Parson Hubbard House, Old Village Road, 625-9730
West Hawley (01339):
 Stump Sprouts Guests, West Hill Road, 339-4265
Whately (01093):
 Sunnyside Farm, 11 River Road, 665-3113

2. **Hampden County**
 (Greater Springfield Bed and Breakfasts, (739-7400)
Blandford (01008):
 Trianoag/McKenna Place, Chester Road, 848-2083
Holland (01550):
 Alpine Haus, Mashapaug Road, 245-9082
Springfield (01100):
 Gnome Crossing B&B, 11 Ingersoll Grove, 739-3133
Wilbraham (01095):
 B&B with Barbara and Bob, 153 Rivers Road, 596-6258

3. **Hampshire County**
 (Berkshire Bed and Breakfast Homes, (268-7244)
Cummington (01026):
 B&B, Main Street, 634-5556
 Cumworth Farm B&B, Route 112, 634-5529
 The Hill Gallery, Cole Street, 238-5914
 Windfields Farm, Bush Road, 634-3786
Florence (01060):
 The Knoll B&B, 230 North Main Street, 584-8164
Goshen (01032):
 The Whale Inn, Route 9/Main Street, 268-7246
Huntington (01050):
 Paulson B&B, Allen Coit Road, 667-3208
Northampton (01060):
 The Beeches, Hampton Terrace, 586-9288
 The Knoll, 230 North Main Street, 586-8164
Ware (01082):
 The Wildwood Inn, 121 Church Street, 967-7798
Westhampton (01027):
 Outlook Farm, Route 66, 527-0633
Williamsburg (01096):
 B&B, 9 South Street, 268-7283
 Twin Maples B&B, 106 South Street, 268-7925
Worthington (01098):
 B&B, Williamsburg Road, 238-5817
 Franklin Burrs, Kinne Brooke Road, 238-5826
 Worthington Inn at Four Corners Farm, Route 143, 238-4441

4. **Worcester County**
 (Folkstone Bed and Breakfast, 617/869-2687)

Sturbridge:
Colonel Ebenezer Crafts Inn, c/o Publik House,
Fiske Hill Road, PO Box 1771, Sturbridge, MA 01566
617/347-3313
Commonwealth Inn, 11 Summit Avenue, 01518
617/347-7603

Boats and Snowmobiles

The state Division of Marine and Recreational Vehicles is located at 64 Causeway Street in Boston 02114. It determines rules and regulations for boats and snowmobiles. For specific information on registration and laws, call 617/727-3900.

In general, snowmobiles can be used in state parks and forests, with these restrictions:
1. There is a minimum of four inches of packed snow.
2. They can be used only between the hours of 6:00 a.m. to 11:00 p.m.
3. Snowmobiles and recreational vehicles cannot be operated within 300 feet of a residence without permission.
4. There is a $15.00 registration fee for out-of-state residents.

Massachusetts calls itself "Water Wonderland" for its 1,980 miles of coastline along the Atlantic Ocean, 4,230 miles of rivers, 1,100 of lakes and ponds, and its many islands in Boston Harbor and off Cape Cod. All motorboats must be registered, and all boaters must follow these rules:
1. When crossing, boat to starboard (on right) has the right of way.
2. When passing, boat being overtaken has the right of way.
3. When meeting (head-on), both vessels turn to starboard (right) and pass port to port.
4. International rules prohibit sailboats and other small craft from hindering the passage of large boats that cannot move out of a channel.
5. Departure from the rules: it shall be the duty of every operator to abide strictly by the rules of the road. However, when immediate danger exists, the operator shall, if necessary, depart from the rules to the extent necessary to avoid collision.

Covered Bridges in Western Massachusetts

The Vacationland Map that is published by the Massachusetts Department of Commerce and Development includes these covered bridges in the western part of the state:
1. **Charlemont,** one-quarter mile north of Route 2, features a 60-foot span over Mill Brook on Heath Road.
2. **Colrain** has a 100-foot span over North River on Lyonsville Road off Route 66.
3. **Conway's** South River bridge has a 107-foot span. It is located one mile from the Post Office.
4. **Greenfield,** near the Leyden Town line, has a 95-foot span over the Green River on Eunice Williams Drive off Leyden Road.
5. **Hadley** has a bridge on Old Road, leading from Hadley to Hockanum.
6. **Sheffield** has two bridges. The upper one spans 93 feet over the Housatonic River, three-eighths mile east of Route 7 at Sheffield Plain. The lower bridge, three-eighths mile east from Route 7 in the village on County Road, has a 100-foot span over the Housatonic River.

Fairs and Festivals in Western Massachusetts

In typical New England tradition, fairs and festivals are an integral part of Western Massachusetts. Most of these events are listed under individual towns, but here are some of the key ones:

1. **Berkshire County:** Adams Agricultural, Mill Street, Adams; Barrington Fair, South Main Street, Great Barrington; Berkshire County Fair; Lenox 4th of July parade and square dance, Lenox; Monterey Arts Festival, Monterey; Pittsfield Grange, Richmond Grange, Stockbridge Grange, and Williamstown Grange.

2. **Franklin County:** Franklin County Agricultural, Wisdom Way, Greenfield; Franklin County Jersey, David Fisk Farm, Shelburne; Heath Agricultural, Colrain Stage Road, Heath; Shelburne Grange, and Yankee Doodle Days chicken barbecue in Charlemont.

3. **Hampden County:** Connecticut Valley Flower Show, Springfield; Eastern States Exposition, West Springfield; Western Massachusetts Goat Breeders, Montgomery Road, Westfield; Hampden County Beekeepers, Hampden County 4-H, Memorial Avenue, West Springfield; Littleville Fair, Kinnebrook Road, Chester; Ludlow Grange; Palmer Grange; Massachusetts Grange at the Avenue of States in West Springfield; Union Agricultural and Horticultural, North Street, Blandford; Wales County Fair, Main Street, Wales; Westfield Fair, Russelville Road, Westfield.

4. **Hampshire County:** Goshen Flower Show, Route 9, Goshen; Highland Agricultural, Bell Road, Middlefield; Hillside Agricultural, Fair Street, Cummington; Massachusetts 4-H Lamb Show, Northampton Fairgrounds; Hampshire, Franklin, and Hampden Agricultural, Bridge Street, Northampton; Massachusetts 4-H Dairy, Fairgounds Road, Cummington; Pioneer Jr. Black and White, Cummington Fairgrounds; Ware Grange; and Williamstown Grange.

For more information and a current list of Massachusetts agricultural fairs, contact the Massachusetts Department of Goods and Agriculture at the Leverett Saltonstall Building, 100 Cambridge Street in Boston, 02202.

Fishing and Hunting
in Western Massachusetts

These popular sports come under the auspices of the state Division of Fisheries and Wildlife at the Leverett Saltonstall Building Government Center, 100 Cambridge Street, Boston 02202. (Telephone: 617/727-3151). The Educational Section can be reached at 617/366-4470, and Field Headquarters, with general information on fishing, hunting, and wildlife conservation, is at Westboro, Massachusetts 01581. In the western part of the commonwealth, there are two wildlife districts: Western Wildlife District, Hubbard Avenue, Pittsfield 01201. (Telephone: 413/447-9789), and the Connecticut Valley Wildlife District, East Street, Belchertown 01007,

413/323-7632.

Fishing and hunting places are listed separately in this guide under individual cities and towns, camping sites (under Extras), and state forests, parks, and reservations. Both require licenses (usually $8.25 for residents of at least six consecutive months of the state), which are issued by city and town clerks or through the Division of Fisheries and Wildlife. All Division lands and facilities are open to the general public without regard to race, color, creed, sex, handicap, or age. Sporting, hunting, fishing and trapping licenses must be displayed in a visible manner on outer clothing when hunting, fishing, or trapping.

The fishing season usually runs from mid-April to late October. Be sure to have a proper license, and know your limit. There are state fish hatcheries in Belchertown, Sunderland, and Turners Falls, all open to the public from 9:00 a.m. to 4:00 p.m. While the fishing season changes from year to year, bass, pickerel, pan fish, and most trout fishing continues to the end of February.

Be sure to read over the state game laws about hunting, which is usually allowed during the season from one-half hour before sunrise to one-half hour after sunset, mid-October to March. There is a limit to one per year, and no hunting permitted on beaver hawk, fisher, mink, moose, muskrat, owl, otter, coyote, turkey, or birds and mammals listed under state regulations. Also, remember there is a one-year mandatory jail sentence for gun violations. Check out the Massachusetts "Abstracts" of Fish and Wildlife Laws.

Golf Courses

The Bay State's Division of Tourism has 294 golf courses listed with it, 60 of them in Western Massachusetts, including:

1. **Public courses:** Agawam Country Club in Agawam, Par 71, 413/786-2194; Ashfield Community Golf Club, Ashfield, Par 33, 628-4413; Cherry Hill Golf Course, North Amherst, Par 37, 253-9935; Chicopee Municipal Golf Course, Chicopee, Par 72, 592-4156; East Mountain Country Club, Westfield, Par 71, 568-1539; Franconia Municipal Golf Club, Springfield, Par 71, 734-9349; Jug End Golf Club, South Egremont, Par 35, 528-0434; Mill Valley Golf Links, Belchertown, Par 36, 323-4079; Mohawk Meadows Golf Club, Deerfield, Par 36, 773-7710; Oak Ridge Golf Club, Gill, Par 36, 836-2010; Pine Grove Golf Club, Northampton, Par 72, 584-4570; Pine Knoll Golf Course, East Longmeadow, Par 54, 525-7647; St. Anne Country Club, Agawam, Par 72, 786-2088; Skyline Country Club, Lanesboro, Par 36, 447-9363; Southampton Country Club, Southampton, Par 70, 527-9815; Veterans Golf Club, Springfield, Par 72, 783-7264; Waubeeka Springs Golf Course, South Williamstown, Par 72, 458-5869; and Whippernon Club, Russell, Par 29, 862-3606.

2. **Semi-private courses:** Amherst Golf Club, Amherst, Par 35. Telephone: 413/256-6894; Beaver Brook Country Club, Haydenville, Par 36, 268-7229; Blandford Country Club, Blandford, Par 33, 848-2414; Cranwell Golf Course, Lenox, Par 70, 637-1030; Edgewood Golf Course, Southwick, Par 69, 569-6826; Elmcrest Country Club, East Longmeadow, Par 70, 525-6641; Forest Park Country Club, Adams, Par 34, 743-0775; GEAA Golf Club, Pittsfield, Par 35, 442-3585; Great Barrington Golf Course, Great Barrington, Par 64, 528-9764; Greenock Country Club, Lee, Par 35, 243-3323; Hickory Ridge Country Club, South Amherst, Par 72, 256-6638; Holyoke Country Club, Holyoke, Par 72, 539-9133; Mt. Everett Golf Course, Great Barrington, Par 72, 528-4222; North Adams Country Club, Clarksburg, Par 36, 664-9011; Northfield Country Club, East Northfield, Par 36, 498-5311; Orchard Golf Course, South Hadley, Par 71, 538-2543; Pittsfield Gen. A. A., Pittsfield, Par 69, 442-3585; Pontoosuc Lake Country Club, Pittsfield, Par 70, 445-4217; Southwick Country Club, Southwick, Par 71, 569-9081; Stockbridge Golf Club, Stockbridge, Par 71, 298-3423; Tekoa Country Club, Westfield, Par 35, 562-9859; The Orchards Golf Club, South Hadley, Par 72, 533-3861; Country Club of Wilbraham, Wilbraham, Par 36, 596-8897; and Worthington Golf Club, Worthington, Par 35, 238-9731.

3. **Private courses:** Berkshire Hills Country Club, Pittsfield, Par 72, 442-1451; Country Club of Greenfield, Greenfield, Par 72, 773-7530; Crestview Country Club, Agawam, Par 72, 786-2593; Hampden Country Club, Hampden, Par 72, 566-3096; Longmeadow Country Club, Longmeadow, Par 70, 567-3381; Ludlow Country Club, Ludlow, Par 72, 583-3434; Northampton Country Club, Northampton, Par 68, 584-9852; Oxford Country Club, Chicopee, Par 71, 598-8363; Country Club of Pittsfield, Pittsfield, Par 70, 443-1896; Quaboag Country Club, Monson, Par 35, 267-5588; Springfield Country Club, West Springfield, Par 72, 734-5677; Taconic Golf Club, Williamstown, Par 71, 458-3997; Thomas Memorial Golf and Country Club, Turners Falls, Par 34, 863-4366; Twin Hills Country Club, Longmeadow, Par 71, 567-0321; Wahconah Country Club, Dalton, Par 71, 684-9752; Westover Golf Club, Ludlow, Par 72, 557-3830; Wyantenuck Country Club, Great Barrington, Par 70, 528-0350; and Wyckoff Park Golf and Country Club, Holyoke, Par 69, 536-5364.

Historic American Buildings (HABs)

Throughout this book you will note that certain dwellings are official Historic American Buildings. Permission was obtained to include these places from Charles Scribner's Sons, publishers of the Scribner Historic Buildings Series of 1976 that included the Massachusetts Catalog of the "Historic American Buildings Survey," with a list of measured drawings, photographs, and written documentation. It was compiled and edited by the Historic American Buildings Survey at the Eastern Office Design and Construction, National Park Service, Department of the Interior, with John C. Poppeliers as editor.

According to the book's preface, "The Historic American Buildings Survey, organized in 1933 by the National Park Service in collaboration with the American Institute of Architects and Library of Congress, is a long-range program to assemble an archives of American architecture." The basic criteria for selection of buildings are architectural interest and merit, as well as historical associations. Buildings chosen can be private or public, large or small, wtih priority given to buildings threatened with demolition or alteration.

State Campgrounds
in Western Massachusetts

Key:
- B—boating
- F—fishing
- H—hunting
- L—lodgings
- P—picnicking
- S—swimming
- T—trails

Camping area Location	B	F	H	L	P	S	T
Berkshire County:							
Beartown State Forest (SF), Rt. 23, Monterey	X	X	X		X	X	X
Clarksburg State Park (SP), Rts. 2 & 8, Clarksburg	X	X	X		X	X	X
Greylock Mt. State Reservation, Routes 2, 7, 8, Adams		X	X		X		X
Historic Valley Park, Rt. 2, North Adams	X	X			X	X	
October Mt., SF, Routes 7 & 20, Lee/Lenox		X	X				X
Pittsfield SF, West Street, Pittsfield	X	X	X		X	X	X
Savoy Mt.-Florida SF, Rt. 2, Florida	X	X	X		X	X	X
Tolland Otis S, Rts. 8 & 23, Otis	X	X	X		X	X	X
Windsor SF, Rt. 16, Savoy		X	X		X	X	X
Franklin County:							
Erving SF, Rt. 2, Erving	X	X	X		X	X	X
Mohawk Trail SF, Rt. 2, Charlemont	X	X	X		X	X	X
Hampden County:							
Granville S, Rt. 57, Granville		X	X		X	X	X
Hampshire County:							
D.A.R. SF, Rt. 9, Goshen	X	X	X		X	X	X X

All campsites are open to the public on an unreserved basis, limited to a two-week period between the last Saturday in June and the Saturday before Labor Day. Register at the camp headquarters and pay a rental fee of about $3.00 to $5.00 per night. Abide by the local rules and enjoy all the facilities!

Private Campgrounds
in Western Massachusetts

Camping area Location	B	F	H	L	P	S	T
Berkshire County:							
Bonnie Brae, Rt. 7, Pittsfield		X	X	X	X	X	X
Camp Karu, Washington Mt. Rd., Washington				X	X	X	X
Camp Overflow, PO Box 150, Otis	X	X			X		
Camp Thunderbird, Rt. 71, N. Egremont		X	X		X	X	X
Chilson's Pond, Rt. 2, Florida				X	X	X	
Lauren Ridge Farm, Old Blandford Rd., E. Otis	X	X	X	X	X	X	X
Prospect Lake, Rts. 23 & 71, N. Egremont	X	X	X	X	X	X	
Shady Pines, Loop Rd. (Rt. 116), Savoy		X			X	X	X
Skyview, Old Middlefield Rd., Washington		X				X	X
Franklin County:							
Barton Cove, Rt. 2, Gill	X	X			X	X	
Bernardston KOA, off Rt. I-91, Bernardston		X				X	
Colony Travel, Rt. 5, Whately						X	
Lakeridge, Jct. Rts. 122 & 202, Orange	X	X			X	X	X
Lake Wyola, off Rt. 202, Shutesbury	X	X				X	X
Mohawk Park, Rt. 2, Charlemont	X	X				X	X
Pikes Camping, Rt. 2, Charlemont	X	X	X		X	X	X
Sleepy Hollow, off Shutesbury Rd., E. Leverett		X			X	X	X
Springbrook, Tower Rd., Shelburne						X	X
Wagon Wheel, Wendell Depot Rd., Orange						X	X
White Birch, North St., Whately		X				X	X
Hampden County:							
Frain-Derosa, Rt. 19, Wales						X	X
Golden Acres, Rts. 20 & 202, Southwick		X				X	
Long-Vue, Rt. 20, Brimfield						X	
Partridge Hollow, Sutcliffe Rd., Monson		X			X	X	X
Quinnebaug Cove, off Rt. 20, Brimfield	X	X			X	X	X
Sodom Mt., Rt. 57, Southwick						X	
Sunnyside, Rts. 10 & 202, Westfield						X	
Sunsetview Farm, Tower Farm Road						X	X
Walker Island, Rt. 20, Chester		X				X	X
Hampshire County:							
Berkshire Green Acres, Grant St., Plainfield						X	X
Berkshire Park, Old Post Rd., Worthington		X				X	X
Cummington Farm, South Rd., Cummington					X	X	X
Mountain View, Rt. 9, W. Cummington	X	X			X		
Windy Acres, South Rd., Westhampton						X	X

Maple Sugaring in Western Massachusetts

Ever had hot, pure maple syrup on cold, clean snow? It is surely one of the rites of spring practiced in Western Massachusetts, a delicacy in a class all its own! You can see maple syrup being made (about 35-60 gallons of sap for one gallon of syrup) on many farms throughout the area, and are welcome to visit these maple camps during the Maple Sugaring season (mid-March to early April) that the Pioneer Valley Association in cooperation with the Massachusetts Maple Producers' Association of Shelburne, has identified:

1. **Berkshire County:** Newton's Maple Sugar House, Baily Road (off of Route 71), Lanesborough, 413/443-4235; Sunset Farm, Tyringham Road, Tyringham, 243-3229; West Wind Farm, Washington Mountain Road, Washington, 623-8348.

2. **Franklin County:** Beaver Meadow Farm, Baptist Corner Road (off Route 116), Ashfield 625-6559: Howes Sugar House, Route 112, Ashfield, 628-3296; Lesure Farm, off Route 116 (Four miles west of town), Ashfield—be sure to check out their Maple Sugaring Museum!, 628-3268; Roger Scott, Apple Valley Road, (off of Route 112), Ashfield, 625-2250; River Maple Farm, Route 5, Bernardston, 648-9676; A. N. Purington & Son, E. Hawley Road (off of Route 112), Buckland, 625-2780; Roy A. Hicks, Maxwell Road (off of Route 8A), Charlemont, 339-4787; Hill House Farm, Warner Hill Road (right at three-way fork on Route 8A), Charlemont, 339-8348; Hager Bros., Heath Road, Griswoldville in Colrain, 624-3214; W. R. Hillman & Son, Adamsville Road, Colrain, 624-3310; Harold Truesdell, Jacksonville Road (Route 112), Colrain, 624-3980; Boyden Bros., Route 116, Conway, 369-4637; Burnett's Sugar House, Route 116, Conway, 369-4626; Kenneth Graves, Sr., Bardwells Ferry Road (off of Route 116), 369-4490; Hickory Ridge Farm, Hickory Ridge Road (off of Route 116), Conway, 369-4447; Walter Truce, South Shirkshire Road (off of Route 116), Conway, 625-6840 (after 7:00 p.m.); Harold White, Jr., West Hawley Road (Route 8A), West Hawley, 339-4426; Elmer L. Sherman, Judd Road (off of Route 8A), Heath, 337-4855; R. Carlyle Field & Sons, Long Plain Road (Route 63), Leverett, 549-1788; Don Herron, Glen Road, Leyden, 772-0083; Herbert H. Maynard, Winchester Road (off of Route 63), Northfield, 498-2403; Philip Johnson, Wheeler Avenue (off of Route 2A), Orange, 617/544-3614; Gerald A. Truesdell, Hoosic Tunnel Road (off of Route 2), Rowe, 413/339-4780; Davenport's Sugar House, Little Mohawk Road via signs (off of Route 2), Shelburne, 625-2866; Gould's Sugar House, Route 2, Shelburne, 625-6170; Graves' Sugar House, Wilson Graves Road (off of Route 2), Shelburne, 625-6174; Mt. Toby Sugar House, Route 47, Sunderland, 665-3127; Mt. Esther Sugar House, Haydenville Road (west at Whately Inn), Whately, 665-4973; Bob Bergeron, Whately, 532-4530.

3. **Hampden County** Maple Corner Farm, Beech Hill Road (off of Route 23), Blandford, 357-8829; Windy Mountain Farm, Birch Hill Road, Blandford, 848-2277; Countryside Farm, Burthill Road (off of Route 57), Tolland, 258-4412; Little Red Sugar House, Colebrook River Road (off of Route 57), Tolland, 258-4457.

4. **Hampshire County:** Hubbard Farm, Route 116 (next to State Fish Hatchery), Amherst, 549-1894; Ledge Line Farm, South Street, Chesterfield, 296-4745; Wilma's Little Sugar House, Sugarhill Road (off of Route 143), Chesterfield, 296-4275; Alfred Morey, Cummington Hill (off of Route 9), Cummington, 634-5441; Snow's Sugar House, between Routes 9 and 116, 634-5415; Francis Wells, Cummington Hill, Cummington, 634-5342; Hillwood Farm, Route 9, Goshen, 268-7036; Twin Maples, one mile west of center, Goshen, 268-7124; Walter Steins, Church Road (off Route 66), Huntington, 667-5792; Leo Aloisi, North Road three miles west of Leeds PO), Westhampton, 527-0710; Daniel B. Krug, North West Road (off of Routes 66 and 9), Westhampton, 527-9408; Philip J. Norris & Sons, South Road, Westhampton, 527-5887; Mahlon K. Parsons, Easthampton Road, Westhampton, 527-1342; Paul's Little Sugar House, Route 9, Williamsburg, 268-7063; Robert D. Carr, Cummington Road (off of Routes 142 and 112), Worthington, 238-5504; Cook Family, Bashan Hill Road (off of Route 143), Worthington, 238-5827; Echo Valley Farm, Route 112, Worthington, 238-5518; Windy Hill Farm, Sam Hill Road (off of Route 112), Worthington, 238-5869.

Massachusetts Audubon Society

"Conservation, education, and research" are the key concerns of the Massachusetts Audubon Society. Headquartered in Lincoln, Massachusetts (telephone: 617/259-9500) it is one of the oldest conservation groups in the world, the largest in New England. It is a nonprofit organization dependent upon volunteers with a goal "to educate the public about the environment so that they can act intelligently at national, state, and local levels."

This book has dealt with three Massachusetts Audubon wildlife sanctuaries and nature centers:
1. Arcadia Wildlife Sanctuary in Easthampton, Hampshire County. Telephone: 413/584-3009.
2. Laughing Brook Education Center in Hampden, Hampden County. Telephone: 566-3571.
3. Pleasant Valley Wildlife Sanctuary at Lenox, Berkshire County. Telephone: 637-0320.

People wishing specific information on tours and programs should contact each sanctuary directly. For more information about the Society and a free map of its sanctuaries across the state, contact Massachusetts Audubon Society in Lincoln, 01773.

The Mohawk Trail

The state's Route 2, the Mohawk Trail, calls itself "The Highway of History"—the four-season vacation area. Running 63 miles from Greenfield to North Adams east to west, the legendary Indian trail has over 50,000 acres of state forests, parks, and reservations for recreational enjoyment, in addition to some of the most breathtaking views in New England. Of particular note is the spectacular fall foliage, Greenfield Mountain, *Hail to the Sunrise* monument, Hairpin Turn at Clarksburg (where Mt. Greylock can be seen to the southwest, the Green Mountains of Vermont to the northwest), and Western and Whitcomb summits, the latter being the highest point on the trail at 2,100 feet. There are numerous places to visit along the Mohawk Trail, as indicated separately in the various town write-ups in this book. For more information on the Mohawk Trail itself, contact Pat Fritz, Executive Director of the Mohawk Trail Association in Charlemont, 01339. Telephone: 413/339-4962.

Native Sons and Daughters
of Western Massachusetts

Allen, Joel Asaph (1838-1921) Springfield. Author, zoologist, and curator of birds at the Harvard Museum of Comparative Zoology and the American Museum of Natural History in New York.

Allen, William (1784-1868) Pittsfield. Congregational clergyman, educator, and author who served as president of Dartmouth and Bowdoin Colleges and who compiled, in 1809, the *American Biographical and Historical Dictionary.*

Anthony, Susan Brownell (1820-1906) Adams. Social

reformer involved in temperance, anti-slavery, and women's rights movements who served as president of the National Woman Suffrage Association from 1890-1900.

Bancroft, Edward (1744-1821) Westfield. Secret agent who started his career by volunteering his services as a spy for Benjamin Franklin during the American Revolution.

Barnard, Frederick Augustus Porter (1809-1889) Sheffield. Educator who, as president of Columbia College, did so much to advance higher education for women that Barnard College was named after him.

Beach, Alfred Ely (1826-1896) Springfield. Owner of *Scientific American* magazine, plus a patenter of a regular typewriter, a typewriter for the blind, a cable railway system, and pneumatic tube systems.

Beach, Moses Sperry (1822-1892) Springfield. Owner of *New York Sun* newspaper, inventor of a web press and a cutting device for continuous printing on rolls of paper, and the first to print simultaneously on both sides of paper.

Bellamy, Edward (1850-1898) Chicopee Falls. Journalist and author concerned with social reform, Bellamy wrote the utopian novel *Looking Backward, 2000-1887,* established the *Nationalist* and the *New Nation,* and as such influenced the Populist Party of 1892.

Benjamin, Asher (1773-1845) Greenfield. Architect of the Carew and Alexander houses in Springfield, the Old South Meeting House in Windsor, Vermont, and the First Congregational Church in Bennington, Vermont. Benjamin was also the author of illustrated guide books on architecture.

Boltwood, Bertram Borden (1870-1927) Amherst. Scientist with a specialty in the field of radioactivity, discoverer of the element ionium.

Bowles, Chester Bliss (1901-) Springfield. Statesman who served as governor of Connecticut and ambassador to India and Nepal.

Bowles, Samuel II. (1826-1878) Springfield. Editor who carried to great heights his father's newspaper, the *Springfield Republican,* by his independent reportage. Through the newspaper's offices, one of the first schools for journalism was opened in the 1880s.

Bridgman, Herbert Lawrence (1844-1924) Amherst. A journalist, Bridgman was business manager for the *Brooklyn Standard Union* from 1887-1924. He was a friend and patron of arctic explorer Robert Peary, and was the first person notified of the 1909 discovery of the North Pole.

Brown, Henry Billings (1836-1913) South Lee. Justice of the Supreme Court named by President William Henry Harrison, Brown was the nation's foremost authority on maritime law in his day.

Brown, Henry Kirke (1814-1886) Leyden. Sculptor of the equestrian statues of Washington and Lincoln at West Point and the Capitol, Generals Winfield Scott and Nathaniel Green in Washington, and *Angel of the Resurrection* at the Greenwood Cemetery.

Bryant, William Cullen (1794-1878) Cummington. Poet best known for his work *Thanatopsis,* Bryant was editor and part owner of the *New York Evening Post.*

Chapin, Chester William (1798-1883) Ludlow. Railroad promoter who developed the Connecticut River Valley Railroad, serving as its president from 1850-54, then president of the Boston and Albany Railroad from 1854-77.

Clark, Alvan (1804-1887) Ashfield. Astronomer and, with his sons, telescope lens-maker of the 26-inch lens for the US Naval Observatory, the 30-inch lens for the Pulkovo Observatory in Russia, and the 36-inch lens for the Lick Observatory at Mt. Hamilton, California.

Clark, Hubert Lyman (1870-1947) Amherst. Zoologist on the staff of the Museum of Comparative Zoology at Harvard; associate professor of zoology at the university.

Conwell, Russell Herman (1843-1925) South Worthington. Lawyer and clergyman who founded the *Minneapolis Daily Chronicle* and the *Somerset Journal,* Conwell was the first president of Temple University in Pennsylvania. He is famous for his "Acres of Diamonds" speech.

Cross, Whitman (1854-1949) Amherst. A member of the US Geological Survey from 1880, he is the person for whom the mineral crossite was named.

Davis, George Breckenridge (1847-1914) Ware. Army officer and author of books on international and military law.

Davis William Stearns (1877-1930) Amherst. Author and educator, his books have included *A Friend of Caesar, A Day in Old Athens, The Roots of the War, Life on a Medieval Barony,* and *Europe Since Waterloo*

Dawes, Henry Laurens (1816-1903) Cummington. Public official who served in both the House and Senate, a supporter of daily weather bulletins that eventually became the National Weather Service, and author of the 1887 Dawes Act to help Indian status.

Day, Benjamin Henry (1810-1889) West Springfield. Printer, journalist, and publisher-owner of the *New York Sun,* which at one point had the highest circulation in the world—catering to the workingman. Day introduced the use of newsboys and pioneered street vending.

DeMille, Cecil Blount (1881-1959) Ashfield. Motion picture director and producer whose *The Squaw Man* was the first full-length movie made in Hollywood. Others of his pictures included: *The Ten Commandments, King of Kings, Sign of the Cross, Cleopatra, The Crusades* and *The Greatest Show on Earth* (Academy Award for best picture, 1952).

Dickinson, Emily Elizabeth (1830-1886) Amherst. One of America's foremost poets, Emily Dickinson was the author of several series of poems which were published posthumously.

Dickinson, Jonathan (1688-1747) Hatfield. A leading clergy defender of Presbyterianism, he helped obtain the charter for the College of New Jersey (Princeton), serving as its first president in 1747.

Dodge, Theodore Ayrault (1842-1909) Pittsfield. Military historian and army officer, Dodge was the author of biographies of war leaders such as Alexander the Great, Hannibal, Caesar, and Napoleon.

DuBois, William Edward Burghardt (1868-1963) Great Barrington. Founder of the Niagra Movement that led to the establishment of the National Association for the Advancement of Colored People (NAACP), editor of the *Encyclopedia of the Negro,* DuBois was an author and reform leader who was highly influential in promoting black independence both in the US and in Africa.

Durant, Thomas Clark (1820-1885) Lee. Railroad official and financier, president of the Credit Mobilier of America, Durant took a leading role in organizing and constructing the Union Pacific Railroad, linking it with the Central Pacific in 1869.

Durant, Will (1885-) North Adams. Educator and, with his wife Ada Kaufman Durant (Ariel), author of *The Story of Civilization* and the Pulitzer Prize-winning *Rousseau and Revolution* of 1967.

Durocher, Leo Ernest (1906-) West Springfield. Baseball great, both as player of the NY Yankees, St. Louis Cardinals, and Brooklyn Dodgers, then as Dodger and NY Giant manager; also a sports announcer on television.

Dwight, Harrison Gray Otis (1803-1862) Conway. Congregational missionary to the Armenians from 1834-62.

Dwight, Timothy (1752-1817) Northampton. The grandson of Jonathan Edwards and a religious leader in his own right. Dwight was the author of poems and travel books, one of the "Hartford Wits" (as was his brother Theodore (1764-1846), and an educator who served as president of Yale from 1795-1817.

Edwards, Jonathan (1745-1801) Northampton. Son of the famous theologian of the same name, this Jonathan Edwards was president of Union College in Schenectady, New York.

Edwards, Pierpont (1750-1826) Northampton. Another of Jonathan Edwards' sons. Pierpont was a delegate to the Continental Congress from Connecticut, judge of District Court in that state, and a member of the Constitutional Convention in 1818.

Fairbanks, Thaddeus (1796-1886) Brimfield. Inventor of the first platform scale, Fairbanks formed what became the Fairbanks Scale Company in 1874.

Fairchild, James Harris (1817-1902) Stockbridge. Taught at and then became president of Oberlin College from 1866-1889.

Field, Cyrus West (1819-1892) Stockbridge. Businessman and financier involved in laying a transatlantic cable, Field later became president of the NY Elevated Railway Company, and was responsible for bringing the rapid-transit system to New York City.

Field, Erastus Salisbury (1805-1900) Leverett. Painter of portraits and scenes from mythology and biblical history, Field was an outstanding 19th century American folk artist. One of his most famous pieces, the *Historical Monument of the Amercian Republic,* is housed in Springfield's Museum of Fine Arts.

Field, Henry Martin (1822-1907) Stockbridge. Another son of lawyer David Dudley Field of International Code fame, and a clergyman and editor of the *Evangelist.*

Field, Marshall (1834-1906) Conway. Organized Marshall Field and Company of Chicago, which became the largest wholesale and retail dry-goods establishment in the world. He gave the grounds for the University of Chicago site and funds for the Columbian Museum at the Chicago World's Fair of 1893, which later became the Field Museum of Natural History.

Finklehoffe, Fred (1911-1977) Springfield. A playwright and producer, he was the co-author of *The Egg and I* and the screenplay author of *Meet Me in St. Louis, Babes on Broadway, Strike Up the Band, Best Foot Forward,* and *Brother Rat.*

Foster, Johns Wells (1815-1873) Brimfield. A geologist who assisted in the surveys of Ohio (1837) and Lake Superior and conducted paleontological and ethnological studies in the Mississippi Valley.

Fowler, Harold North (1859-1955) Westfield. Teacher and translator of Greek and Latin classics.

Fuller, George (1822-1884) Deerfield. Artist with paintings in Worcester and the Metropolitan Museum in New York.

Geisel, Theodor Seuss (1904-) Springfield. Known as Dr. Seuss, the author and illustrator of political cartoons, Academy Award-winning film documentaries, and educational children's books such as *The Cat in the Hat,* Geisel is the president of Beginner Books.

Gillet, Frederick Huntington (1851-1935) Westfield. Lawyer and public official who served for 32 years in the House of Representatives, where he supported economy in government, the merit system of civil service, and constructive partisanship.

Goodale, Elaine (1863-1953) and Dora Read (1866-1953) Berkshire County. Sisters, both were poets.

Goodrich, Chauncey (1836-1925) Hinsdale. Missionary to China from 1865 until his death in 1925.

Hall, Granville Stanley (1844-1924) Ashfield. Psychologist and educator, Hall established one of the first psychological laboratories in the U.S., was the first president of the American Psychological Association, edited various psychological journals, and was the first president of Clark University, where he founded the first institute of child psychology in the country and established graduate studies for education and pyschology.

Harding, Chester (1792-1866) Conway. Portrait painter whose works of Daniel Boone, Robert Owen, John C. Calhoun, Timothy Pickering, Daniel Webster, John Marshall, and General William T. Sherman today hang in major galleries throughout the country.

Hayden Ferdinand Vandeveer (1829-1887) Westfield. Geologist whose explorations and scientific investigations in the West were forerunners of the 1879 US Geological Survey and the 1872 establishment of Yellowstone National Park.

Hitchcock, Edward (1793-1864) Deerfield. State geologist of Vermont, professor of chemistry and natural history and later president of Amherst College, Hitchcock conducted a geological survey of the state, investigating dinosaur tracks in Connecticut Valley sandstone.

Holland, Josiah Gilbert (1819-1881) Belchertown. Author and editor of a book on Western Massachusetts, also wrote poetry, moral essays, lectures, and novels. He helped found and was the first editor of *Scribner's Monthly* (later, *The Century*).

Hooker, Joseph (1814-1879) Hadley. Known as "Fighting Joe," a soldier who saw action in the Seminole Wars, Mexican War, Peninsular Campaign of 1862, Williamsburg, South Mountain and Antietam, retiring as a Major General in 1868.

Hopkins, Mark (1802-1887) Stockbridge. Philosopher of the puritanical "gospel of wealth" school, a professor of moral philosophy and rhetoric at Williams College, then its president from 1826-1872.

Hosmer, James Kendall (1834-1927) Northfield. Unitarian minister and author.

Huntington, Frederic Dan (1819-1904) Hadley. A Protestant Episcopal bishop who was ordained a priest in 1861 and was a consecrated bishop of central New York in

1869. (See the Porter-Phelps-Huntington House in Hadley).

Jackson, Helen Hunt (1831-1885) Amherst. Writer of poems and books, her most famous one being *Ramona,* telling of the plight of American Indians in old California.

Jones, Anson (1798-1858) Great Barrington. President of the Republic of Texas.

Lyon, Mary Mason (1797-1849) Buckland. Educator and champion of higher education for women, she founded the Mount Holyoke Female Seminary at South Hadley in 1837 and served as its principal for 12 years.

MacArthur, Arthur (1845-1912) Chicopee Falls. The father of General Douglas MacArthur, a soldier himself known as "Boy Colonel of the West," he was cited many times, earned the Congressional Medal of Honor, and retired a Lieutenant General of the Army.

Mann, Horace (1796-1859) Franklin. An educator and public official who served in both the House and Senate, best known for his accomplishments as an educational reformer in Massachusetts, then president of Antioch College in Yellow Springs, Ohio. Mann was elected to the American Hall of Fame in 1900.

Mason, Mary Knight (1857-1944) Easthampton. Composer of such songs as "Ashes of Roses," "Egyptian Love Song," "Song of Joy," "Songs of Sleep," and "Songs of Tangier."

McKay, Gordon (1821-1903) Pittsfield. Inventor who purchased the patent on and perfected the machine for sewing soles onto shoes.

Mead, George Herbert (1863-1931) South Hadley. Philosopher and social psychologist of the behaviorist/pragmatic school, author of *Mind, Self and Society,* published posthumously in 1934.

Miller, William (1782-1849) Pittsfield. Religious leader, master of the apocalyptic theme, author of *Evidence from Scripture and History of the Second Coming of Christ, About the Year 1843.* Inspired Millerite Movement of Adventism.

Moody, Dwight Lyman (1837-1899) East Northfield. Evangelist who conducted national and international tours to support the YMCA and foreign missions, the Northfield Seminary for girls (1879) and Mount Hermon School for boys (1881), and the Chicago (later Moody) Bible Institute (1889).

Morgan, Junius Spencer (1813-1890). West Springfield. Organizer and president of the J. S. Morgan Company, he was a benefactor of the New York Metropolitan Museum of Art and other institutions and father of John Pierpont Morgan ("J. P." 1837-1913), who became president of the Met and a renowned collector of art and rare books.

Murphy, Lambert (1885-1954) Springfield. Operatic tenor who sang with the Metropolitan Opera Company from 1911-15, as well as teaching and making concert appearances.

Perry, Bliss (1860-1954) Williamstown. Professor of English at Williams, Princeton, and Harvard, editor of the *Atlantic Monthly* from 1899-1909, and author of books about poetry and poets.

Pomeroy, Seth (1706-1777) Northampton. A volunteer at Bunker Hill, commissioned as a Brigadier General in the Continental Army, this American Revolution officer's "Journals" form an important document on 18th century Bay State history.

Reid, Rober (1862-1929) Stockbridge. A painter with works in the Corcoran Art Gallery in Washington, District of Columbia, and the Metropolitan Museum of Art in New York City.

Rice, William Marsh (1816-1900) Springfield. Merchant and philanthropist whose profitable store in Houston, Texas, led him to bequeath his fortune to what became Rice Institute in 1912.

Riddell, John L. (1807-1865) Leyden. Inventor of the binocular microscope.

Ripley, George (1802-1880) Greenfield. Editor of *Specimens of Foreign Standard Literature,* the transcendentalists' *Dial,* and Brook Farm's *Harbinger.* Ripley also was literary critic of the *New York Tribune,* founder of *Harper's New Monthly Magazine,* producer (with Charles Dana) of the 16-volume *New American Cyclopedia,* and president from 1872 until his death of the Tribune Association.

Shaw, Henry Wheeler (1818-1885) Lanesborough. Humorist known as "Johs Billings" who wrote for the *New York Weekly,* published several books, and contributed to *Century* magazine under the name "Uncle Esek."

Sibley, Hiram (1807-1888) North Adams. Businessman and financier, president of the Western Union Telegraph Company (in 1861 having the first transcontinental telegraph line), and benefactor of the Sibley College of Mechanic Arts at Cornell University and Sibley Hall at the University of Rochester.

Strong, Caleb (1745-1819) Northampton. One of the first two persons elected to the Senate from Massachusetts (1789-96), Strong later served as governor of the commonwealth from 1800-07 and 1812-16.

Symington, Stuart (1901-) Amherst. First Secretary of the Air Force (1947-50), later serving in the Senate from the state of Missouri.

Tappan, Arthur (1786-1865) Northampton. With his brother Lewis (1788-1873), Tappan was a philantropist and social reformer, founder of the Mercantile Agency (the first rating agency for commercial credit in the country) and the *New York Journal of Commerce.* The Tappans were deeply involved in the abolitionist movement, Arthur being president of the American Anti-Slavery Society and founder of *The Emancipator* and *National ERA* journals and the American Missionary Association.

Thomas, Albert Ellsworth (1872-1947) Chester. Playwright and journalist.

Thompson, James Walter (1847-1928) Pittsfield. A name synonymous with advertising, as Thompson entered the field and revolutionized it, increasing advertising 300 percent from 1880-90, representing such companies as Eastman Kodak, Pabst Blue Ribbon, and Prudential Insurance.

Thorndike, Edward Lee (1874-1949) Williamsburg. Educator and psychologist, Thorndike was a teacher at Columbia Teachers' College who pioneered in the field of experimental and animal psychology, devised standard testing measurements and intelligence tests for the Army during World War I, and wrote widely in both books and journals.

Thorpe, Thomas Bangs (1815-1878) Westfield. Humorist who was both a painter (*Ichabod Crane*) and writer (*The Big Bear of Arkansas*), as well as co-owner and editor of the *Spirit of the Times* in New York.

Tyler, John Mason (1851-1929) Amherst. Biologist and author of books on evolution.

Wade, Benjamin Franklin (1800-1878) Springfield. Lawyer and public official, member of the Senate from Ohio, he was co-sponsor of the Wade-Davis Bill declaring reconstruction of the Southern state governments a legislative concern and condemning Lincoln's usurpation of powers.

Warner, Charles Dudley (1829-1900) Plainfield. Author of essays, travel books, and (with his neighbor, Mark Twain) of *The Gilded Age.* Warner was editor of the *Hartford Evening Press,* the 22-volume *American Men of Letters* series, co-editor of the 30-volume *Library of the World's Best Literature,* and contributing editor to *Harper's New Monthly Magazine.*

Warner, Francis Emory (1844-1929) Hinsdale. First governor of the state of Wyoming (1890), he was known as the "Father of Reclamation" for his interest in arid lands. Warren's daughter Helen married General John J. Pershing.

Wells, David Ames (1828-1898) Springfield. Economist and author, chairman of the National Revenue Commission under President Abraham Lincoln and an adviser on tariff matters to Presidents Garfield and Cleveland, Wells was head of the NY State Tax Commmission and member of the board of arbitration of the Associated Railways; he was internationally recognized for his work in economics.

Whiting, William Fairfield (1864-1936) Holyoke. President of the Whiting Paper Company, he succeeded Herbert Hoover in 1928 as U.S. Secretary of Commerce.

Whitney, Josiah Dwight (1819-1896) Northampton. Geology author and educator, he taught at Iowa, California, and the Lawrence Scientific School at Harvard. Josiah Dwight was the discoverer of what became known as the Calaveras (California) skull in 1886.

Whitney, William Collings (1841-1904) Conway. Businessman and public official who helped break up Boss Tweed's "Ring" in New York City, served as corporation counsel there, and was Secretary of the Navy under Grover Cleveland, when he modernized it as a military force.

Whitney, William Dwight (1827-1894) Northampton. Younger brother of Josiah, he was a linguist who was a professor of Sanskrit and philology at Yale, served as editor-in-chief of the six-volume *Century Dictionary,* and was the first president of the American Philological Association.

Wright, Chauncey (1830-1875) Northampton. Philosopher and mathematician, Wright was a member of the American Academy of Arts and Sciences and the Metaphysical Club of Cambridge, in addition to being a supporter of Darwin, a precursor of the pragmatic movement, and an exponent of John Stuart Mills utilitarianism.

Yale, Linus (1821-1868) Shelburne. Inventor and manufacturer of Yale Lock Manufacturing Company, making bank and dial locks and small cylinder locks that became known as "Yale locks."

Old Sturbridge Village

A living history museum re-creating a New England town of the early 1800s, **Old Sturbridge Village** (OSV) in Sturbridge, Massachusetts, is an educational, nonprofit center covering 200 acres with more than 40 restored houses, gardens, craft shops, meetinghouses, and mills and a farm. Its collections, exhibits, and programs present the story of everyday life in a small New England town during the years 1790 to 1840.

OSV's express purpose is: "to provide modern Americans with a deepened understanding of their own times through a personal encounter with the New England past. Old Sturbridge Village offers a historical perspective on the present based on the preservation and re-creation of the acts, thoughts, and material resources of those who lived in rural New England in the early 19th century."

The museum was first opened in 1946 by Albert B. Wells and Joel Cheney Wells, executives at the American Optical Company in Sturbridge, Massachusetts. In the early 20th century, the Wells family had opened to the public the Wells Historical Museum, which housed their collection of antiques. Eventually the collection outgrew the quarters of the original museum, and the family decided to display their objects in a setting that would reveal how they were made and originally used; thus, the idea of a museum village—Old Sturbridge Village—developed.

At the heart of the early 19th century New England community was the Center Village, with houses, shops, stores, and meetinghouses clustered around a common. Some of the OSV buildings include:

1. **A country bank**—which usually issued its own bank notes and made loans to merchants, farmers, and manufacturers
2. **Blacksmith Shop**—made and repaired farm implements and other hardware, and usually shod oxen and horses for farmers
3. **Carding mill**—one of the steps in the cloth-making process
4. **Center Meeting House**—where worshippers would gather each Sunday; also, the site of town meetings, elections, lectures, political events, and musical performances
5. **Cider Mill**—pressing apples into the favorite domestic beverage

6. **Clock gallery**—an extensive collection of clocks and timepieces
7. **Cooper Shop**—the making of staved containers, like barrels, and pails was one of the many woodworking skills
8. **District School**—an ungraded school
9. **Fitch House**—furnished as the home of a country printer's family
10. **Freeman Farm**—a typical 70-acre farm
11. **Grant Store**—offering 20th century shopping
12. **Gristmill**—waterpowered mill, grinding rye and corn into flour and meal
13. **Knight Store**—a rural store
14. **Law office**—usually dealing with property litigation, inheritance, and debt collection
15. **Pottery**—redware pottery
16. **Powder House**—stored powder and ammunition used by town militia companies
17. **Printing Office**—for printing, binding, and selling books, broadsides, bills, and pamphlets
18. **Richardson House/Parsonage**—the minister's home
19. **Sawmill**—predecessor of the modern water turbine, where logs are cut into boards and planks for further shaping or for use in building
20. **Shoe Shop**—producing footwear for distant markets
21. **Society of Friends Meeting House**—Quakers
22. **Tin Shop**—making tin products
23. **Town Pound**—confined livestock found running at large or in other farmers' fields until they could be reclaimed by their owners
24. **Town House**—a Federal-type dwelling

In addition, meals are available in the Bullard Tavern year-round. Telephone: 617/347-3362. New England crafts and gifts are available at the Museum Gift Shop.

There are Special Events and programs planned throughout the year, such as: the George Washington's Birthday celebration, maple sugaring, Wool Days, Independence Day activities, Garden Days, cider making at the Cider Mill, fall foliage, turkey shoots, magic shows, family workshops, Dinner in a Country Village, antiques identification and care, Thanksgiving Weekend, concerts, spinning, hog butchering, Town Meeting, historic wood finishing, Militia Day, haying contests, and seasonal exhibits.

More than 500,000 people from all over the United States and the world visit OSV each year. Approximately 400 individuals are employed there during the summer months, 325 during the winter, and there are also many volunteers. The staff is made up of historically costumed men and women who interpret a past way of life.

Admission prices for 1987 are $9.50 for adults, $4.00 for children 6 to 15; under 6 admitted free. Prices are subject to change, and group rates are available. All major credit cards are honored. Leashed pets are welcome, but must be carried in all buildings. Visitor services include restrooms, telephones, first aid, security, and lost and found. Conferences, weddings, social and business gatherings can all be arranged.

Open year-round: Fall 9:00 a.m. to 5:00 p.m. daily through the end of October; winter, 10:00 a.m. to 4:00 p.m. until early April (closed Mondays); spring and summer,

9:00 a.m. to 5:00 p.m. It is closed winter Mondays, Christmas, and New Year's Day. The Village is located on Route 20 West in Sturbridge. It can be reached by car via I-84's exit 3 or Massachusetts Turnpike's exit 9. Parking is free. There is bus service from Boston on Peter Pan Lines. Telephone: 617/426-7838. Amtrak train service to Worcester from New York and Boston. Telephone: 800/872-7245. By air, you might fly into Bradley International Airport at Hartford/Springfield or Worcester Airport.

Lodging is available at the Old Sturbridge Village Motor Lodge and the Oliver Wright House (Telephone: 617/347-3327) or any number of hotels or bed and breakfast places nearby.

For more information on Old Sturbridge Village, write them at Sturbridge, Massachusetts 01566. Telephone: 617/347-3362.

The Society for the Preservation of New England Antiquities

The initials SPNEA after certain buildings listed in this architectural, educational, historic, and recreational guide, indicate properties of the Society for the Preservation of New England Antiquities. The oldest and largest regional preservation organization in the nation, SPNEA is located at the Harrison Gray Otis House, 141 Cambridge Street, Boston MA 02114. Telephone: 617/227-3956. The Society owns and maintains over 60 historic properties throughout New England, many of them open to the public from June 1 through September 30 on Tuesday, Thursday, and Sunday afternoons from 1:00 p.m. to 5:00 p.m. unless otherwise noted. Its Western Massachusetts holdings include:

1. Alexander House, Linden Hall, (c. 1811), 284 State Street, Springfield.
2. Colton House, 787 Longmeadow Street, Longmeadow.
3. Merrell Tavern, South Lee.
4. Merwin House, Tranquility, (c. 1825), 39 Main Street, Stockbridge.

SPNEA members are admitted free of charge to the various buildings, as are children under 12 years of age when accompanied by an adult; otherwise, there is an admission of $.50 per person. The Society invites the public to "visit these tangible records of how past generations have lived."

Alpine/Downhill Ski Areas

Ski Area and Location		Facilities and facts	E	F	I	N	R	S	T
Berkshire East (413) 339-6617	Box O, South River Road Charlemont 01339 (On Mohawk Trail)	1,180-foot drop, 20 trails. "Most challenging terrain in the Berkshires."	X	X	X	X	X	X	3 chairs 1 t-bar, 1 j-bar
Berkshire Snow Basin (413) 634-8808	W. Cummington 01265 (18 m. east of Pittsfield on Route 9)	Open Wed.-Sun. & vacation weeks.		X	X		X	X	3 T-bars for different levels
Bousquet Ski Area (413) 442-2436	Tamarack Road Pittsfield 01201	One of oldest ski schools in U.S. Among first in New England to make snow.		X	X	X	X	X	1 chair 1 T-bar, 2 pomas 6 ropes
Brodie Mt. Ski Area (413) 443-4752	Route 7 New Ashford 01237	Claims largest single night skiing in the world. "Kelly's Irish Alps."	X	X	X	X	X	X	4 double chairs
Butternut Basin (413) 528-2000	Great Barrington 01230 (on Route 23)	Named for butternut trees all around area. Uphill capacity of 7,200 skiers/hour.		X	X	X	X	X	4 double chairs 1 triple chair 1 T-bar
Catamount (413) 528-1262 (518) 325-3200	Route 23, South Egremont Borders Hillsdale, NY	NASTAR races. Straddles Mass./NY border on Route 23		X	X	X	X	X	3 double chairs
Chickley Alps Ski Center (413) 339-4802	W. Hawley Road, Charlemont (Mass. 8A off Mass. 2)	Open weekends and holiday weeks.		X	X		X	X	3 ropes 1 T-bar
Eastover **(413) 637-0625**	East Street, Lenox 01240	Novice slopes for registered guests only.		X	X		X	X	1 chair 1 rope

Nordic/Cross-Country/Ski-Touring Areas

Ski Area and Location		Facilities and facts	E	F	N	R	S	T
Alice's at Avaloch (413) 637-0897	Rt. 183, 224 West Street Lenox 01240	Pkg. of lunch and 3 hr. instruction. Reserve 1 day in advance.		X	X		X	3 trails
Arcadia Wildlife Sanctuary (413) 584-3009	Easthampton	Open year-round during daylight hours.						5 miles
Blantyre (413) 637-0475	Rt. 20 & East St., Lenox (PO Box 717)	82 acres of land open to the public. Fine restaurant.		X				4-5 miles
Brodie Mt. Ski Area (413) 443-4752	Rt. 7, New Ashford 01237	Hundreds of acres of meadows, miles of woods.		X	X		X	Prepared.
Bucksteep Manor (413) 623-5535	Ski Touring Center at Camp Karu, Washington Mt. Road, Washington 01223	Weekend & holidays 8am-4pm, weekdays, 9am-4pm. Home cooking in lodge.		X	X		X	15 miles marked & groomed
Burt Hill Natural Area	Tolland	Magnificent views.				X	X	8 miles

Nordic/Cross-Country/Ski-Touring Areas (Continued)

Ski Area and Location		Facilities and facts	E	F	N	R	S	T
Butternut Ski Touring (413) 528-0610	Route 23, Great Barrington 01230	Part of Butternut Basin Ski area.		X		X		
Cummington Farm Ski Touring Center (413) 634-2111	South Rd., Cummington 01026 (off Rt. 9, W. of Northampton)	700 acres of farmland. Open daily. Full moon night tours. Special events. Season membership. Winter camping.	X	X	X		X	X 25 miles
Egremont Country Club (413) 528-4222 (413) 528-4232	Route 23, Great Barrington 01230	18-hole snow-covered golf course. 300 acres of trails.			X		X	
Egremont Inn (413) 528-2111	Old Sheffield Rd., S. Egremont (off Rt. 23)	200-yr. old inn, second oldest in Mass. Adjacent to network of 18 miles of trails.		X	X		X	7 miles
Flying Cloud Inn (413) 229-2113	Star Route 70, New Marlboro 01230 (12 m. se of Great Barrington)	Inn dates to 1771. Meals & Skiing for lodging guests only.						200 acres
Center at Foxhollow (413) 637-2000	Route 7, Lenox 01240	285-acre historic estate. Also—sliding, skating rink, horsedrawn sleighs.		X	X	X	X	Public.
Hitchock Center for Environment (413) 256-6006	525 S. Pleasant Street, Larch Hill, Amherst	Open to public.						19 acres
Jug End (413) 528-0434	Box 68X, S. Egremont 01258 (Routes 23 & 41)	Open weekends 9am-4pm.		X			X	8 miles
Laughing Brook (413) 566-3571	789 Main Street, Hampden 01036	Education center and wildlife sanctuary of Mass. Audubon. Former home of author Thornton Burgess.						84 acres for novices
Look Park (413) 584-5457	Route 9, Florence/ Northampton	200 acres of rec. pleasure. Open year-round.						Public.
Lost Wilderness Range, Inc. (413) 258-4872	Route 57, Sandisfield	Miles of unplowed roads.						Marked & maintained
Matt's Ski & Sport Shop (413) 562-9841 (413) 568-9002 shop	Route 20, Westfield	Daily 9am-4pm during ski-touring season.		X			X	15 miles
Northfield Mt. Ski Touring Center (413) 659-3713	Route 63, Northfield (10 min. from exit 27 on I-91)	Run by Northeast Utilities. Wed.-Sun. 9am-5:30 pm. 6 mi. snowshoe trails.		X			X	25 miles groomed & scenic
Notchview Reservation	Route 9, Windsor	3,000-acre preserve.						25 miles
Oak 'N Spruce Resort (413) 243-3500	Meadow St., S. Lee 01260	440 acres of woodland trails and open meadowland. Open 9am to dusk, weekends and holiday weeks.		X	X		X	Public.
Oak Ridge Ski Touring Center (413) 786-9693	Oak Ridge Golf Club South Westfield St., Feeding Hills/Agawam	Run by Paddlers and Packers, 1615 Riverdale Rd., W. Spfld. 413/737-0267. Open daily 9am-5pm.		X	X		X	15 miles
Otis Ridge Touring Center (413) 269-4444	Route 23, Otis 01253	Associated with Otis Ridge ski area.			X		X	3 miles

Nordic/Cross-Country/Ski-Touring Areas (Continued)

Ski Area and Location		Facilities and facts	E	F	N	R	S	T
Petersburg Pass	Route 2, w. of Williamstown	Williamsburg Outing Club, Box 627, Williamstown. Trail guide & map book. $1.25.						Novices & intermediates.
Pleasant Valley Wildlife Sanctuary (413) 637-0320	Dugway Road, Lenox 01240	700 acres of Mass. Aububon Society trails & museum. Wooded and open trails.						12 miles
Twining Lake Village Ski Touring Center (413) 258-4767	East Otis Road, Tolland 01034	Scenic area.						
Tyringham Cobble Reservation	Tyringham 01264	Owned by Trustees of Reservations. 222 acres of pasture and woodland.						
Wheatleigh (413) 637-0610	PO Box 824 West Hawthorne Street Lenox 01240	Year-round inn dating to 1894. 22 acres.						Practice area.
Wilder Ski Track (413) 783-4411	Veterans Golf Course, South Branch Pkwy., Springfield	Part of Wilder Family Outdoor Center (Carol and Jim Anderson). Club memberships. Open 9am-5pm daily.	X	X	X		X	10 km. groomed

Ski touring is also available at these state campgrounds: Beartown, Clarksburg, D.A.R., Erving, Granville, Greylock Mountain, Mohawk Trail State Forest, October Mountain, Pittsfield State Forest, Savoy, Tolland, Otis, and Windsor.

State Forests, Parks, and Reservations for Day Use

Many state forests, parks, and reservations are open to the public from May 1 through October 15, 10:00 a.m. to 8:00 p.m., with facilities other than camping. The general fee schedule is $2.00 for cars, $20.00 for buses, $15.00 for a seasonal pass, and $.25 for walk-ins. This fee covers the use of recreational facilities and the two-hour use of picnic facilities and fireplaces. There are special passes for senior citizens. Some of these areas in Western Massachusetts include:

State facility Location	B	F	H	P	S	T
Berkshire County:						
Bash Bish Falls State Forest (SF), Rts. 23 & 41, Mt. Washington		X	X			X
Campbells Falls SF, Rt., 272, Southfield, New Marlboro		X	X	X		X
Cookson Property, Rt. 183, New Marlboro		X	X			X
East Mt. SF, Rt. 23, Great Barrington			X		X	
Mt. Everett State Reservation, Mt. Washington		X				X
Otis SF, Rt. 23, Otis	X	X	X			X
Peru SF, Rt. 143, Peru		X	X			X
Sandisfield SF, Rt. 57, Sandisfield	X	X	X	X	X	X
Taconic Trail State Park (SP), Rt. 2, Williamstown						X
Wahconah Falls SP, Rts. 8A & 9, Dalton		X	X	X		X
West Lake Recreation Area, West Rd., Sandisfield	X	X	X			X
Franklin County:						
Catamount SF, Rts. 2 & 112, Colrain		X	X			X
Conway SF, Rt. 116, Conway		X	X			X
H. O. Cook SF, Rt. 8A, Colrain			X	X		X
Hawley SF, Rt. 8A, Hawley			X	X		X
Monroe S, Rt. 2, Monroe		X	X			X
Mt. Grace SF, Rt. 78, Warwick		X	X	X		X
Mt. Sugarloaf SR, Deerfield						X
Northfield SF, Rt. 2A, Northfield		X	X		X	
South River SF, Rt. 116, Conway		X	X	X		
Warwick SF, Athol Road, Warwick		X	X			X
Wendell SF, Wendell Rd., Wendell	X	X	X		X	X
Hampden County:						
Brimfield SF, Rt. 20 (Dean Pond), Brimfield		X	X	X	X	X
Chester SF, Rt. 20, Chester			X	X	X	X
Chicopee SP, Exit 6 off Mass. Tpk., Chicopee			X	X	X	X
Hampton Ponds, SP, Rt. 202, Westfield	X	X		X	X	
Holland SP, Rt. 20, Holland		X	X	X	X	
Ludlow SP, via Plumbley St. & Tower Rd., Ludlow				X		X
Robinson SP, North St., Feeding Hills, Agawam		X	X	X	X	X
Hampshire County:						
Deer Hill SP, Cummington/Plainfield						
Charles M. Gardner SP, Rt. 112, Huntington		X		X	X	X
Holyoke Range SP, Hadley, S. Hadley/Amherst/Granby						X
Skinner SP, Rt. 47, South Hadley				X		X

Key:
B—boating   P—picnicking
F—fishing   S—swimming
H—hunting   T—trails

Trustees of Reservations

The notation TOR after certain places in this guide signifies ownership and maintenance by the Trustees of Reservations, located at 224 Adams Street in Milton, MA 02186. Telephone: 617/698-2066. TOR is a privately administered charitable corporation that was founded in 1891 for conservation purposes and "to preserve for the public, beautiful and historical places and tracts of land within the Commonwealth of Massachusetts." Among its properties in the western part of the state, all fully described in this book, are:

1. Colonel John Ashley House, Ashley Falls/Sheffield
2. Bartholomew's Cobble Reservation, Ashley Falls on the Housatonic River, Sheffield
3. Bear Swamp Reservation, Ashfield
4. William Cullen Bryant Homestead, Route 112, Cummington
5. Chapelbrook Reservation, Williamsburg Road, South Ashfield
6. Chesterfield Gorge Reservation, River Road, West Chesterfield
7. Dinosaur Footprints Reservation, off Route 5, Holyoke
8. Glendale Falls Reservation, Middlefield
9. Mission House, Main Street, Stockbridge
10. Monument Mountain, Reservation, Route 7, Great Barrington
11. Naumkeag, Prospect Street, Stockbridge
12. Notchview Reservation, Route 9, Windsor
13. Petticoat Hill Reservation, south of Route 9, Williamsburg
14. Tyringham Cobble Reservation, off Route 102, Tyringham

Index

A
Adams 2
Agawam 42
Airports 98
Alexander House 55
Alford 2
Alpine slides 6, 49
Amherst 76
Amherst College 76
American International College 55
Appalachian National Scenic Trail 98
Apple Orchards 98
Arcadia Nature Center and Wildlife Sanctuary 82
Arena Civic Theatre 31
Armory Museum 55
"The Arsenal at Springfield" 56
Arrowhead 14
Ashfield 26
Ashley, Colonel John House 17
Aston Magna Foundation for Music 5

B
Balloon School of Massachusetts 43
Barrington Fair 5
Bartholomew's Cobble 17
Barton Cove Nature Area 30
Basketball Hall of Fame 57
Bay Path Junior College 50
Baystate Medical Center 62
Baystate West 57
Bear Swamp Project 5
Becket 2
Bed and Breakfasts 98
Belchertown 80
Bellamy Homestead 44
Bellefontaine 9
Bement School 28
Berkshire Athenaeum 14
Berkshire Balloonfest 81
Berkshire Community College 14
Berkshire Country Day School 9
Berkshire Garden Center 17
Berkshire Museum 14
Berkshire Scenic Railway 8
Berkshire School 17
Berkshire Theatre Festival 18
Bernardston 26
Blandford 43
Boats and snowmobiles 100
Bridge of Flowers 37
Brimfield 43
Bryant Homestead 82
Buckland 26
Buxton School 21

C
Campanile 59
Camping 102
Canoe Meadows Wildlife Sanctuary 15
Carnegie Library Museum 34
Chapelbrook 26
Clarlemont 27
Cheese Press 3
Cheshire 3
Chester 43
Chesterfield 81
Chesterwood 18
Chicopee 44
Child's Park 87
Children's Chime Tower 18
Children's Museum of Holyoke 47
Civic Center (Springfield) 58
Clapp Memorial Library 80
Clark Art Institute 21
Clark-Chapman House 94
Clarke School for the Deaf 87
Clarksburg 3
Cobble Mountain Reservoir 43
Colrain 27
Connecticut Valley Historical Museum 64
Conway 27
Coolidge, Calvin 88
Court Square 58
Covered bridges 100
Crane Museum of Papermaking 4
Cummington 81

D
Damon, Isaac House 89
Dalton 3
Day, Josiah House 70
Deerfield 28
Deerfield Academy 28
Devil's Football 92
Dinosaurland 92
Dinosaur tracks 48, 84
Dickinson Homestead 76
Dickinson Library 39
Dunn, Olga Dance Company 5

E
Eaglebrook School 28
Eastern States Exposition ("Big E") 70
Easthampton 82
East Longmeadow 45
Edwards Memorial Museum 81
Edwards, Jonathan 88
Egremont 4
Elms College 44
Erving 30

F
Fairs and festivals 100

114

Farm Museum   84
Field Memorial Library   27
Fishing   100
Florida   4
Forbes Library   88
Forest Park   60
Fort Massachusetts   12
French King Bridge   34

G
Gill   30
Golf courses   101
Goodwin Memorial Library   84
Goshen   83
Granby   84
Granville   45
Great Barrington   5
Greenfield   31
Greenfield Community College   31
Greylock War Memorial   2
Gunboat Monitor   11

H
Hadley   84
Hail to the Sunrise Monument   27
Hall School   15
Hampden   46
Hampshire College   77
Hancock   6
Hancock Shaker Village   7
Harambee Holiday   60
Hatfield   86
Hawley   32
Hawthorne Cottage   9
Heath   32
Hinsdale   7
Historic American Buildings   101
Historic Deerfield, Inc.   28
Hitchcock Center for the
   Environment   77
Holland   77
Holyoke   47
Holyoke Canal   47
Holyoke Community College   48
Holyoke Dam   48
Holyoke Heritage Park   48
Hoosac Tunnel   4
Hopkins Trust   85
Hopkins Memorial Forest   21
Hubbard Memorial Library   52
Hunting   100
Huntington   86

I
Indian Motocycle Museum   61
Indian House Memorial   28
Institute of Open Education/West   87

J
Jacob's Pillow Dance Festival, Inc.   3
Jones Library   77

K
Kingman Tavern Historical
   Museum   82
Knightville Dam   87
Knox Trail   11
Kolburne School, Inc.   11

Kripalu Center   9

L
Lanesboro   7
Laughing Brook   46
Lee   8
Lenox   9
Lenox Arts Center   18
Leverett   33
Leverett Craftsmen and Artists, Inc.   33
Leyden   33
Linden Hill School   34
Longmeadow   50
Look Memorial Park   89
Ludlow   52

M
MacDuffie School for Girls   62
Maple sugaring   102
Massachusetts Audubon Society   103
Mattoon Street   62
McCann Technical School   12
McCarthy, Helen Memorial Museum   37
Meekins Library   95
Memorial Hall   29
Merwin House   19
Metacomet-Monadnock Trail   42
Middlefield   87
Mission House   19
Mohawk Trail   103
Mohawk Trail Concerts   32
Monroe   33
Monson   53
Montague   34
Monterey   11
Montgomery   53
"The Mount"   10
Mountain Park   48
Mount Holyoke   93
Mount Holyoke College   93
Mount Tom   49
Mount Tom State Reservation   49
Mount Washington   11
Museum of Fine Arts (Springfield)   64
Music Inn   10

N
Native sons and daughters   103
Natural Bridge   12
Naumkeag   19
New Ashford   11
New Marlboro   11
New Salem   34
Norcross Wildlife Sanctuary   68
Northfield   34
Northfield Mount Hermon School   35
Northfield Mountain   36
North Adams   11
North Adams State College   12
Northampton   87
Notchview Reservation   24

O
Old Bloody Brook Tavern   28
Old Field Tavern   33
Old First Church   59
Old Sturbridge Village   107
Orange   36

Ornamental Tree Association 78
Otis 13

P
Palmer 54
Parsons House 89
Pelham 91
Peru 13
"Pesky Sarpent" Legend 72
Petticoat Hill 95
Pine Cobble School 22
Pittsfield 13
Plainfield 92
Pleasant Valley Wildlife Sanctuary 10
Pocumtuck Valley Memorial
  Association 29
Poison Oyster Stone 91
Poet's Seat Tower 32
Porter-Phelps-Huntington House 85
"Pot Holes" 37
"The Puritan" 63
Pynchon, William 63

Q
Quabbin Reservoir 81
Quadrangle 63
Quinnetukut 36

R
Rattlesnake Gutter 33
Rice, Dorothy Frances Sanctuary 13
Richmond 16
Riverside Park 42
Rockwell, Norman Museum at
  Stockbridge 19
Rowe 36
Russell 54

S
Sandisfield 16
Sand Springs Mineral Springs 22
Savoy 16
Schweitzer, Albert Friendship House 6
Shaw-Hudson House 92
Shays, Daniel 92
Sheffield 16
Shelburne 37
Shutesbury 38
Simon's Rock Early College 6
Skiing—alpine and nordic 109
Skinner Museum 93
Skinner Park 93
Smith's Agricultural and Vocational
  High School 90
Smith College 90
Smith College Campus School 90
Smith College Observatory 39
Smith, George Walter Vincent Art
  Museum 65
Smith, Sophia Homestead 86
Society for the Preservation of New
  England Antiquities 108
South Hadley 92
Southampton 94
South Mountain Association 15
Southwick 54
Springfield 55
Springfield College 66

Springfield Heritage State Park 66
Springfield Indians (hockey) 61
Springfield newspapers 62
Springfield Museum of Fine Arts 64
Springfield Science Museum 65
Springfield Symphony Orchestra 59
Springfield Technical Community
  College 66
Springfield Women's Club 67
St. Patrick's Day parade (holyoke) 49
Stage/West 67
Stanley Park 69
State forests, parks, and
  reservations 112
Steerage Rock 43
Stevens School of the Bible 9
St. Hyacinth College and Seminary 84
Stockbridge 17
Stone House Museum 81
Stoneleigh-Burnham School 32
Storrowton Village 71
Stockbridge 17
Storrs House 51
Storrs Library 52
Strong Houe Museum 78
Sunderland 38
Symphony Hall 59

T
Tanglewood 18
Titan's Piazza 93
Three-County Fair 90
Tolland 68
Trustees of Reservations 113
"Twin Spires" 34
Tyringham 20
Tyringham Galleries and Gingerbread
  House 20

U
University of Massachusetts 79

V
Volleyball 49

W
Wales 68
"Warbeek" 38
Ware 94
Warwick 38
Washington 20
Wendell 38
Western Gateway Heritage State
  Park 13
Western New England College 67
Westfield 69
Westfield Athenaeum 70
Westfield State College 70
Westfield White Water Canoe Races 70
Westhampton 94
West Springfield 70
West Stockbridge 20
Whately 39
Whitaker-Clary House 34
Wilbraham 72
Wilbraham and Monson Academy 73
Williamsburg 95
Williams College 22

Williamstown 21
Williamstown Theatre Festival 23
Williston Northampton School 83
Windsor 24
Wistariahurst 50
Woolman Hill 30
Worthington 95

Y
Yankee Atomic Electric Power Plant 37

Date: _____

Please send _____ copies of *Trips and Trivia* at $15.95 each, plus $1.50 postage and handling. I enclose a check in the amount of $_____, payable to The Donning Company/Publishers, 5659 Virginia Beach Blvd., Norfok, VA 23502.

Name _____

Address: _____

City and State: _____ Zip _____

About the Author

Linda K. Fuller, author, is a resident of Wilbraham, Massachusetts. She earned a B.A. in American Studies from Skidmore College, an M.A. in Human Relations and Community Affairs from American International College, and a Ph.D. in Communication Studies from the University of Massachusetts. Currently, she teaches in the Media Department of Worcester State College.

In addition to serving nearly a dozen years as Executive for the World Affairs Council of the Connecticut Valley, Linda has been very active on local community boards, including Child and Family Services, Inc.; Stage/West Theatre Guild; Springfield Adult Education Council; and the Junior League of Springfield, Massachusetts; she has just completed a term as President of the Springfield Women's Club. She is the author of *Public Access Cable Television; Popular Cultural Perspectives on Western Massachusetts; Springfield, Massachusetts: Microcosm of Popular Culture;* and numerous publications and conference reports on media.

Linda is married to Eric Fuller, President of the Holyoke Card and Paper Company. They have three sons: William, Keith, and Alexander—plus two Siamese cats and a chocolate Labrador dog. *TRIPS & TRIVIA* is dedicated to the family, "Who tripped all around Western Massachusetts with me collecting trivia..."